Making the American Home

Making the American Home

Middle-Class Women
&
Domestic Material Culture
1840-1940

edited by
Marilyn Ferris Motz and Pat Browne

Bowling Green State University Popular Press
Bowling Green, Ohio 43403

Contents

Introduction

Marilyn Ferris Motz

The transformation of a house, a physical structure, into a home, with its resonant emotional meanings, has been in our culture a traditional task of women. The importance of this work has frequently been overlooked, in part because the work process is hidden from public view, often even from the view of other family members. In the late nineteenth and early twentieth centuries, even many working-class women were able to achieve some degree of decoration of the home. Anzia Yezierska records in her 1912 novel, *Bread Givers*, the pride with which the mother of a poor Jewish family in New York City would lay out a white tablecloth every Friday night, a symbol not only of the importance of the Sabbath dinner as a religious ritual but also of the mother's ability to own and keep clean a piece of white linen—to create, even in the midst of poverty, a sense of control of the environment, an illusion of beauty and security. It was, however, the middle-class and upper-class married woman of the period who was the primary focus of what has come to be known as the "cult of domesticity," the belief that women should devote themselves to home and family since such attention would satisfy women's natural desires as well as fulfill their duty to society (Welter; Cott).

Both popular fiction and didactic literature glorified the role of women in altering the household environment, raising the task to the status of an almost holy endeavor. The articles collected here examine this process of the making of a home, the adaptation and decoration of the house itself and the creation, selection, and arrangement of the objects within it as they reflected the role of American middle-class women as homemakers in the years from 1840 to 1940.

Throughout the nineteenth century, and to a lesser extent during the first half of the twentieth century, women were expected to devote themselves to home and family. Indeed the atmosphere of the home was seen as having an almost mystical effect on its inhabitants, determining their moral standards, happiness, and success in the outside world. It was the responsibility of the homemaker to create this aura of well-

1

being and security that was associated with the home, and her skill and diligence as a wife and mother were judged in part by the condition of her house. The care and decoration of the home was a major aspect of the daily work of most married women. Even those women who were forced to seek employment outside the home to support the family, almost always at low wages and long hours, were still expected to maintain a minimum standard of household cleanliness and decoration. The relegation of women to the domestic sphere, and the meanings encoded in the image of the home, were reinforced by women's magazines, guidebooks for housewives, sermons, and popular songs.

Homemaking and domestic culture have traditionally been disdained or overlooked by historians in inverse proportion to their glorification in popular literature. Decades of scholarship, following prevailing attitudes in our society, have placed a higher value on customary male activities than on customary female activities. The creative domestic products and processes for which women traditionally have been responsible have been most commonly relegated to the devalued category of the merely decorative or functional, if indeed they are accorded any artistic status at all. From the standpoint of economic, as opposed to aesthetic, evaluation, traditional women's domestic tasks have frequently been viewed as outside the realm of useful production, as leisure rather than work activities.

Recently, many scholars have begun to question these assumptions and to attempt to view the unpaid domestic activities of women as valid and valuable in aesthetic as well as economic terms. Patricia Mainardi has examined previous scholarship about quilts and concluded that assessments of their artistic merit are often based on aesthetic criteria formulated to evaluate works of art created in a male tradition and thus reflect a bias against the aesthetic choices most commonly made by female artists. The question of whether or not such a "female" aesthetic exists remains a matter of debate among feminist scholars. Several articles in *Heresies* have proposed the existence of a set of aesthetic principles characteristic of women's art in general and American women's domestic art in particular (Bovenscen; Lippard; Meyer and Shapiro). A few articles and books published by folklorists in recent years discuss the artistic choices made by specific contemporary women working in traditional domestic art forms. In "Quilts and Quiltmakers' Aesthetics," Sandra Stahl examines the aesthetic judgments made by one quilter, while Susan Roach, in "'The Kinship Quilt': An Ethnographic Semiotic Analysis of a Quilting Bee," discusses such evaluations made jointly during a quilting bee. In her study of the makers of rag rugs, Geraldine Johnson considers the artistic criteria they use as well as the economic role the rugs play in their lives.

As the artistic value of women's traditional domestic art has often been ignored, so has the labor that lies behind the creation of an aesthetically pleasing home environment. If the home has traditionally served, as historian Christopher Lasch has suggested, as a "haven in a heartless world," it is through the work of women that this illusion of ease is created. The establishment of a pleasant home environment which helps family members to feel secure and to escape from the tensions of the workplace as well as providing their needs for food, clothing, and shelter requires a great deal of physical labor, even with the help of modern technological devices. In earlier decades, as historians studying housework have shown, exhausting physical work was required for the maintainance of the household. Even the supervisory activities of women with servants and the decorative needlework of the genteel lady were demanding activities that served a practical function in maintaining the status of the household. The association of the home with non-productive activities, in contrast to an outside world of work, created an image of the middle- and upper-class woman as a lady of leisure that hid the true nature of her work activities within the household.

Several books and articles published in recent years have explored the history of housework, particularly the impact of changes in household technology on women's domestic roles. Susan Strasser, in *Never Done: A History of American Housework*, presents an overview of the history of household work, while Ruth Schwartz Cowan, in *More Work for Mother: The Ironies of Household Technology from the Open Hearth to the Microwave*, argues that technological developments have not lessened the workload of the homemaker. Joann Vanek's earlier study indicates that improvements in technology have not decreased the amount of time women spend on housework. Ruth Schwartz Cowan, in "The Industrial Revolution in the Home: Household Technology and Social Change in the 20th Century" and William and Deborah Andrews in "Technology and the Housewife in Nineteenth Century America" also consider the impact of technological changes on the American woman's domestic work. The artistic aspects of housework remain largely unexamined, although folklorist Judy Levin's unpublished paper on the aesthetics of contemporary household work suggests some interesting lines of inquiry. Heidi Hartman has explored the economic importance of household work from a Marxist feminist perspective, considering why and how homemaking came to be devalued in a capitalist society.

While scholars have begun to examine domestic art forms, particularly needlework, and to trace the history of housework and the development of household technology, few studies have looked at the relationship of women to the house itself. The relationship of women to their living space has long been an important issue to feminists as well as to those advocating the continuation of traditional roles for women. The rearing of children requires a secure, relatively climate-controlled enclosure, whether it be temporary or permanent, private or collective, and in many cultures the arrangement of such a shelter is carried out by women. The interaction between women and the houses in which they live is often complex and ambiguous. Many women have transformed drab mass-produced houses into comfortable, individualized environments. But, as one Midwestern woman noted around the turn of the century, a house often leaves its mark on a woman. Her environment may shape her self-image as well as the image others have of her (Keeler, 139).

A few scholars have examined the careers and designs of female architects and advocates of housing reform (Torre; Wekerle, et. al.). Some nineteenth-century reformers considered the impact of housekeeping tasks on women's lives and proposed the creation of kitchenless houses with collective housekeeping facilities, while others suggested more efficient kitchens and baths to make housework easier (Hayden; Sklar). For most women in the past as well as the present, however, significant input into the design of their own houses has been out of reach. They have been limited to minor adaptations to the structure of the houses and to their decoration and furnishing.

Articles in women's magazines from the nineteenth century to the present, as well as advertisements for home furnishings and appliances, have provided advice to women on how to decorate their living spaces. But the term "decorate" implies the embellishment of an already fixed form rather than the creation of an artistic object. The word carries a pejorative meaning that implies a lack of control of the total artistic effect, an association reflected in the low status accorded the decorative arts and home decoration in comparison to other artistic activities. Aesthetic considerations aside, however, home decoration often serves an important economic and social function for the family as well as contributing to the psychological well-being of its members.

In earlier generations, as today, the decorating and redecorating of the home provided a medium for the display of the upper-middle-class family's financial resources as well as for the homemaker's skill as a consumer and her knowledge of current styles in home decor. Such decorating often represents an attempt to project an image of the family's social status rather than to express their personal taste. Home decoration may thus serve a practical function in providing a display of the family's wealth and its ability to follow current design trends: it is often a means of increasing the family's social status and even, through the husband's— or, more recently, the wife's—professional advancement, the family income level. The house becomes a monument to the willingness of the family to conform, usually at great expense, to accepted standards of style and taste.

At a more modest economic level, the labor-intensive work of creating hand-made decorative items out of household scraps has long provided women with the opportunity to display their awareness of current trends, often as reflected in women's magazines, and the creation of such objects denotes that time can be spared from the essentials of providing food, clothing, and shelter. Seasonal decorations or those made of ephemeral materials such as live flowers need to be replaced regularly and thus provide a continuous display of the availability of leisure time as well as creative skill.[1] The space required to exhibit and store decorative items and the time needed to keep them clean further reflect the family's ability to afford such non-essential items. These displays symbolically suggest the woman's artistic role in the embellishment of the home and her economic role in managing and conserving the family's resources so as to allow an excess for decorative purposes.

For many women, home decoration has represented a limitation of their skills, a painful cramping of creative and organizational capabilities that have been denied access to a more public forum. Certainly, it both reflects and reinforces the traditional relegation of women to the house, their banishment from wider arenas of productive activity. Yet for many women the decoration of the home has provided a relatively satisfying creative activity. Middle- and upper-class women without access to artistic training or markets could present their creations to an appreciative audience, particularly during the various rituals of social entertaining. While the decorations and artistically presented food for such social events are ephemeral, they are shared with a community of women and assessed according to local artistic standards. These activities can provide women with the opportunity to affiliate with others, exchange goods and services, and gain recognition for their achievements.

Women's literature provides abundant examples of the positive and negative imagery of the house and its decor, from the oppressive wallpaper symbolizing the woman's confinement in Charlotte Perkins Gilman's short story, "The Yellow Wallpaper" and the cryptic messages conveyed by the quilt in Susan Glaspell's play "Trifles" to the sentimental visions of home in nineteenth- and twentieth-century popular poetry. For many women the house has both protected and entrapped, expressed and concealed. Houses have long formed a common subject matter for women's traditional art from quilts to samplers. When amateur photography became widely available in the late nineteenth century, many women took pictures of their own houses and those of their friends. Some of these images show families in their domestic settings while others simply portray house interiors (Motz). Twentieth-century photographs frequently create permanent documentation of ephemeral holiday decorations or the table settings for social events. Houses thus not only provide a medium for creative expression—an object to be decorated—but also serve as a symbol of a complex web of emotional meanings—a subject of artistic comment.

Considering the significance and pervasiveness of the association of women with the home, it is logical to wonder what the house and the objects used in its decoration can tell us about women's lives. Much of the recent research that has been conducted on the history of women has examined women as actors—altering their environment, adapting the advice they received, and expressing their own views, albeit often covertly—rather than as passive consumers and followers. The articles included in this volume represent an interdisciplinary approach to the study of women's transformation of the domestic environment: their making of the American home from 1840 to 1940. Several of the articles explicitly discuss methodological issues in material culture study, while the remaining articles use a wide range of source materials and methods to examine American women's domestic material culture in the nineteenth and early twentieth centuries. In the collected articles, scholars in history, interior design, home economics, literature, American studies and women's studies examine household objects, photographs of houses, popular magazines, domestic manuals, government documents, and popular fiction to determine what these sources can tell us about the relationship of women to the homes they created.

Susan Arpad considers the question addressed by many feminist scholars: does there exist a separate women's culture and, if so, what characteristics define such a culture? Using secondary and primary sources, Arpad summarizes how both women's personal writings, such as diaries, and their domestic material culture, such as needlework and gardens, can provide evidence of the nature of women's experiences and the meaning women assigned to them. Arpad explores the themes common to the artifacts she discusses—family, home, death, and female friendship—and describes the way nineteenth-century women used their quilts, gardens, and other domestic forms of expression to create a sense of order and control in their lives and to express their own vision of reality.

In "American Women and Domestic Consumption, 1800-1920: Four Interpretive Themes," Jean Gordon and Jan McArthur discuss the role of American women as purchasers of household goods. Using literary sources, domestic manuals, and secondary historical works, Gordon and McArthur trace changes in women's domestic consumption patterns. They describe the development during the nineteenth century of consumption by middle-class women designed to enhance one's social status, in contrast to working-class and earlier middle-class patterns of selecting goods considered appropriate to one's social level.

Gordon and McArthur, like Arpad, consider a wide range of domestic objects. Several other scholars represented here focus on a single aspect of the home: fancywork, the front porch, the garden, and aspects of interior decor. Beverly Gordon examines the penwipers, pincushions and similar items made by women in the nineteenth century, looking primarily at the articles in women's magazines describing such items. She considers the factors that have led to the devaluation of such work by scholars and demonstrates how fancywork provided women with a means of creative expression that was compatible with socially accepted roles for middle-class women but also allowed for a limited transcendence of those roles through a temporary escape into fantasy and a whimsical transformation of mundane objects into fanciful ones.

Using concepts developed by sociologists and anthropologists, Sue Bridwell Beckham examines women's allocation of space within the house, particularly southern women's use of the front porch as an area transcending the boundary between public and private domains. While women were relegated to the domestic sphere in the nineteenth and early twentieth centuries, Beckham argues, they developed strategies for assuming a more public presence. The front porch, which was clearly domestic space, but was also visible from the street, enabled women to participate in community life while symbolically remaining at home. Beckham bases her analysis on information provided by early photographs of houses, on literary sources, and on the houses themselves as they exist today.

Arpad, Beckham and Gordon view domestic material culture as an expressive tool which enabled women to transcend the limitations of their roles: Beverly Seaton views gardens as representative of women's traditional sphere. Using as source material nineteenth- and early twentieth-century novels and gardening guides written by women and apparently designed for a female readership, Seaton traces the changing nature of vegetable and flower gardens and compares the rural woman with the upper-class woman who spent hours every day creating indoor flower arrangements. In both cases, she finds, women's gardening work was viewed as decorative or peripheral, underlining women's dependent status. Since gardens are by nature ephemeral, even less evidence remains of them than of porches and quilts. Published gardening manuals and novels can be used, as Seaton shows, at least to describe the ideal situation presented to the upper-class or middle-class woman who read such books.

In "Interior Decorating Advice as Popular Culture: Women's Views Concerning Wall and Window Treatments, 1870-1920" Jean Gordon and Jan McArthur examine the interior decorating advice of women writers published in popular magazines and decorating guides from 1870 to 1920. Gordon and McArthur conclude that home decoration was by this period considered a responsibility of the middle-class woman, who was told how to purchase new household products and how to display her house, which she had no power to change structurally, to best advantage. They trace the biographical backgrounds of the authors and the evolution of decorating taste in the context of women's roles during the period.

Jane Converse Brown examines the late nineteenth-century decorating trend known as the "Japanese Taste." On the basis of articles published in popular and trade magazines, Brown considers the ways in which the decorating style reflects prevalent attitudes and values of the time period, particularly those espoused by prominent intellectuals. She views the style as a means by which women could indicate their assimilation of these attitudes and inculcate these values in their children. The objects women selected and the ways in which they combined them thus served to perpetuate a set of values which were promulgated through the popular literature directed at the middle-class woman.

As Nancy Cott has noted regarding written sources, scholars examining the lives and artistic products of ordinary women, as Arpad and Beckham do, are likely to find evidence of women using such forms as strategies to enhance their power and express their perceptions, while those who base their argument on published prescriptive literature, as Seaton, Brown and Gordon and McArthur do, tend to view women as following in real life the roles outlined in the literature (197). Beverly Gordon uses women's magazines as source material; however, on the basis of the analysis of the objects themselves, she finds women using fancywork as an escape from their constricted lives. While all seven authors examine ways in which women attempted to alter their immediate environment, the differing types of source material consulted reflect differing emphases on women as overcoming constricting roles versus women as acting within constricting roles.

The final three articles use case studies of specific artifacts and women to illuminate methodological and theoretical concerns. Patricia Cunningham examines the ways in which a nineteenth-century weaver's account book can be used to learn about her craft. Cunningham discusses the relative value of analysis of objects themselves and of the written documentation that surrounds them. She describes the context of the weaver's life and her role in the community as they relate to her weaving.

Ricky Clark analyzes in detail a single quilt, illustrating the depth of information that can be derived from an artifact and its surrounding documentation. Clark presents biographical information about the quilt's creators and outlines its transmission between generations. She discusses the quilt's relationship to the family and community in which it was produced and, using secondary sources, relates these to broader issues concerning the nature of women's experiences in the mid-nineteenth century.

Mary Sies examines the activities of several "privileged" women from three exclusive suburbs and concludes that they influenced not only the nature of their own architect-designed houses but also, indirectly, more general trends in the design of houses for the less affluent. She views the impact of these women on domestic material culture as extending to the alleviation of uncomfortable and unsanitary housing for the urban poor and the support of progressive architectural innovations aimed at making houses more functional for middle-class families. Sies presents these women as stretching the traditional limitation of their activities to the home and family to encompass charitable, reform and artistic activities intended to improve the homes of working-class and middle-class families.

All of these articles treat objects as texts which reveal the thoughts and attitudes of their creators and their subsequent users. They explore the ways in which women transformed raw materials and everyday objects—flower seeds, walnut shells, patches of cloth, houses—into expressive forms. In the decoration of their homes and the selection of objects to be used within them, women were not simply expressing their own taste but were reacting to—interpreting, adapting, displaying, rejecting—values of the broader culture. The articles included in this volume make use of a wide range of sources—popular literature, decorating and gardening handbooks, decorative objects themselves, photographs, biographical data derived from a variety of sources, diaries and account books, interviews, secondary sources establishing historical context—to determine the meanings attributed to the objects by their creators and users. Whether they examine a single individual or a broad cultural group, the articles place the objects within the context of the culture in which they were created and used. The objects therefore tell us not only about themselves but also about the society in which they existed.

Note

[1]In unpublished research, folklorists Lucy Long and Jack Santino have investigated the importance to contemporary women of seasonal home decorations.

Works Cited

Andrews, William and Deborah. "Technology and the Housewife in Nineteenth Century America." *Women's Studies* 2 (1974): 309-328.
Bovenscen, Silvia, "Is There a Feminine Aesthetic?" *Heresies* 1: 4 (1978): 10-12.

Cott, Nancy. *The Bonds of Womanhood: "Woman's Sphere" in New England, 1780-1835*. New Haven: Yale Univ. Press, 1977.

Cowan, Ruth Schwartz. *More Work for Mother: The Ironies of Household Technology from the Open Hearth to the Microwave*. N.Y.: Basic Books, 1983.

_____ "The 'Industrial Revolution' in the Home: Household Technology and Social Change in the 20th Century." *Technology and Culture* 17 (1976): 1-23.

Gilman, Charlotte Perkins. *The Yellow Wallpaper*. 1899. N.Y.: Feminist Press, 1973.

Glaspell, Susan. *Trifles*. N.Y.: Frank Shay: The Washington Square Players, 1916.

Hartmann, Heidi I. "The Unhappy Marriage of Marxism and Feminism: Towards a More Progressive Union." *Capitalism and Class* 8 (1979): 1-33.

Hayden, Dolores. *The Grand Domestic Revolution: A History of Feminist Designs for American Homes, Neighborhoods, and Cities*. Cambridge, Mass.: The MIT Press, 1981.

Johnson, Geraldine. *Weaving Rag Rugs: A Women's Craft in Western Maryland*. Knoxville: Univ. of Tennessee Press, 1986.

Keeler, Lucy. Notebook XXXIV: 139. Rutherford B. Hayes Presidential Center, Fremont, Ohio.

Lasch, Christopher. *Haven in a Heartless World: The Family Besieged*. New York: Basic Books, 1977.

Levin, Judy. "A Woman's Work is Never Done: Aesthetics in the Occupational Lore of Housewives." Presented at American Folklore Society Annual Meeting, October 1985.

Lippard, Lucy R. "Making Something from Nothing (Toward a Definition of Women's 'Hobby Art')". *Heresies* 1:4 (1978): 62-65.

Mainardi, Patricia. "Quilts: The Great American Art." *Radical America* 7 (1973): 36-68.

Meyer, Melissa, and Shapiro, Miriam. "Waste Not, Want Not: An Inquiry into What Women Saved and Assembled, Femmage." *Heresies* 1:4 (1978): 66-69.

Motz, Marilyn Ferris. "Turn of the Century Midwestern Women's Photograph Albums as Social Commentary." Presented at Popular Culture Association/American Culture Association Annual Meeting, April 1984.

Roach, Susan. "The 'Kinship Quilt': An Ethnographic Semiotic Analysis of a Quilting Bee." *Women's Folklore, Women's Culture*. Ed. Rosan A. Jordan and Susan J. Kalcik. Publications of the American Folklore Society. Philadelphia: Univ. of Pennsylvania Press, 1984. 54-64.

Sklar, Kathryn Kish. *Catharine Beecher. A Study in American Domesticity*. New Haven: Yale Univ. Press, 1973.

Stahl, Susan. "Quilts and Quiltmakers' Aesthetics." *Indiana Folklore* 11 (1978): 105-132.

Strasser, Susan. *Never Done: A History of American Housework*. N.Y.: Pantheon Books, 1982.

Torre, Susana, ed. *Women in American Architecture: A Historic and Contemporary Perspective*. N.Y.: Whitney Library of Design, 1977.

Vanek, Joann. "Time Spent in Housework." *A Heritage of Her Own*. Ed. Nancy F. Cott and Elizabeth Pleck. N.Y.: Simon and Schuster, 1979. 499-506.

Wekerle, Gerda R., Peterson, Rebecca, and Morley, David, eds. *New Space for Women*. Boulder, Colo.: Westview Press, 1980.

Welter, Barbara. "The Cult of True Womanhood, 1820-1860." *American Quarterly* 18 (1966): 151-174.

Yezierska, Anzia. *Bread Givers*. 1925. N.Y.: Persea Books, 1975.

"Pretty Much to Suit Ourselves": Midwestern Women Naming Experience Through Domestic Arts

Susan S. Arpad

In 1916 Susan Glaspell published a play about rural and small town midwestern women called "Trifles." The play begins when three men, the sheriff, the county attorney, a neighbor and two women, the Sheriff's wife and the neighbor's wife, enter the gloomy kitchen of John Wright's farmhouse.

The men are there to investigate the murder of John Wright, who had been found by his wife when she awakened the previous morning, lying beside her, strangled by a rope. When asked who did this, Mrs. Wright said she didn't know, even though she was sleeping in the bed with her husband. "I was on the inside," she said, and "I sleep sound."

Mrs. Wright has been charged with murder and locked in jail; the three men have come to her house to find evidence and a motive for the murder. The two women have come to the farmhouse to straighten up and to pack some things to take to Mrs. Wright in jail. As the women go about their work, one of the men dismisses their concerns about preserves and quilts with the comment, "Well, women are used to worrying over trifles." The men move authoritatively through the house, yard, and barn looking unsuccessfully for clues.

In the meantime, the women reconstruct Mrs. Wright's life by reading the domestic clues with which they are familiar. When they gather her worn clothes to take to the jail, one woman comments,

Wright was close. I think maybe that's why she kept so much to herself...I suppose she felt she couldn't do her part, and then you don't enjoy things when you feel shabby. She used to wear pretty clothes and be lively when she was Minnie Foster, one of the town girls singing in the choir.

Reprinted from Vol. IV, No. 4, Fall, 1984, pp. 15-27 of the *Hayes Historical Journal: A Journal of the Gilded Age*. Reprinted with permission.

When they look at Minnie's partly finished quilt top, they noticed something wrong:

All the rest of it had been so nice and even. And look at this! It's so all over the place! Why, it looks as if she didn't know what she was about!

They find a bird cage with the door partly pulled off and remember a man selling canaries last year. They notice how lonely and bleak the house is and they speculate about what Minnie's life was like. As they sort through the quilt pieces, they discover a fancy box, inside of which, wrapped in a piece of silk, is a dead canary, its neck wrung. Again, the women discuss what Minnie's life must have been like and they talk about their own similar experiences:

Mrs. Peters: (In a whisper) When I was a girl—my kitten...there was a boy took a hatchet, and before my eyes...and before I could get there...(covers her face an instant). If they hadn't held me back I would have...(catches herself, looks upstairs where steps are heard, falters weakly)...hurt him.
Mrs. Hale: If there'd been years and years of nothing, then a bird to sing to you, it would be awful—still, after the bird was still.
Mrs. Peters: (Something within her speaking) I know what stillness is. When we homesteaded in Dakota, and my first baby died—after he was two years old, and me with no other then—
Mrs. Hale: Oh, I wish I'd come over here once in a while! That was a crime! That was a crime! Who's going to punish that?... I might have known she needed help! I know how things can be—for women. I tell you, it's queer, Mrs. Peters. We live close together and we live far apart. We all go through the same things—it's all just different kind of the same thing—

One of the women takes the erratic stitches out of the quilt top; they carry the fancy box containing the canary's body away from the house in a coat pocket. As they leave the house, the men joke facetiously that even though they haven't found the clues they sought they did learn something about quilting.

Glaspell's play is currently undergoing a revival of popularity among feminist scholars because it illuminates a problem that many women have experienced, but few have been able to articulate. Women, particularly those women who devote themselves to domestic work, live in a symbolic universe that is very different from the symbolic universe inhabited by most men.[1] The symbols that make up these two disparate worlds, including material culture, language, arts, customs, habits, and beliefs, appear strange and unimportant to members of the other sex. The men in Glaspell's story could dismiss the women's conversation and work as "trifling" and without significance. What makes Glaspell's story so interesting to feminist scholars is the unusual suggestion of the story that the men's inability to understand the women's world is a handicap; it causes them to fail in their quest. On the other hand, familiarity with and respect for this woman's world allows the women to reconstruct the motives and events leading up to the murder. The play's ending suggests, further, that the failure of the men to understand the women's world and the women's point of view causes such an alienation between men and women that wives will lie to their husbands to protect a woman who has murdered her husband. The play reminds us that reality is perceived from many points of view and that the dominant point of view is not necessarily the most valuable or useful one.

For the past several decades feminist historians have been collecting evidence about women's historical experiences in an effort to reconstruct the story of the American past from women's points of view. The result may be a radically different story than the one to which we are accustomed. As Annette Kolodny points out, for instance, the conventional popular literary history of American frontiers from a male point of view has told the story as the psycho-erotic journey of conquest of a lone frontiersman into a virgin wilderness, while the same story from a female point of view has imagined the frontier experience as idealized domesticity, "locating a home and familial human community within a cultivated garden" (Kolodny, *The Lay of the Land* and *The Land Before Her.*)

For the past several years, I have been examining domestic arts created by rural midwestern women between approximately 1830 and 1920 in order to reconstruct these women's experiences from their own points of view. I have looked at both literary artifacts (diaries, letters, reminiscences, and oral histories) and material cultural artifacts (especially quilts and other needlework, photographs, and gardens). These arts have been labelled as the lesser arts or domestic arts by art experts and, partly because of this denigration, these arts have been left mostly to women. Because these domestic arts were largely controlled by women, they provide a valuable indication of women's experience—what happened to them and what meaning they found in their experiences.

Needlework is, perhaps, the primary woman's art. Women have been defined by the needlework they do and, in turn, they use the major metaphors of their lives to shape their needlework. For instance, in many reminiscences, a woman's needlework is an index of her role and status in the community. An Ohio woman who was a pioneer in the Firelands area was memorialized with these words:

> Her life has been one continual round of work. She wove and spun long after the hum of the wheel and the clash of the loom had died away in most homes. In the last fourteen years she has pieced and quilted 102 quilts, and many are the homes that possess a quilt, or rug, doll, or some other piece of her handiwork (Wickham 284).

Marguerite Ickis recorded this story from her great-grandmother, who lived in Ohio, and who talked about a quilt she had made that was later handed down in the family:

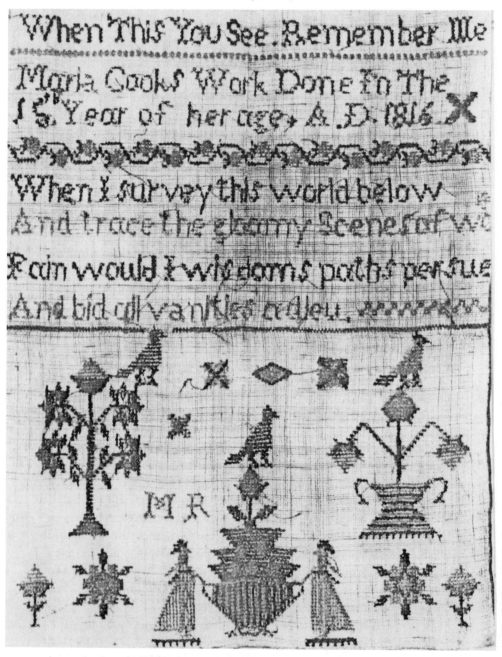

When This You See, Remember Me
Maria Cooks Work Done In The
15 Year of her age, A.D. 1816 X

When I survey this world below
And trace the gloomy Scenes of w[o]
[F]ain would I wisdoms paths persue
And bid all vanities adieu,

M R

A sampler done in 1816 by Lucy Webb Hayes' mother, Maria Cook Webb, as a young girl of fifteen. This sampler is on display in the Hayes Presidential Center Museum.

It took me more than twenty years, nearly twenty-five, I reckon, in the evening after supper when the children were all put to bed. My whole life is in that quilt. It scares me sometimes when I look at it. All my joys and all my sorrows are stitched into those little pieces. When I was proud of the boys and when I was down-right provoked and angry with them. When the girls annoyed me or when they gave me a warm feeling around my heart. And John too. He was stitched into that quilt and all the thirty years we were married. Sometimes I love him and sometimes I sat there hating him as I pieced the patches together. So they are all in that quilt, my hopes and fears, my joys and sorrows, my loves and hates. I tremble sometimes when I remember what that quilt knows about me. (Safford and Bishop 88)

Another woman, a nineteenth-century farm woman, said about the importance of her needlework, simply, "I would have lost my mind if I had not had my quilts to do." (Mainard 40)

Far from being the mindless work that quilts are often thought to be, women carefully chose their patterns, piecing small and varied bits of fabric in a way that created order out of chaos, giving meaning to lives that, for many women must have been experienced as fragmented and chaotic. A late nineteenth century fictional character, Aunt Jane of Kentucky, talked about this process of women controlling their arts:

You see, you start out with just so much caliker; you don't go to the store and pick it out and buy it, but the neighbors will give you a piece here and a piece there, and you will have a piece left every time you cut out a dress, and you take what happens to come and that's predestination. But when it comes to cuttin' out why you're free to choose your patterns. You can give the same kind o' pieces to two persons, and one will be a Nine Patch and one'll make a Wild Goose Chase and there'll be two quilts made out o' the same kind of pieces, and jest as different as they can be, and that is just the way with livin'. The Lord sends in the pieces, but we can cut 'em out and put 'em together pretty much to suit ourselves. (Hall 74)

In addition to sewing, gardens seem to have provided women with an important outlet for their creativity and a form for expressing their view of the world. Certainly, in women's records of their pioneering experiences, they write in detail about the specific plants they carried to their new homes and the arrangements of those plants. Mary Dodge Woodward of North Dakota, wrote lovingly in her diary in 1888.

My red, old-fashioned peonies have stuck their pink noses out of the ground. I covered them up last night. I have watched them ever since I was a little girl: in Vermont, in Wisconsin, and now in Dakota Territory where they still thrive. Anything that can live in this cold country should be reverenced. The rose-colored one and the white one are not up yet. I shall see them later. (Hampsten 232)

Again, women were defined by their communities in symbolic language of flowers and textiles, as was this Ohio woman in a reminiscence:

> Mrs. Holiday lived to a good old age, loved and respected by all who knew her. Hollyhocks and other old time flowers bloomed around her, and loom and spinning wheel made merry music within her humble dwelling.... (Wickham 644)

The connection between quilting and flowers seemed a natural one. One quilter described her first quilt this way:

> Before we was old enough to sew, Mama taught us to garden...when we were just small, we each had a little flower garden to tend. Mama loved flowers, but she didn't have time to work them herself, so she put us little kids to learning gardening on flowers.
>
> Well, we quilted in the winter mostly. And when it came time for me to piece my first quilt, it was a Flower Garden. My fingers just wanted to work flowers. All the pieces in my first quilt was flowered prints. (Cooper and Buferd 68)

Women used the imagery of flowers and gardens to express their fantasies of orderliness, control, and renewal and their dreams of beauty and gaiety.[2]

Among literary forms, diaries, letters, and reminiscences have been the primary genres that women have used to record their experiences and the meaning they found in those experiences; in recent decades, oral histories of women have provided additional verbal record of women's lives. In my survey of all of these artifacts, certain themes and images are repeated; it became evident that women did have an aesthetic—a universe of symbolic meanings—that caused them to shape their art work in certain ways, to repeat certain themes, and to value certain ideas.

The first and most obvious of the themes prominent in women's domestic arts is the focus on home and family. With the advent of the industrial revolution, men's and women's roles along with their workplaces diverged dramatically. Men went out into the "world" to work, while women's roles and women's work was confined to the home. During the nineteenth century a so-called "cult of domesticity" defined a woman's role as responsibility for keeping the home and family. When Mary Samuella Curd left Virginia in 1860 to live with her husband in the frontier state of Missouri, this is what she wrote in her diary on the day she and her husband left her relatives and headed west:

> from this time the Scenes & whole Tenor of my life would change. I would soon turn my face Westward away from the scenes of home and childhood, a new sphere of action would open before me, and on me in great measure must depend the making of a home happy or miserable. (Arpad 46)

A woman who emigrated to Kansas in 1879 remembered making the trip against her will. She went because, as she said, "the characteristic disposition of the male prevailed." But as soon as she arrived at what must have appeared a rough and bleak frontier, she began to transform it in her mind's eye into a new home. In her reminiscence, written fifty years after the event, she wrote:

> We arrived in Winfield one beautiful Sabbath morning, and to the ringing of the church bells, we wended our way through the attractive hamlet to...a beautiful spot on a mound south of the town. As we gazed with rapture over the beautiful valley, encircled by a fine stream of water, we felt that instead of the wild West, we have found God's own country, and were quite content to accept it as our future home. (Stratton 45)

Women's art work shows this same concern for homes and domestic themes. Again and again we see houses, domestic animals, domesticated land depicted in the subjects portrayed in the needlework, as well as in the names given to patterns. Homes, families, and homey objects are depicted with a humor characteristic of a woman's vision.

In fact, the theme of humor belies a common stereotype of women as prudish nags. As an example, here is a quote from Ellen Aultman's diary, written by a rural northwestern Ohio woman who shows great forbearance for her husband's weaknesses.

> February 22, 1901. Friday. Cold. This is Washington's Birthday. There is no school today, it is a holiday. We went over to Payson's entertainment. Baked cookies and pie. I and Theora walked over to the Beeker School House. Payson put the entertainment off 2 weeks so we had our walk for nothing. Payson brought us home in the cutter...Geo's back was so lame that he couldent go to the entertainment but after I had gone, he and Grace and Blanche went over to Jim Brandeberry's to a dance. Diden't get back till after 3 o'clock the next morning. That is a new cure for lame back. He hasent had any sign of it since. What do you suppose I think of such work. They had an oyster supper. His back was so lame before that he couldent do only certain things. I had to rub it with linement and keep hot plates on it. I believe I will have the receipt published in the county paper for the benefit of others that is troubled with lame back.

Women's art celebrates life, home, and family. The motif of the tree of life is one of the most common in early needlework. But the tree of death—the willow tree—also appears frequently because women's lives were deeply touched by death. Death was experienced differently by men and women. As the caretakers of the dying and the bodies of the dead, women probably experienced death more immediately. Deaths of husbands frequently left women feeling useless as well as vulnerable. When Sam Curd's husband died in 1863, barely three years after their marriage, she stopped writing in her diary and only after a year had passed did she write a final entry about her grief.

The designs and motifs of women's needlework were used by a Bowling Green, Ohio, stone mason to shape this tombstone. Photographed by Susan Arpad.

June 15, 1863 Since I last wrote, time to me has not been measured by the brief span of days & weeks; it has draged its "weary length along" with such heaviness, that I can scarcely be convinced that only 13 months have passed away since the death of my dear husband. Oh! God what hours of gloom & thick darkness, of loneliness bordering at times on despair, of weariness, feeling at night as if my days, had been of toil, & awakening with the same crushing consciousness, that I was widowed, a feeling which if language were exhausted no idea could be given of its full import. God & myself only know what I have felt to be—a widow. (Arpad 129)

Women frequently experienced a life-long grief at the death of an infant child. This story, told in reminiscence of a woman in Huron County, Ohio during pioneer days, was probably true of the feelings of many women:

During their early life in the woods a little child, the baby, sickened and died. Upon retiring for the night, the broken-hearted mother had placed the little form of her baby in the drawer of the old-fashioned bureau, that it might be safe and undisturbed.

Missing her baby in the night, though still asleep, she had arisen from her bed, and, taking the baby from its resting place, began to fondle and caress it, when she suddenly awakened, to find but a cold and lifeless image, instead of the living, breathing baby of which she had dreamed. (Wickham 548-549)

The large number of photographs of dead infants extant in private and public collections attests to the importance of infant deaths in the world of women. Scholars who have studied diaries of women written during the mid-nineteenth-century migration west indicate that women were greatly concerned with death (for instance, many women diarists counted the number of graves they passed on their journey westward) and that they frequently used language of death and dying to indicate their intense grief at parting from loved ones who stayed home. (Hampsten; Riley; Schlissel).[3] When Lodisa Frizzel began the overland trip west with her husband, she wrote in her diary:

Who is there that does not recollect their first night when started on a long journey, the well known voices of our friends still ring in our ears, the parting kiss feels still warm upon our lips, and that last separating word Farewell! sinks into the heart. It may be the last we ever hear from some or all of them, and to those who start. . .there can be no more solemn scene of parting only at death. (Jeffrey, 37)

Another central theme in women's art is the theme of friendships with other women—mothers, daughters, sisters, and friends. Carroll Smith-Rosenberg has written that as men's and women's roles diverged in the nineteenth century, husbands and wives had less and less in common and each tended to bond with same-sex friends. Women performed important tasks with and for each other: in sickness, in childbirth, in the rituals of death as well as birth, and in friendship and laughter. Life on the frontier was especially lonely for women, who missed the company of other women. Mollie Sanford wrote in her diary soon after she moved to Nebraska:

I do try to feel that it is all for the best to be away off here. I can see and feel that it chafes mother's spirit.... If the country would only fill up.... We do not see a woman at all. All men, single or bachelors, and one gets tired of them. (Jeffrey 56)

Interestingly enough, the communion that women shared often included the doing of art work, such as at a quilting bee. A woman from Ohio described in a letter in 1841, such an event after a long, cold winter when women were forced to stay at home:

We have had a deep snow. No teams passed for over three weeks, but as soon as the drifts could be broken through, Mary Scott sent her boy Frank around to say she was going to have a quilting. Everybody turned out. Hugh drove on to the Center, where he and several other men stayed at the Tavern until it was time to come back to the Scotts' for the big supper and the evening.... One of Mary's quilts she called 'The Star and Crescent'. I had never seen it before. She got the pattern from a Mrs. Lefferts, one of the new Pennsylvania Dutch families, and pieced it this winter.... Her other quilt was just an old fashioned 'Nine Patch'. (Mainard 60)

The design of some quilts expressed this pattern of women's friendships directly in what was called the friendship quilt. These were made when a woman married or when she moved away; her friends each created one or more blocks that were sewed together and quilted.

The act of doing communal work with other women was an important part of women's lives. One young Iowa pioneer reported, "I went to Mrs. Low's quilting. There was 15 to quilt. Had 2 quilts and there was indeed merry faces about them." (Jeffrey 86-87). Another woman wrote: "This afternoon I go to Sewing Society at Mr. Pierces. I suppose the affairs of the town will be discussed over the quilt." (Jeffrey 86-87). It was at meetings such as these that women could share their anxieties without being told that their concerns were trifling; here they could communally affirm women's view of the world and, perhaps, even attack male society. When we see the startling effects created by Amish women in their quilts, it is difficult to avoid the speculation that in their domestic artwork these women make a statement in opposition to their male-dominated culture.

It is, in part, the communality of quilting—the sharing of designs, plans, patterns, innovations, even materials and methods—that have designated women's arts as not "high art." At the same time, the emotional attachments that the artwork symbolized gave meaning to their art for many women. Aunt Jane of Kentucky expressed this feeling when she said,

There is a heap of comfort in making quilts, just to sit and sort over the pieces and call to mind that this is of the dress of a loved friend. (Hall 76)

Out of these disparate pieces of their lives, women used their arts to create meaning and order. This is the way one woman quilter expressed that meaning:

You can't always change things. Sometimes you don't have no control over the way things go. Hail ruins the crops, or fire burns you out. And then you're just given so much to work with in a life and you have to do the best you can with what you got. That's what piecing is. The materials is passed on to you or is all you can afford to buy...that's just what's given to you. Your fate. But the way you put them together is your business. You can put them in any order you like. (Cooper and Buferd 20)

Through their arts women gained a sense of integrity and order in what many of them must have experienced as a fragmented existence.[4] In a recent article about a farm woman's work in 1850, John Mack Faragher lists the tasks of women:

Nearly all of the food consumed by farm families was a direct product of women's work in growing, collecting, and butchering. An acre or so of improved land near the house was set aside for the domestic garden...that required daily attention.... Wives and daughters were also traditionally responsible for the care of henhouse and dairy.... Women milked, tended, and fed the animals. The milking and the manufacture of butter and cheese was one of their central tasks.... Food preparation was, of course, women's work.... Women cooked on the open hearth, directly over the coals; it was low, backbreaking work that went on forever; a pot of corn mush took from two to six hours with nearly constant stirring.... Water had to be carried to the house, sometimes from quite a distance, and that invariably was women's work. Domestic work—house cleaning, care of the bedding, all the kitchen work, in addition to responsibility for decorating and adding a 'woman's touch'—was a demanding task under the best of circumstances, and farms offered far from the best. The yard between the kitchen and barn was always covered with enough dung to attract hordes of summer houseflies. In those days before screen doors, kitchens were infested; men and women alike ignored the pests. In wet months the yard was a mess of mud, dung, and castoff water, constantly tracked into the house. (119-120)

The form of both diaries and quilts—fragmented into small, discrete segments—reflects the fragmentation of women's lives. Here is a single diary entry from the life of an Ohio woman—the same Ellen Aultman whose husband's backache was miraculously cured by a dance and oyster supper.

"Album Block," a pieced quilt made by several people, c. 1895, from Columbia Station, Ohio; now owned by the Lorain County Historical Society. Photographed by Patricia and John Glascock.

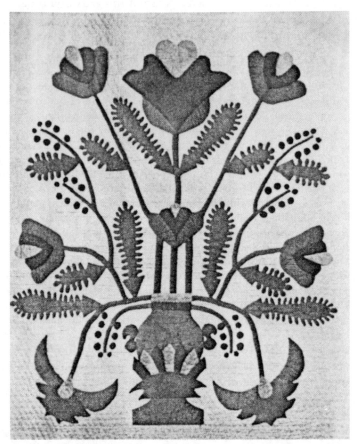

"Michigan Flowerpot," an appliqued quilt made by Metta Peard, 1929, Oberlin, Ohio; now owned by Gene Smith. Photographed by Marcia Roberts.

Saturday, January 26, 1901. Cloudy, Snowing this aft. The old black sow had pigs today. I made 4 pies, baked cookies, ironed. Blanche mopped, Grace cleaned front room and up stairs. The men went to corners tonight. Geo. got 4 lb. sugar, 24 c, butter, 2 lb. 36 c, tablecloth 50 c, tea 15 c, coffee 18 c, thread 5 c...Blaine hauled feed and wood; cleaned stable. Geo. cut wood. Lew Householder is about dead with consumsion.

Birth, economics, work, family, and death are all mentioned in this one small fragment of a woman's life—a single day.

For these women, their domestic arts provided forms and symbols that allowed them to create order in lives they may have experienced as disordered—a way of integrating the fragments of their lives and expressing its meaning. Quilters frequently talk about art work immortalizing the artist, as does Aunt Jane of Kentucky:

I've been a hard worker all my life,...but 'most all my work has been the kind that' perishes with the usin', as the Bible says. That's the discouragin' thing about a woman's work. Milly Amos used to say that if a woman was to see all the dishes that she had to wash before she died, piled up before her in one pile, she'd lie down and die right then and there. I've always had the name o' bein' a good housekeeper, but when I'm dead and gone there ain't anybody goin' to think o' the floors I've swept, and the tables I've scrubbed, and the old clothes I've patched, and the stockin's I've darned. Abram might 'a' remembered it, but he ain't here. But when one o' my grandchildren or great-grandchildren sees one o' these quilts, they'll think about Aunt Jane, and, wherever I am then, I'll know I ain't forgotten. (Hall 78)

Quilts also immortalize memories of individuals and communities important to the quilter—those who make up the human context within which the artwork was created.

Different ones of my family are always appearing from one of these bags. Just when you thought you'd forgotten someone, well, like right here...I remember that patch. That was a dress that my grandmother wore to church. I sat beside her singing hymns, and that dress was so pretty to me then. I can just remember her in that dress now. (Cooper and Buferd 75)[5]

For these women, domestic arts had an integrative function. Early in Agnes Smedley's novel, *Daughter of Earth*, the heroine states, "I shall gather up these fragments of my life and make a crazy-quilt of them. Or a mosaic of interesting pattern—unity in diversity" (8). In their studies of pioneer women's diaries, Lillian Schlissel and Elizabeth Hampsten found a decided emphasis on continuity and pattern in women's writing.

They write in order to assert a pattern and to blur distinctions between recurring and unique events. In this view, keeping the pattern intact day after day is the mark of a well regulated and successful life...their writing emphasizes patterns because patterns compose their days, and they do not see time as a succession of discrete or climatic events....

The success of a woman's life traditionally is judged by the skill with which she manages to keep undisturbed the smooth pattern of daily living. (Hampsten 68-69, 71)

At times of emotional despair and disorder, quilting restored a sense of order and control.

After my boy Razzie died when he was fourteen, I began to quilt in earnest, all day sometimes. There was still the two younger ones to take care of but losing my oldest just took away something. I lost my spirit for housework for a long time, but quiltin' was a comfort. Seems my mind just couldn't quit planning patterns and colors, and the piecing, the sewing with the needle comforted me. (Cooper and Buferd 107)

Another of the ways women expressed their need to impose order and control was to enclose the spaces and to carefully border the edges.

Whether in quilts or gardens, most of the designs are within carefully enclosed spaces. The quilt has a border just as women's other spaces—houses, rooms, gardens, barnyards—are bordered, enclosed, defined. This confined space can represent either a woman's vocation—the center of her meaningful activities—or her confinement. This potential tension gives women's art work much of its artistic vitality. Its beauty centers around certain repeated images: houses and domestic images are frequent, as are flowers. We sense that the flowers, in riotous but controlled display, are an attempt to see beyond the dirt of the dooryard, the flies on everything, the mud that was being tracked onto a clean kitchen floor.

For many women living in the rural midwest between 1850 and 1920, their worlds must have appeared fragmented, disordered, lonely, bleak, filled with dirt, flies, dung and mud. Women's art created a world of order, cleanness, integrity, beauty, and community—one that incorporated the meaningful experiences of their lives.

Notes

[1]The idea that people construct the reality in which they live is certainly not new. Cultural anthropologists and historians have long recognized that groups of people share "social constructions of reality." Traditionally, however, these scholars have tended to distinguish the separate cultural groups by national or ethnic origins or by class. Feminist scholars are suggesting that gender also determines distinctly different world views; further, they suggest that the dominant class will rarely bother to understand or value the symbolic universe of the oppressed classes, although the oppressed classes will have to understand the symbolic universe of the dominant class in order to survive. W.E.B. DuBois recognized this same split in consciousness among American black men at the turn of the century when he described "...a world which yields him no true self-consciousness, but only lets him see himself through the revelation of the other world. It is a peculiar sensation, this double-consciousness, this sense of always looking at one's self through the eyes of others." (45)

[2]Annette Kolodny, *The Land Before Her*, believes gardens were a central metaphor used by women in their effort to domesticate the American frontier. Julia Bader, "The 'Rooted' Landscape," notes that gardens are central images in women's private writings, providing "sources of independent existence and self-expression."

[3]Hampsten believes that women's writings indicate an obsession with death and that for many women, contemplation of death offered them an erotic experience denied them by sexuality.

[4]Feminist scholars in many fields have explored repeatedly this theme of the fragmentation and discontinuity of women's lives (Moffat and Painter; Wescott; Kalcik 347; and Hammond 66).

[5]The authors of this book of oral histories of quilters note that quilts frequently act as triggers to memories: "As the quilters talked about quilts they were constantly reminded of some other parts of their lives, a story about pioneering times, an anecdote about a family member, or some technical detail of quilting. The quilts seemed to be the format in which they had condensed much of the personal, family, and

community history. Talking about the quilts often triggered memories of stories they had heard from their mother or grandmother over the quilting frame. That common task which had brought them together to sew also brought them together to talk and exchange stories. In a similar setting they passed on to us what they had heard." (18-19).

Works Cited

Arpad, Susan S. ed., *Sam Curd's Diary: The Diary of a True Woman*. Athens, Ohio: The Ohio University Press, 1984.

Aultman, Ellen Cornelia Kelly. Diaries, MMS. 18. Center for Archival Collections, Bowling Green State University.

Bader, Julia, "The 'Rooted' Landscape and the Woman Writer." *Teaching Women's Literature from a Regional Perspective*. Ed. Leonore Hoffman and Deborah Rosenfelt. New York: The Modern Language Association of America, 1982.

Cooper, Patricia and Norma Bradley Buferd. *The Quilters: Women and Domestic Art*. Garden City, N.Y.: Doubleday, 1977.

DuBois, W.E.B., "Of Our Spiritual Strivings." *The Souls of Black Folk*. Greenwich, Conn.: Fawcett, 1961.

Faragher, John Mack. "The Midwestern Farming Family, 1850," Ed. Linda K. Kerber and Jane De Hart Mathews. *Women's America: Refocusing the Past*. New York: Oxford University Press, 1982.

Glaspell, Susan. *Trifles*. New York: Frank Shay: The Washington Square Players, 1916.

Hall, Eliza Calvert. *Aunt Jane of Kentucky*. Boston: Little, Brown, and Company, 1907.

Hammond, Harmony. "Feminist Abstract Art—A Political Viewpoint." *Heresies* (1977).

Hampsten, Elizabeth. *Read This Only to Yourself: The Private Writings of Midwestern Women, 1880-1910*. Bloomington: Indiana University Press, 1982.

Jeffrey, Julie Roy. *Frontier Women: The Trans-Mississippi West 1840-1880*. New York: Hill and Wang, 1979.

Kalcik, Susan. "'...like Ann's gynecologist or the time I was almost raped': Personal Narratives in Women's Rap Groups." *Journal of American Folklore* 88 (Jan.-Mar. 1975).

Kolodny, Annette. *The Lay of the Land: Metaphor as Experience and History in American Life and Letters*. Chapel Hill: The University of North Carolina Press, 1975. *The Land Before Her: Fantasy and Experience of American Frontiers, 1630-1860*. Chapel Hill: The University of North Carolina Press, 1984.

Mainardi, Patricia. "Quilts: The Great American Art." *Radical America* VIII, 1 (1973).

Moffat, Jane and Charlotte Painter, eds. *Revelations: Diaries of Women*. New York: Vintage Books, 1975.

Riley, Glenda. *Frontierswomen: The Iowa Experience*. Ames: The Iowa State University Press, 1981.

Safford, Carleton L. and Robert Bishop. *American Quilts and Coverlets*. New York: Weathervane Books, 1974.

Schlissel, Lillian. *Women's Diaries of the Westward Journey.* New York: Schocken Books, 1982.

Smedley, Agnes. *Daughter of Earth,* (reprinted by The Feminist Press, 1973).

Stratton, Joanna L. *Pioneer Women: Voices from the Kansas Frontier.* New York: Simon and Schuster 1981.

Smith-Rosenberg, Carroll. "The Female World of Love and Ritual: Relations Between Women in Nineteenth-Century America." *Signs* I (Autumn 1975).

Wescott, Marcia. "Feminist Criticism of the Social Sciences." *Harvard Educational Review* 49, 4 (Nov. 1979).

Wickham, Mrs. Gertrude Van Rensselaer, ed. *Memorial to the Pioneer Women of the Western Reserve.* Women's Department of the Cleveland Centennial Commission, 1896 and 1924.

American Women and Domestic Consumption, 1800-1920: Four Interpretive Themes

Jean Gordon & Jan McArthur

In 1953 Betty Friedan, searching for a cause for the perpetuation of what she termed the "feminine mystique" long after it should have become obsolete, found her answer in American business. "Why is it never said," she asked, "that the really crucial function, the really important role that women serve as housewives, is to *buy more things for the house*... the perpetuation of housewifery, the growth of the feminine mystique, makes sense (and dollars) when one realizes that women are the chief customers of American business. Somehow, somewhere, someone must have figured out that women will buy more things if they are kept in the under-used, nameless-yearning, energy-to-get-rid-of state of being housewives."[1]

In this statement Friedan called attention to issues that were the theme of much scholarly writing in the 1960s and 1970s. It was agreed that America is a consumer society. It was also noted that much of our GNP was directed to providing Americans with elaborately furnished, single-family, detached suburban dwellings. The responsibility for equipping and maintaining these homes belonged to married women. For many it was their *raison d'etre*.[2]

How such a situation came about is less clearly understood. Historians have not given a great deal of attention to the specifics of American consumer behavior. In the colonial and early national periods much that was consumed by families was also made by them. Economic and social historians have made thorough investigations of the mechanism of subsistence agriculture, domestic production and the pattern of life which these fostered in rural areas and small town communities. At the same time they have emphasized the fact that, from the first settlements in Virginia, many Americans were engaged in production for export and imported much of what they required. The habits of mind fostered by this commercial activity were given a tremendous impetus by the industrial revolution. By the 1880s and 90s

Reprinted from Vol. 8, No. 3 of the *Journal of American Culture*. Reprinted with permission.

domestic consumption had become the norm for most Americans. Although values associated with a simpler, small town way of life persisted, these were challenged by the mores of the newer, urban, commercial, secularized communities. In the 1920s mass production, popular culture and modern advertising had all but prevailed over rural values and traditional patterns of gentility. America was well launched into "the culture of consumption."[3]

How all this affected women remains to be determined. So far historians have been content to point out in a general way the importance of women's ceasing to be domestic producers and becoming domestic consumers.[4] However, little has been written explaining in detail how this shift came about. It is important to establish, for example, when men abandoned the role of primary domestic consumer and women assumed that function. As women became the primary domestic consumers, we need to know what their tastes and priorities in expenditure were. Related to this matter is what kinds of furnishings were present in households at different periods and how women managed these possessions.

We do have considerable information concerning domestic consumption for the seventeenth and eighteenth centuries. Over the past ten years social historians, historical archeologists and historic preservationists have used excavated remains and inventories to determine in a quantifiable manner precisely what people owned at a given site or region at a particular time.[5] In addition, historic preservationists have documented in great detail the furnishings of particular nineteenth century homes.[6] However, with the advent of the industrial revolution, the quantity and variety of available goods has become too complex for easy tabulation. This fact and the abandonment of the practice of taking inventories have discouraged extending the quantifiable study of domestic material culture to the nineteenth and twentieth centuries. Scholars interested in the consuming habits of nineteenth and twentieth century Americans must rely, for the most part, on histories of the decorative arts, studies of folk art and histories of technology.[7] With the advent of sociology as a scholarly discipline, specific studies have been published concerning women's behavior as consumers. However, these are highly selective in the groups of women covered. Much remains to be learned with regard to women's opportunity to buy furnishings for the home as well as their priorities in spending the money available to them.[8]

It is not the purpose of this study to attempt anything like the historical equivalent of a modern study of consumer behavior. Rather it is to suggest some general characteristics of the relationship of American women to their domestic possessions from the early nineteenth century to the early twentieth century based on the authors' study of American material culture and popular books and magazines published during that period. These characteristics are not intended to be taken as definitive or even as the most important ones that could be identified. They are behavior patterns that we have found significant. We offer them in the hope that they may suggest further lines of research by other scholars working in related areas.

We have chosen to discuss the consumption habits of American women within four categories. These are traditional consumption, consumption based on upper-class European models, rationalized consumption and consumption for personal gratification. Paralleling these four types of consumer behavior is a recognition of the difference between consumption that has as its goal the preservation of a stable way of life and consumption that is self-consciously upwardly mobile. In addition one must recognize differences in consumer habits based on ethnicity and social class. It should also be pointed out that the four categories of consumption we have identified do not take place in a clear chronology of historical progression. All four behavior patterns have existed throughout our history, sometimes two or more being exhibited in the same individual at a given time. However, in general, it can be said that traditional consumption grounded in a relatively stable way of life characterized America before 1830. Status seeking consumption based on upper-class European models persisted until the early twentieth century. Rationalized consumption was important in the late nineteenth and early twentieth centuries. As for consumption for personal gratification, it exists wherever there is enough wealth to support it. There are examples of what one writer refers to as "domestic sensualism" as early as the eighteenth century. However, buying for personal gratification has been particularly prevalent since the 1920s.[9]

The primary characteristic of traditional consumption is that it takes place within clearly defined, stable classes and communities of people. Families seek to acquire what is appropriate for their class and group. Before the industrial revolution traditional consumption was marked by an economy of scarcity and few consumer choices were possible. Householders had to be content with what could be acquired from local craftsmen and importers or purchased through overseas factors. Even after the industrial revolution when far more goods were available, traditional consumers were guided by what was thought suitable for their group.

The most important fact concerning women's consumption behavior within a traditional context was that it was severely restricted. During the first two and a quarter centuries of our history most consumption decisions were made by men. Married women, legally subsumed by their husbands, were considered part of a man's household. If a wife had any influence in what was bought it was usually through persuasion rather than by exercising what was an acknowledged right. Unless a woman was acting as an agent for her husband or as a widow, most of her consumption choices were confined to her personal clothing.[10] It was not uncommon for either the husband or the father of the bride to provide a young wife with a completely furnished house. Caroline Gilman in *Recollection of a Housekeeper* described how a newlywed [very likely herself] was taken to a house in the North Square of Boston completely furnished with "new carpet, new chairs, new mahogany with its virgin hue, undimmed by wax and turpentine...." Everything was provided, even the kitchen pots and pans and a fresh sanding of the kitchen floor.[11]

Only the wealthy could afford to provide brides with entirely new household furnishings. It was more common to make use of old possessions which in wealthier families could be considered heirlooms. This was particularly true of the South. John Pendleton Kennedy in *Swallow Barn*, a novel concerning a southside Virginia planter household of the early nineteenth century, describes the family's dining room which in its decoration and furnishings had remained virtually unchanged since the mid-eighteenth century. As other antebellum novels and reminiscences confirm, this kind of conservatism was not at all unusual.[12]

Because household objects were scarce and passed on from generation to generation they could have multiple layers of meaning for the women who looked after them. The furniture and decorative objects in Mary Virginia Hawes Terhune's novels of the antebellum South communicate the same kind of personal association later generations would find in photograph albums. This attitude was also common in the North. Harriet Beecher Stowe, in *The Pearl of Orr's Island*, wrote of two old-maid sisters living in a Maine cottage in the early nineteenth century for whom "every plate, knife, fork, spoon, cup, or glass was as intimate...as instinct with home feeling, as if it had a soul."[13]

In general the taste of America's traditional household tended to favor the plain.[14] The absence of a rigid class structure forestalled the kind of "class appropriate" consumer behavior imposed on Europe's working and middle classes.[15] Yet in earlier American communities, consumption took place in a relatively closed society and made any expenditure that differed too drastically from community taste unlikely. A Hanover, New Hampshire resident wrote in 1859, "Thirty years ago, a carpet in a farmer's house, or a piano, was everywhere spoken against as insufferable pride." However, he went on to admit, "Now both the carpet and the piano adorn many a parlor among the hills and valleys of this comparatively sterile country."[16] Harriet Beecher Stowe, in *Uncle Tom's Cabin*, satirically related the reaction of Miss Ophelia's New England neighbors when the lady was given fifty dollars to buy a new wardrobe:

As to the propriety of this extraordinary outlay, the public mind was divided,— some affirming that it was well enough, all things considered, for once in one's life, and others stoutly affirming that the money had better have been sent to the missionaries; but all parties agreed that there had been no such parasol seen in those parts as had been sent on from New York, and that she had one silk dress that might fairly be trusted to stand alone....[17]

It was almost as if Miss Ophelia's clothes were common property.

The most extreme example of traditional consumption, one in which virtually all family assets were employed by the male head of the household to further the joint family enterprise, was subsistence farming. The object of these precommercial farmers was to save as much currency as possible to buy more land.[18] Even when commodities were available for purchase it was often preferable to make them or do without. Minimum consumption and recycling were a way of life. Lydia Maria Child in *The Frugal Housewife* advised: "Nothing should be thrown away so long as it is possible to make any use of it, however trifling that use may be."[19] When, in the 1850s commercial agriculture became the norm, farm families still consumed as a household unit dominated by the husband. First priority was given to increasing the farm's productivity. And, although farmers were willing to invest in labor-saving machinery for field or barn they were less inclined to spend money to ease the work of their wives. As Dr. W.W. Hall, in the first (1862) annual report of the Department of Agriculture wrote:

In plain language, in the civilization of the latter half of the nineteenth century, a farmer's wife, as a general rule, is a laboring drudge.... It is safe to say, that on three farms out of four the wife works harder, endures more, than any other on the place; more than the husband, more than the 'farm hand,' more than the 'hired help' in the kitchen.[20]

The conditions Dr. Hall denounced in a government document formed the theme of many late nineteenth-century women's magazine short stories. One example is Mary Wilkins Freeman's "The Revolt of Mother" which tells how a normally patient wife, when she discovers that her husband has spent their life savings on a new barn instead of the long-wished-for new house, protests by moving the family and the furniture into the barn. To Freeman the action of the farmer, which would have been regarded as perfectly normal a generation earlier, was now hopelessly out of step with the consideration shown by urban middle-class husbands for their wives' desire for domestic comfort.[21] As late as the 1940s farm families lagged far behind the rest of the nation in terms of household modernization and in the housewife's opportunity to engage in domestic consumption to suit her needs and tastes.[22]

Another group of nineteenth century women who can be considered within the category of traditional consumers are the wives of artisans and working class men. In contrast to the households of early rural Americans which have been painstakingly recreated at outdoor museums like Sturbridge Village and Cooperstown, New York, we know relatively little of the domestic environments of antebellum urban working-class Americans. However, on the basis of studies of traditional working-class culture we do know that the consumption habits of artisans and working-class Americans differed significantly from those of rural Americans. For one thing, working-class wives had more opportunities for consumption than rural women. Although many urban working-class families kept a small garden and a few domestic animals, much of what the family needed had to be bought in the local market. Shopping for this was the responsibility of the wife.[23]

Among immigrant families, according to studies made at the end of the nineteenth century, it was customary for the husband to turn his paycheck over to his wife after he had taken out enough for his personal needs.[24] One can assume that this was less likely to be true of native born artisans who had started out as part-time farmers and only later moved on to full-time craft or factory work.

Exactly what antebellum working-class wives bought for their homes remains to be determined. How much money was available for such expenditures depended not only on the husband's income but the family's life style. If an artisan lived in a more traditional manner, spending much of his free time in all male sociability—drinking at the tavern, playing sports or spending time at the hall of the voluntary fire department—it is reasonable to conjecture that less money would be allocated for household furnishings.[25] If, on the other hand, an artisan had middle-class aspirations it would be reflected in a larger, more elaborately furnished house.[26] For the poorest working-class wives, according to the writers of nineteenth-century fiction, the only opportunity to demonstrate respectability was through scrupulously neat housekeeping. A few class-appropriate embellishments—a potted plant at the window or a pretty piece of china—were regarded as evidence of finer feelings.[27] Popular writers agreed, however, that the working-class woman must not attempt a cheap approximation of the consumption habits of the affluent. Black women who dressed with a picturesque flair were regarded as quaint or absurd and Irish girls, who tried to look like Broadway belles, were set down as ignorant or possibly immoral.[28]

Mary Terhune in a serialized story published in *Godey's Lady's Book* in 1871 provides us with one of the few instances of a detailed description of a respectable working-class family home. A young couple has rented three rooms on the second floor of a house a mile from the factory where the husband works. Their superior taste is shown by the fact that they have moved beyond the smoky, squalid environs of the factory itself and that the wife has bought simple cottage furniture instead of the showy mahogany preferred by her sister and mother. In this story the wife's fault is that her taste is too good. When her husband prospers she uses her knack for buying the right thing, particularly fashionable clothes, to marry her daughter to a scion of one of the city's oldest families. But even though the daughter is accepted the mother is not. Her consumption tastes have cut her off from her own family but her working-class origins cause her to be snubbed by the fashionable families into which her daughter has married. Because of the daughter's false social success through consumption the mother has become a woman without a class.[29]

Most working-class women had neither the means, the knowledge, nor the desire to aspire to this kind of social metamorphosis. Their primary goal was to live comfortably among family and friends.[30] Because the husband's wages were usually insufficient to make this possible it was often necessary to use the home itself to make more money. Family funds might be allocated to taking in boarders with expenditures for extra beds, linens, tableware, etc. Or money might be spent on the tools of sweatshop production—for example, a sewing machine.[31] Yet by the beginning of the twentieth century, according to social investigators, more prosperous working-class wives were able to embellish their crowded flats and houses in a highly decorated manner with fancy wallpaper, lace curtains and cheap, ornamented furniture bought on the installment plan. Although social workers complained that such things were inappropriate and unsanitary—the wallpaper harbored bugs and the lace curtains dust—the working-class women were probably merely trying to achieve their own, albeit outdated version, of the taste for opulence displayed by the middle and upper-classes a generation earlier.[32]

Our second category, an upwardly mobile consumption based on European, upper-class models, was given an impetus with the great increase in manufactured goods that began in the nineteenth century. Mass production made available to middle and upper-class families the styles of household furnishings originally designed for Europe's wealthy and aristocratic classes.[33] Men still controlled the purse strings in antebellum homes, but women's influence in purchasing became increasingly evident, particularly in such thriving commercial centers as New York City.

Although a variety of styles of furnishings were available in the 1830s and 40s, by far the most popular was the French. It was both aristocratic and feminine. Mrs. Trollope described New York interiors of the 1830s as resembling those of a "European petite maitresse."

Little tables, looking and smelling like flower beds, portfolios, nick-nacks, bronzes, busts, cameos, and alabaster vases, illustrated copies of lady-like rhymes bound in silk, and, in short, all the pretty coxcomalities of the drawing-room scattered about with the same profuse and studied negligence as with us.[34]

George William Curtis in *The Potiphar Papers*, wrote satirically of New York residences that were all just alike, each furnished by ambitious wives in the style of Louis Quatorze or Louis Quinze according to the advice of the "best upholsterers and fancy-men in town."[35] In Anna Cora Mowatt's play, "Fashion," it is Mrs. Tiffany, with the help of her French maid, who makes all the consumer choices. Mr. Tiffany has become a mere income-earning appendage to domestic display.[36]

Curtis and Mowatt were both critical of the new taste for French elegance, considering it a symptom of impersonal social climbing. As Curtis made his spokesman, Mr. Potiphar, say, "We have each got to re-furbish every few years, and, therefore, have no possible opportunity for attaching ourselves to the objects about us."[37]

Curtis was typical of many genteel Victorians in emphasizing the falseness and hypocrisy of lavish domestic expenditures.[38] An additional concern was the effect of luxury on women. William Dean Howells expressed a general anxiety when he worried that the lack of meaningful work made middle-class women overly nervous and prone to depression.[39] Recent historians have joined in the censure of women's expanded involvement in domestic consumption.[40] Many have also taken the position that women enjoyed a higher social status as domestic producers and that their status fell when they became consumers.

This idea seems to have had its origin in two intellectual traditions. One is the nineteenth-century Puritan-Jacksonian suspicion of luxury as leading to aristocratic privilege and self-indulgent sin. Antebellum women writers were in the habit of contrasting the selfish materialism of city women with the hard-working virtue of small town and rural housewives. Harriet Beecher Stowe, throughout her literary career, wrote admiringly of the heroic housekeeping skills of her grandmother's and mother's generations. In her *House and Home Papers* she expressed a wish "for the strength and ability to manage my household matters as my grandmother of notable memory managed hers..."but she feared "that those remarkable women of olden times are like the ancient painted glass,—the art of making them is lost; my mother was less than her mother, and I am less than my mother."[41]

A second intellectual tradition to question the merits of consumerism was the socialist labor theory of value which considered making things to be of more social worth than buying them. Ann Douglas is a recent exponent of this view. In her *Feminization of American Culture* she accuses nineteenth-century women, particularly women writers, of falling victim to the blandishments of a second-rate culture of consumption which, with its tawdry sentimentality was greatly inferior to the plain living, tough-minded religiosity which preceded it.[42]

But for nineteenth-century women, raised amidst austere surroundings and unceasing work and threatened with eternal damnation by a judgmental Calvinist God, domestic luxuries and a forgiving, if sentimental religion, came as a welcome change. Even Harriet Beecher Stowe was not willing to imitate the nun-like existence of her domestically efficient Aunt Esther. Instead she took an unabashed delight in pretty clothes, pretty china and handsome Episcopal churches.[43] Sarah Hale, similarly raised within the tradition of Calvinism, did not regard fine clothes as a lure of Satan. To her, adorning the body was analogous to clothing the soul in grace. She agreed with the English that "only backward" cultures like the Hindus and the Chinese never changed their styles.[44]

The most extreme phase of consumption based on European upper class models came at the end of the nineteenth century. The year 1870 marked the highest per capita expenditure on furniture in America.[45] Census figures for the same year indicate that one half of all women wage earners in the United States had been domestic servants.[46] Contemporary photographs of the period reveal an amazing proliferation of objects, even in fairly modest homes.[47] For most Americans, the goal of this large commitment of money and time was to create an ideal environment for private middle-class families. The unspoken assumption was that in a democratic society, virtuous families deserved the same kind of luxury previously available to the rich, just as in a democracy virtuous citizens were entitled to a share in public power which formerly had been the monopoly of the privileged.[48] This being the case, it was only natural that the most popular styles were princely. Kenneth Ames has said that when today's children visit a museum exhibit of Grand Rapids furniture made for the Philadelphia Centennial of 1876 they are sure it belonged to royalty.[49]

With the advent of the department store, shopping itself became an occasion to enjoy opulent surroundings. In the 1890s the largest department stores of Philadelphia, New York and Chicago were as grandly spacious as the Louvre. Although most women could afford only modest purchases, the message conveyed by these vast palaces of merchandise was that value was inexorably linked to both elaborate embellishment and to sheer quantity.[50]

Still, no matter how ornate, most late nineteenth-century American interiors conveyed a sense of individuality and comfort. Except for the extremely ostentatious, American homes were for the private enjoyment of their owners, not for public display. As Henry James wrote of Olive Chancellor's Boston drawing-room, "he [Basil Ransom] had never felt himself in the presence of so much organized privacy or of so many objects that spoke of habits and tastes...and he had never before seen so many accessories."[51]

Many of the accessories enjoyed by James' heroines came from Europe. In the post Civil War decades Europe became a great bazaar for American women. The Grand Tour was now well within reach of upper middle-class school girls, brides and matrons. Wealthier women often maintained separate residences abroad. Men, preoccupied as they were with the postwar expansion of business, left buying and cultural matters to women. The generation of Edith Wharton agreed it was the duty of American men to make money and the right of American women to spend it. Yet as Wharton's heroine, Lily Bart, was ruefully aware, for a girl to have the chance to re-do the parlor she must first marry.[52] Those women who did marry well, Berthe Honore Palmer, Isabella Stewart Gardner, Louisine Havemeyer, Alva Vanderbilt Belmont, to name a few, furnished their houses on a scale worthy of royalty. Much of what they bought is now in museums. To them belongs some of the finest examples of American "conspicuous consumption."[53]

The phrase, of course, is from Thorstein Veblen's *Theory of the Leisure Class.* Yet as Veblen admitted most turn of the century American women, even the more prosperous ones, were not leisured in the sense of being idle. It was just that the activity of rich women was often directed toward status seeking display. Veblen considered work as something that led to the production of necessities or of luxuries that were enjoyed as ends in themselves, not as a means of social climbing.[54] Even so, as recent historians have pointed out, a high level of domestic consumption, whether conspicuous or not, can be as labor intensive as the earlier domestic production. Although the industrial revolution eliminated major domestic tasks, others appeared to take their place. Ruth Schwartz Cowan in *More Work for Mother* demonstrates that each "labor saving" innovation brought with it higher expectations for the housewife. The manufacture of less expensive, factory-made cloth resulted in more clothes, table and bed linens. These in turn required more hours of sewing and laundry. The availability of milled white flour and refined sugar led families to expect an unceasing supply of cakes and pastries. Spacious Queen Anne houses crammed with furniture, rugs, curtains and decorative objects posed herculean housekeeping chores.[55]

John Kenneth Galbraith has dealt with this phenomenon in his book *Economics and the Public Purpose.* Consumables, to be of value, he pointed out, must be managed. Otherwise they become a burden. In the early years of the industrial revolution when goods became more abundant there was a parallel increase in the need for servants. But, ironically, the same factories which produced more goods also provided jobs for the very people whose only previous work was domestic service. Eventually, when factory wages increased beyond the subsistence level, working class wives became major domestic consumers in their own right.[56]

However, before that transition could take place a situation existed full of frustration for the housewife and the women who worked for her. Mistresses, wishing to live at the highest possible level of consumption, were determined to extract as much work as possible from their servants. Servants retaliated by moving to another family or by leaving household service altogether. By the 1870s most maids were unskilled immigrants and blacks. Immigrants, once acclimated to American ways, usually left domestic service for other kinds of work or for marriage. Black women, having fewer options, continued to do housework even after marriage. Like women who worked as teachers, they were often overqualified for the job. Unfortunately for housewives, with the exception of the South, there were not enough black servants to go around.

A library could be compiled of the complaints of nineteenth and early twentieth century American housewives against transient servants. They could wreck havoc with a woman's most prized possessions. They disrupted family routine. Furthermore, by their presence they constituted a violation of the family's cherished privacy. It was clear to the more analytical that transient servants had to be banished from the household if the family was to be a complete world unto itself.[57]

The problem was how to minimize the need for servants and still maintain the style of consumption appropriate for a middle or upper-class way of life. Housework, when performed by servants, was generally viewed as even more demeaning than factory work.[58] No middle-class woman wanted to be thought of as a domestic drudge. Yet somehow the ever proliferating household tasks had to be performed. As it turned out, American women were particularly resourceful in meeting the challenge. Women writers and scientists, with the help of advertisers, were able to instill in the popular mind the concept of home-making as an activity suitable for an educated, upper-class woman as distinct from housework that was arduous, repetitious and low in status. They achieved this metamorphosis within the parameters of our two remaining categories of consumption—rationalized consumption and consumption for personal gratification.

Rationalized domestic consumption had its roots in the New England version of the Calvinist work ethic. New England housewives, the grandmothers so admiringly celebrated by Harriet Beecher Stowe, lacking servants and eager for a little free time to themselves, made a fetish of household efficiency. For farmers' wives these calculated work habits, known locally as "faculty," were essential just to get through everything that had to be done. Rural women had few resources with which to modify their work spaces and equipment. But small town and city women, with a little money to spare, could adopt labor saving household arrangements and appliances. Before the Civil War the motive of such women was often evangelical. It was Catherine Beecher's conviction that better designed, properly ventilated houses and more efficient work habits would permit the housewife to assume her proper role as spiritual guide, or as Beecher put it as "Christ's representative in the home."[59] Another reformer, Melusina Fay Peirce, was more efficiency oriented. During the Civil War, in a series of articles published in the *Atlantic Monthly*, she urged the formation of women's cooperatives to provide both the services and the manufactured goods necessary for family life.[60]

It was not, however, until the 1880s and 90s when domestic consumption based on European styles reached its most full-blown development that the newer women's magazines began to propagandize the program of the domestic rationalizers. The "homemaker," a newly coined term, was pictured as the domestic counterpart of the professional man. She was responsible for the proper management of her household as he was responsible for the direction of his business. She handled servants with the same impersonal authority with which he presided over his subordinates. She, like the professional man, was knowledgeable in all branches of her job. She knew which modern appliances were best suited to her family's needs. She was prepared to take responsibility for properly installed plumbing so avoid the menace of sewer gas. If she followed the advice of Ellen Swallow Richards, a pioneer of the Home Economics movement, she was willing to consider the entire community an extension of the domestic environment and rightfully under her purview. When, in the early twentieth century servants became scarce and expensive, experts like Christine Frederick, urged the housewife to rationalize herself as well as her house by adopting the techniques of industrial efficiency pioneered by Frederick Taylor.[61] Although decked out in the language of science, Frederick's recommendations were in many ways no more than an updated version of the New England housewife's step-saving "faculty."

At the same time, home magazines popularized what may have been the first truly middle-class aesthetic. In the mid-nineteenth century it had not been thought inappropriate for upper middle-class families to furnish their homes in Louis Quinze or Renaissance Revival styles. Even Mark Twain, whose professional stock in trade was ridiculing the pretentious, saw nothing absurd in the grandiose furnishings of his Hartford, Connecticut, home.[62] But when tenement dwellers began to gratify a taste for fussy lace curtains and heavily carved parlor pieces it was clear that domestic consumption based on aristocratic styles was on its way out. Middle-and upper-class women were only too happy to move in the direction of simplicity. For the daring it might be the dark, jewel-like colors and geometric shapes of the Arts and Crafts movement. For the more conventional there was colonial revival furniture, white painted woodwork and chintz.[63] Both styles complemented the rationalized approach to homemaking of plain living and informed thinking in which home making was conceptualized as the appropriate sphere of an up-to-date professional woman.

At least that is how it was presented in the women's magazines.[64] The actual experience of most turn-of-the-century women was undoubtedly much more diverse. It was, after all, one thing to read about rationalized methods of housework and quite another to implement them. Organizational techniques which made sense for business and factories could quickly become ludicrous when applied to the normal confusion of family life. One has only to look at contemporary photographs to realize how hodge podge most houses were. In addition many women, particularly southerners and immigrants, considered the rationalization of housework both alien and undesirable—especially when its precepts were associated with self-righteous Yankees and meddling middle-class do-gooders.[65]

Domestic rationalization did not really come of age until the 1920s when it was thoroughly institutionalized in schools and colleges by the profession of home economics. By then it was no longer the boldly innovative movement it had once been with Catharine Beecher, Melusina Fay Peirce or Ellen Swallow Richards. Instead it complemented the goals of American industry. The ideal housewife, as defined by educational institutions and the media, was the informed but essentially passive consumer. She was to know where to go to find the best information, not only concerning domestic products but also domestic skills and wisdom—how to buy appropriate furnishings, how to properly clothe, feed and take care of all the members of the family.[66] It was a far cry from Catharine Beecher's vision of the wife as an incarnation of Christ in the home or Ellen Swallow Richard's concept of women as guardians of the environment.

One final category, consumption for personal gratification, is rather more elusive than the other three. It began to assume its modern character with the privatization of experience that accompanied the expansion of cities in the eighteenth and nineteenth centuries.[67] The object of consumption for personal gratification was to acquire possessions which gave the owner pleasure or a sense of personal fulfillment. Such possessions might also carry the connotation of higher social status but this was not the primary reason for their acquisition. In fact, consumption for personal gratification was more likely to help the buyer put up with the social status she occupied. One way of coming to terms with being a housewife was to make housekeeping seem more like a pleasurable avocation than demeaning drudgery.

Consumption for personal gratification has had a long history. In the eighteenth century there were certain household tasks that were thought of as appropriate for ladies. These included fine needlework, the higher branches of cookery and washing the silver, crystal and fine china.[68] In the late nineteenth century when servants became more scarce, a logical strategy was to expand the categories of enjoyable, lady-like housework. Adeline Whitney, in a novel published in 1874, gives a fictional example of how this could be done. A family of young women decide they can do without a servant if household tasks are made more pleasant. Their first decision is to move the basement kitchen to the first floor dining room. Their second is to throw away all the old, unsightly pots and pans used by the maid and replace them with aesthetically pleasing new ones. In the refurbished dining room/kitchen they contrive to make the work itself aesthetically pleasing. As the author observed parenthetically, "A lady will no more make a jumble or litter in doing such things [cooking] than she would at her dressing table."[69]

Although Whitney wrote at a time when the employment of household servants was at its height, her book correctly forecast future consumption priorities. As long as servants were available, most families spent minimal funds on making housework easy or attractive. Kitchens were located in the basement or in the back of the house. They were usually old fashioned in their appointments. Housewives preferred to spend money on rooms used by the family and their guests. Ironically, servants themselves might object to the introduction of labor saving devices regarding them as an unfair attempt to increase the work load.[70]

But when the housewife did her own cooking and cleaning all this changed. Cooking schools became popular to train women in all branches of cookery. Kitchens were moved upstairs where they were more centrally located. Their decor became almost as important as that of the more public rooms. Marion Harland in her 1905 novel *The Distractions of Martha* described how her heroine created an "art kitchen" in grey and blue with a monumental cast iron stove, satirically referred to as "the shrine."[71] By the 1920s kitchens illustrated in women's magazines combined the attributes of a sitting room, boudoir and a laboratory. They were presented under such titles as "The One Room Exclusively a Woman's." In fact, one might infer from the advertisements of this period that the house itself was the private preserve of women. Men, when shown at all, were depicted with the self-conscious politeness of guests rather than the relaxed informality of members of the family.[72]

In reality, housework as a self-fulfilling activity was not plausible as long as it involved hard physical drudgery. But in the 1920s, with the widening availability of gas and electric appliances, chores like doing the dishes and cleaning the rugs could be made to seem, at least in advertisements, the delightful activities of a lady. Once manufacturers had developed appliances for the performance of such basic tasks as laundry, cooking and vacuuming they moved on to other devices like dishwashers and food processors whose time-saving capabilities might be marginal but which gave the housewife a sense of pampered affluence. As recent historians have demonstrated such appliances can actually increase work. They also reinforce the assumption that cooking and household maintenance are the responsibility of the housewife and should be carried out in the home. With home washing machines there is no need for commercial laundries. Expensively equipped kitchens eliminate the necessity of dining out.[73]

Concurrent with the proliferation of home appliances which began in the 1920s there was a shift in the kinds of people who represented models of desirable consumer behavior. In the nineteenth century such persons belonged to the genteel or aristocratic, European classes.[74] By the 1920s trend-setters were more likely to be the new rich, celebrities and movie stars. Because the lifestyle of these persons was based on money, as opposed to inherited status, it was more accessible to upwardly mobile persons or people who merely wished to make their present status more pleasurable. In contrast to the consumption tastes of the genteel and aristocratic which often required a highly sophisticated education, those of the trend-setters could be learned through advertising. Advertisers, in the 1920s, responded accordingly. They invented a new kind of advertisement which appealed to the consumer's subjective desires and fears as opposed to his or her rational judgments.[75] They also helped create a society in which people were defined, not by who they were but by what they owned. As Daniel Boorstin pointed out, by the 1950s we had become a "Consumption Community."[76] In this society, domestic expenditures were awarded a high priority. When Nixon touted the blessings of American capitalism at the 1959 Moscow trade fair, he chose to illustrate the superiority of private enterprise, not by an achievement in science or art, or even the latest car from Detroit, but by a "state of the art" kitchen.[77]

Given this official conservative endorsement of domestic expenditure, it is not surprising that Betty Friedan saw domestic consumption and the feminine mystique on which it was based as a trap imposed on women by capitalists in search of markets. However, that explanation is too simple. Domestic consumption in America began as an activity closely linked to community and class norms. When the industrial revolution caused these community and class ties to break down, the private family emerged as a major focus of economic and cultural life. As men left for work outside the home, women became the chief domestic consumers. It was a situation caused by industry which met industry's needs. But it was not the result of a self-conscious capitalist conspiracy. Nor has women's role as primary domestic consumer and family consumer manager been a static one. We have seen how these roles went through a series of changes in the nineteenth and early twentieth centuries.

At present, women's role as domestic consumer is undergoing yet another change. Married women are now entering the job market in unprecedented numbers primarily to pay for the consumables which advertising has caused them to believe essential to the good life, but whose escalating prices require a second income. But even though women now have the money to increase family consumption, they no longer have the time to act as full time consumption managers.

In many ways what is happening to today's housewife is similar to what happened to earlier American domestic servants. When these servants left private households for work elsewhere it meant that even wealthy women had to function as the consumption managers of their families. Now housewives are leaving the home for outside work. And, like the servants before them, as soon as other alternatives become available, the negative aspects of domestic service begin to be perceived as outweighing its benefits. Many working wives (in a manner similar to the nineteenth-century servants who considered their mistresses too demanding) are finding their personal interests in conflict with the demands of husband and children. When women had no other work options, loyal service meant security for both servant and wife. But when paid work outside the home became available such service was often perceived as leading to economic exploitation and low social status. As more of today's working housewives come to accept this view, women may finally emerge from their role as the last servant class. In any case, domestic consumption, as Betty Friedan described it in 1963, is already becoming a thing of the past. The household as a consuming unit presided over by women is fragmenting into a cluster of consuming individuals. How American industry responds to this fact remains to be seen.

Notes

[1]Betty Friedan, *The Feminine Mystique*, 10th anniversary ed. (New York: W.W. Norton & Co., 1974), pp. 206-207.

[2]See for example, Vance Packard, *The Waste Makers* (New York: David McKay Co., Inc., 1960); George Katona, *The Mass Consumption Society* (New York: McGray-Hill, 1964); David Riesman, *Abundance for What? And Other Essays* (Garden City, N.Y.: Doubleday, 1964), pp. 103-367; John Kenneth Galbraith, *Economics and the Public Purpose* (Boston: Houghton Mifflin, 1973).

[3]See for example, John Demos, *A Little Commonwealth* (New York: Oxford Univ. Press, 1970); Darrett Rutman, *Husbandmen of Plymouth* (Boston: Beacon Press, 1967); Thad W. Tate and David L. Ammerman, eds., *The Chesapeake in the Seventeenth Century* (Chapel Hill: Univ. of North Carolina Press, 1979); J.E. Crowley, *This Sheba, Self The Conceptualization of Economic Life in Eighteenth-Century*

America (Baltimore: Johns Hopkins Univ. Press, 1974); James A. Henretta, "Families and Farms: *Mentalite* in Pre-Industrial America," *William and Mary Quarterly* 35 (Jan. 1978), pp. 3-32; Burton J. Bledstein, *The Culture of Professionalism* (New York: Norton, 1976); T.J. Jackson Lears, *No Place of Grace, Antimodernism and the Transformation of American Culture, 1880-1920* (New York: Pantheon Books, 1981); Richard Wrightman Fox and T.J. Jackson Lears, Eds. *The Culture of Consumerism: Critical Essays in American History, 1880-1980* (New York: Pantheon Books, 1983).

[4]Nancy Woloch in *Women and the American Experience* (New York: Knopf, 1984), provides an excellent synthesis of recent research in the history of American women. Woloch takes the position of more recent historians that women's status became higher when they ceased being domestic producers. The more traditional interpretation is that women's social position declined when they abandoned production for consumption. See, for example, Elizabeth Dexter, *Colonial Women of Affairs* (Boston: Houghton Mifflin, 1931).

[5]Much of this scholarship has been influenced by the work of Fernand Braudel, particularly his *Capitalism and Material Life, 1400-1800*, translated from the French by Miriam Kochan (New York: Harper, Row, 1974). The St. Mary's City commission has made a detailed study based on archeological remains and surviving records of the domestic material culture of the early Chesapeake. The Summer, 1974 issue (69) of the *Maryland Historical Magazine* is devoted to the Commission's earlier findings. Since then a number of important articles have been published by Lois Carr and Lorena Walsh. Of particular interest is "Inventories and the Analysis of Wealth and Consumption Patterns in St. Mary's County, Maryland, 1658-1777," *Historical Methods*, 13 (Spring, 1980), pp. 81-104. See also Cary Carson, N. Barka, W. Kelso, G. Stone and D. Upton, "Impermanent Architecture in the Southern American Colonies," *Winterthur Portfolio*, 16 (Summer/Autumn, 1981), pp. 135-196. James Deetz, in *Small Things Forgotten* (Garden City, N.Y.: Doubleday 1977) has provided a theoretical framework for the domestic material culture of the Northeast, Laurel T. Ulrich, *Good Wives: Image and Reality in the Lives of Women in Northern New England, 1650-1750* (New York: Knopf, 1982), gives a detailed picture of the domestic environments of colonial women.

[6]William Seale, *Recreating the Historic House Interior* (Nashville: American Association for State and Local History, 1979) has established a methodology for such restorations.

[7]Many titles could be cited for these topics. Three representative ones are Edgar de N. Mayhew and Minor Myers, *A Documentary History of American Interiors* (New York: Scribner's, 1980); Henry Glassie, *Pattern in the Material Folk Culture of the Eastern United States* (Philadelphia: Univ. of Pennsylvania Press, 1969); Siegfried Giedion, *Mechanization Takes Command* (New York: Norton, 1948). In addition there are such general works as Edgar W. Martin, *The Standard of Living in 1860, American Consumption Levels on the Eve of the Civil War* (Chicago: Univ. of Chicago Press, 1942); Russell Lynes, *The Tastemakers* (New York: Grosset & Dunlap, 1949); and *The Domesticated Americans* (New York: Harper & Row, 1963); Jan Cohn, *The Palace or the Poorhouse, The American House as a Cultural Symbol* (East Lansing: Michigan State University Press, 1979).

[8]It is interesting to compare Margaret F. Byington, *Homestead, The Households of a Mill Town* (New York: Charities Publication Committee, 1910) with Lee Rainwater, R. Coleman and G. Handel, *Workingman's Wife* (New York: Oceana Publications, Inc., 1959).

[9]The term "domestic sensualist" was used by Carol Shammas to describe patterns of domestic consumption which emerged in the eighteenth century. See her "The Domestic Environment in Early Modern England and America," *Journal of Social History*, 14 (Fall, 1980), pp. 3-24.

[10]Nancy Cott, *The Bonds of Womanhood, "Woman's Sphere" in New England, 1780-1835* (New Haven: Yale University Press, 1977), p. 45.

[11]Caroline Howard Gilman, *Recollections of a Housekeeper* (New York: Harper, 1834), pp. 16-17; Walter Muir Whitehall, *Boston, A Topographical History* (Cambridge: Harvard Univ. Press, 1968), pp. 125-126. Peter Parker of Boston is an example of a father who gave his daughter a fully furnished house as a wedding present. In 1848 he commissioned M. Lemoulnier of Paris to design a handsome brick house in the South End of Boston which was one of the wonders of the mid-century city. It was the son-in-law rather than the daughter who determined the interior appointments. It was also customary for husbands in the early nineteenth century to do the daily marketing. Lily Martin Spencer has documented this practice in her painting "The Young Husband: First Marketing," reproduced in Robin Bolton-Smith and William H. Truettner, *Lily Martin Spencer, The Joys of Sentiment* (Washington: Smithsonian Institution Press, 1973), p. 43.

[12]John Pendleton Kennedy, *Swallow Barn* (New York: Putnam, 1852), p. 24.

[13]Mary Virginia Terhune, *Judith, A Chronicle of Old Virginia* (Philadelphia: Our Continent Publishing Co., 1883); Harriet Beecher Stowe, *The Pearl of Orr's Island* (Boston: Tichnor and Fields, 1862), p. 364.

[14]Henry James in *The Europeans* caused his French bred heroine, the Baroness Munster, to refer to her affluent American cousins, the Wentworths, as "Quakerish" in their simplicity. Henry James, *The Europeans* (New York, 1878; rpt. New York: Penguin Books, 1964), p. 51.

[15]Richard Sennett, *The Fall of Public Man* (New York: Knopf, 1977), pp. 65-72.

[16]Quoted by Clarence H. Dunhof, *Change in Agriculture, The Northern United States, 1820-70* (Cambridge: Harvard Univ. Press, 1969), p. 19.

[17]Harriet Beecher Stowe, *Uncle Tom's Cabin* (Boston, 1852; rpt. New York: Collier Books, 1962), p. 213.

[18]James T. Lemon, "Household Consumption in Eighteenth-Century America and Its Relationship to Production and Trade: The Situation Among Farmers in Southeastern Pennsylvania," *Agriculture History*, 41 (Jan. 1967), pp. 59-70; Danhof, Clarence, *Change in Agriculture: The Northern United States* (Cambridge: Harvard Univ. Press, 1969) pp. 18-20.

[19]Lydia Maria Child, *The American Frugal Housewife* (Boston: Carter and Hendee, 1835), p. 1.

[20]John M. Faragher, *Women and Men on the Overland Trail* (New Haven: Yale Univ. Press, 1979), pp. 59-60.

[21]Mary E. Wilkins, "The Revolt of Mother," in *The Best Stories of Mary E. Wilkins*, Ed. Henry W. Lanier (New York: Harper, 1927), pp. 23-42.

[22]Mary W. M. Hargreaves, "Homesteading and Homemaking on the Plains: A Review," *Agricultural History*, 47 (April, 1973), pp. 156-163; Mary W. M. Hargreaves, "Women in the Agricultural Settlement of the Northern Plains," *Agricultural History*, 50 (Jan. 1976), pp. 179-189; Joann Vanek in "Household Technology and Social Status: Rising Living Standards and Status and Difference in Housework," *Technology and Culture*, 19 (July, 1978), pp. 361-375, cites examples of the undermodernization of rural American homes as late as the 1940s.

[23]Richard L. Bushman, "Family Security in the Transition from Farm to City," *Journal of Family History* 6 (Fall, 1981), pp. 238-256. Sam Bass Warner, *The Private City* (Philadelphia: Univ, of Pennsylvania Press, 1968), pp. 17-19.

[24]Margaret Byington wrote in 1910 "The men are inclined to trust all financial matters to their wives. It is the custom in Homestead for the workman to turn over his wages to his wife on pay day and to ask no questions as to what it goes for. He reserves a share for spending money; otherwise his part of the family problem is to earn and hers is to spend." Margaret F. Byington, *Homestead, The Households of a Mill Town* (New York: Arno Press, 1969), p. 108.

[25]Bruce Laurie writes of the irregularity of work available to artisans in Philadelphia in the 1830s and 40s in "Nothing on Compulsion: Life Styles of Philadelphia Artisans, 1820-1850," *Labor History*, 15 (Summer, 1974), pp. 337-366.

[26]Laurie quotes a Philadelphia artisan who in 1850 spoke of as "necessities" for the "worthy mechanic" "a house...on a front street, three stories high, bath room, hydrant, good yard, cellar...house furniture, bedding, clothing, amusements." "Nothing on Compulsion," p. 373.

[27]Maria S. Cummins, *Mable Vaughn* (Boston: John P. Jewett, 1857), pp. 177-181; Edith Wharton, "Mrs. Manstey's View," in *The Collected Short Stories of Edith Wharton*, ed. R.W.B. Lewis (New York: Scribner's, 1968), I, pp. 3-11.

[28]William Dean Howells described a "young coloured girl...resplendent in a white hat trimmed in orange and purple." He was nonjudgmental but clearly thought the girl's taste very different from upper-class white's. *A Woman's Reason* (Boston: Osgood, 1883), p. 374; Carol Groneman, "Working-Class Immigrant Women in Mid-Nineteenth Century New York, The Irish Woman's Experience," *Journal of Urban History*, 4 (May, 1978), pp. 255-273.

[29]Mary Terhune [pen name Marion Harland] "Getting on in the World," *Godey's Lady's Book*, 82 (Feb. 1871) pp. 135-142.

[30]James M. Patterson, "Marketing and the Working-Class Family," in *Blue Collar World*, eds. Arthur B. Shostak and William Gomberg (Englewood Cliffs: Prentice-Hall, 1964), pp. 76-85.

[31]John Modell and Tamara Hareven, "Urbanization and the Malleable Household," *Journal of Marriage and the Family*, 35 (August, 1973), pp. 467-479.

[32]Lisbeth A. Cohen, "Embellishing a Life of Labor: An Interpretation of the Material Culture of American Working-Class Homes, 1885-1915," in *Material Culture Studies in America*, ed. Thomas J. Schlereth (Nashville: The American Association for State and Local History, 1982), pp. 289-305. Cohen states that immigrant women furnished their homes according to the traditions of their homeland as well as imitating upper-class styles.

[33]For social mobility in the antebellum years see Edward Pessen, *Riches, Class and Power before the Civil War* (Lexington: Heath, 1973).

[34]Frances Trollope, *Domestic Manners of the Americans* (London, 1832; rpt. New York: Vintage Books, 1968), p. 338.

[35]George William Curtis, *The Potiphar Papers* (New York: Harper's, 1900), pp. 99-100.

[36]Anna Cora Mowatt Ritchie, *Fashion* (New York: S. French, 1849).

[37]Curtis, *The Potiphar Papers*, p. 100.

[38]Karen Halttunen, *Confidence Men and Painted Women, A Study of Middle-Class Culture in America, 1830-1870* (New Haven: Yale Univ. Press, 1982), pp. 56-91.

[39]William Dean Howells, *The Rise of Silas Lapham* (New York, 1884; rpt. Boston: Houghton Mifflin, 1912), p. 324.

[40]Mary Beth Norton, "The Evolution of White Women's Experience in Early America," *American Historical Review*, 89 (June 1984), pp. 593-619. For a discussion of the theory that women in the colonial period were better off than their nineteenth-century descendants.

[41]Harriet Beecher Stowe, *Household Papers and Stories, The Writings of Harriet Beecher Stowe*, VIII (Boston: Houghton Mifflin, 1896), p. 98.

[42]Ann Douglas, *The Feminization of American Culture* (New York: Knopf, 1977), chaps. 3,4.

[43]Jean Gordon, "Harriet Beecher Stowe and the Religion of Domesticity in a Consumer Society," unpublished paper given at the conference "Victorian Album, Aspects of American Life 1865-1900" sponsored by the Victorian Society in America and the National Archives, Washington, D.C., March 21-24, 1979.

[44]George Talbot, *At Home, Domestic Life in the Post-Centennial Era, 1876-1920* (Madison: The State Historical Society of Wisconsin, 1976), p. viii.

[45]Kenneth Ames, "Grand Rapids Furniture at the Time of the Centennial," *Winterthur Portfolio*, 10 (1975), pp. 23-50.

[46]David Katzman, *Seven Days a Week: Women and Domestic Service in Industrializing America* (New York: Oxford, 1978), p. 53.

[47]William Seele, *The Tasteful Interlude: American Interiors Through the Camera's Eye, 1860-1917* (New York: Praeger, 1975).

[48]This is the opinion of the authors. A discussion of the middle-class home as a utopian retreat can be found in Kirk Jeffrey, "The Family as Utopian Retreat from the City: The Nineteenth-Century Contribution," *Soundings*, 55 (1972), pp. 21-41; Clifford E. Clark, "Domestic Architecture as an Index to Social History: The Romantic Revival and the Cult of Domesticity in America, 1840-1870," *Journal of Interdisciplinary History, 7 (Summer 1976), pp. 33-56*.

[49]Kenneth Ames, "Grand Rapids Furniture at the Time of the Centennial," p. 31.

[50]John William Ferry, *A History of the Department Store*, American Assembly series (New York: Prentice-Hall, Inc., 1960); Lloyd Wendt and Herman Kogan, *Give the Lady What She Wants!* (Chicago: Rand McNally, 1952).

[51]Henry James, *The Bostonians* (New York, 1886; rpt. New York: Dial Press, 1945), p. 13.

[52]Edith Wharton, *The House of Mirth* (New York, 1905; rpt, New York: Scribner's, 1975), p. 10.

[53]Aline Saarinen, *The Proud Possessors: The Lives, Times and Tastes of Some Adventurous American Art Collectors* (New York: Random House, 1958).

[54]Thorstein Veblen, *The Theory of the Leisure Class* (New York, 1889; rpt. New York: Random House, 1934), chap. 6.

[55]Ruth Schwartz Cowan, *More Work for Mother* (New York: Basic Books, 1983), chap. 3. See also Susan Strasser, *Never Done, A History of American Housework* (New York: Pantheon Books, 1982); Daniel T. Rodgers, *The Work Ethic in Industrial America 1850-1920* (Chicago: Univ. of Chicago Press, 1974).

[56]John Kenneth Galbraith, *Economics and the Public Purpose* chaps. 4, 23.

[57]Faye E. Dudden, *Serving Women: Household Service in Nineteenth-Century America* (Middletown, Ct.: Wesleyan University Press, 1983); Daniel E. Sutherland, *Americans and Their Servants: Domestic Service in the United States 1800-1920* (Baton Rouge: Louisiana State Univ. Press, 1981).

[58]Katzman, *Seven Days a Week,* chap. 1.

[59]Catharine E. Beecher and Harriet Beecher Stowe, *The American Woman's Home* (Hartford: Stowe-Day Foundation, 1975), chap. 1.

[60]Dolores Hayden, *The Grand Domestic Revolution: A History of Feminist Designs for American Homes, Neighborhoods and Cities* (Cambridge: MIT Press, 1981), chap. 4.

[61]Gweldolyn Wright, *Moralism and the Model Home: Domestic Architecture and Cultural Conflict in Chicago, 1873-1913* (Chicago: Univ. of Chicago Press, 1980), chaps. 4-9.

[62]Kenneth R. Andrews, *Nook Farm, Mark Twain's Hartford Circle* (Cambridge: Harvard Univ. Press, 1950).

[63]Robert W. Winter, "The Arts and Crafts as a Social Movement," *Record of the Art Museum Princeton University,* 34 (1975), pp. 36-42; Robert C. Twombly, "Saving the Family: Middle-Class Attraction to Wright's Prairie House, 1901-1909," *American Quarterly,* 27 (March 1975), pp. 57-72.

[64]See for example the early twentieth century issues of *Good Housekeeping, Ladies Home Journal* and *Woman's Home Companion.*

[65]Maxine Seller, "The Education of the Immigrant Woman, 1900-1935," *Journal of Urban History,* 4 (May 1978), 307-30.

[66]Marjorie East, *Home Economics Past, Present and Future* (Boston: Allyn and Bacon, 1980).

[67]Ian Watt, *The Rise of the Novel: Studies in Defoe, Richardson and Fielding* (Berkeley: Univ. of California Press), chap. 6.

[68]Mary Terhune, "Eighty Years of Reminiscence," *Ladies Home Journal,* 37 (Oct. 1920), pp. 128-32.

[69]Adeline Whitney, *We Girls: A Home Story* (Boston: Osgood, 1874), p. 102.

[70]Daniel Sutherland, *Americans and Their Servants,* p. 198.

[71]Marion Harland, *The Distractions of Martha* (New York: Scribner's, 1906).

[72]*Ladies Home Journal,* 42 (August 1925), p. 128; *Ladies Home Journal,* 41 (March 1924), p. 132; *Ladies Home Journal,* 44 (April 1927), p. 1.

[73]Charles A. Thrall, "The Conservative Use of Modern Household Technology," *Technology and Culture,* 23 (April 1982), pp. 175-194.

[74]Stow Persons, *The Decline of American Gentility* (New York: Columbia Univ. Press, 1973).

[75]Stuart Ewen, *Captains of Consciousness: Advertising and the Social Roots of Consumer Culture* (New York: McGraw-Hill, 1976); Stephen Fox, *The Mirror Makers: A History of American Advertising and its Creators* (New York: Morrow, 1984).

[76]Daniel J. Boorstin, "Welcome to the Consumption Community," *Fortune,* 76 (Sept. 1967), pp. 118-138.

[77]"At Our Fair in Moscow," *Newsweek,* 54 (August 3, 1959), pp. 15-20.

Victorian Fancywork in the American Home: Fantasy and Accommodation

Beverly Gordon

Most commentators agree that "fancywork" was an important part of the lives of Victorian American women. By the mid 19th century, notes one contemporary observer, there was scarcely a middle class housewife who did not indulge in some form of this activity (Morris 7). This assertion is supported by evidence from the period. Fancywork "departments" appeared regularly in mid-century women's magazines, and a plethora of fancywork manuals were published at the same time. "Fancy fairs," where fancywork was sold for fundraising purposes, were popular events, and judging from the regular advertisements that suppliers ran in magazines and newspapers, fancywork supplies were in great demand.[1] There are also large numbers of surviving examples of fancy objects, indicating their one-time prevalence or ubiquity.

A satisfactory definition of fancywork is not easy to come by. Present-day popular dictionaries list the term (alternately written as one or two words) as a noun, and define it simply as decorative or ornamental needlework (*Webster's Seventh* 301; *New York Times* 248; *American Heritage* 489). The *Oxford English Dictionary* defines it a little more broadly, stating it is "ornamental, as opposed to plain, work, especially in needlework, crochet and knitting" (*Oxford English Dictionary*, vol. 4: 62); ornamental handcraft in other kinds of media is implied. Nineteenth century usage of the term fancywork was also inclusive, and not only sewn and stitched work but sculptural forms in shell, wax, molded leather, pine cones, fish scales, cardboard and other materials were sometimes referred to in this way. The boundaries of the term were then and are now unclear; there is no exact point where plain becomes ornamental, and few handwork forms that by definition could *not* be fancywork.

The question of definition might seem trivial, but the lack of clarity and precision surrounding the term is an indice both of the great many things that can be classified as fancywork, and of the cavalier or disdainful attitude generally taken to the whole subject. Contemporary scholars speak of this "useless" handwork as a waste of time and intelligence, and as "horrific" and "desperate" "dabbling" (Warren 16; Lichten 170; Green 147). Some late 19th century commentators decried "mere" fancywork, which they did not consider as tasteful as artistic embroidery, and argued that fancywork expressed "little individuality."[2] Epithets used to describe fancywork in the middle of the 19th century also add to present-day disdain or dismissal: words like "trifles," "frivolities," and airy nothings" were used rather fondly and lovingly in *Godey's Lady's Book* and other women's magazines, but have been taken more literally and looked at more disparagingly by subsequent generations that do not perceive them in the same positive way.

Since fancywork was such a ubiquitous feature of Victorian life and was so integral to women's culture of the period, it is important to examine not only the term but the phenomenon and the objects themselves with more care. This paper explores the meanings of fancywork to the mid-19th-century American woman. It reviews the types of objects that were made and the ways in which both the objects and the time spent in making them were part of the accepted image of women and woman's role. It argues that given a limited, constricted arena of acceptable activity and behavior, women's "airy trifles" and "fancies" were imaginative expressions of amusement and play, fantasy, escape and transformation. Specific examples of fancy objects are analyzed in light of this thesis.

An examination of women's magazines and advice manuals published between 1850 and 1880[3] indicates that ornamented objects characterized as fancywork were all artifacts of the domestic sphere. Three main categories emerge, and all three can be further classified as accessories or embellishments—there were personal accessories or embellishments, household accessories or embellishments, and sewing or writing accessories which were themselves embellished.

Instructions for personal accessories were usually limited to small items for women and children, such as bags and purses, handkerchief and glove cases, and ornamented hair combs. Where men's accessories were indicated, they were typically items to be used in the home, such as embroidered smoking caps and slippers, or pockets in which to place watches when not in use. Although trimmings for major garments were sometimes listed, instructions were generally only given for small clothing items such as aprons and hoods.[4]

Household accessories ranged from flat textiles such as table covers, doilies, "tidies" and antimacassars (small furniture coverings ostensibly designed to protect the upholstery from Macassar hair oil); to receptacles constructed of cloth and pasteboard or wood that were hung on the wall and made to hold such diverse items as haircombings, brushes and newspapers; to three dimensional free-standing objects such as firescreens and ottomans. There were also ornaments or "decorations" (wreaths or bouquets of shell, wool or wax flowers, for example) that were framed to hang on the wall or were mounted under glass domes.

The third category, sewing and writing accessories, can be seen as a cross between the first two categories, for objects such as sewing and writing cases, workbags, boxes, needlebooks, pincushions, inkstand mats, letter racks and penwipers were both used by individuals and displayed as ornaments in the home.

The blurred distinction between personal and household use in most of these ornamented handmade fancy objects is appropriate and informative, for there was a concomitant blurred distinction in the mid-19th century between women and the home. In response to the rapid changes that were occurring through industrialization and urbanization, there was a greater separation of the domestic and public realms, and the family home became imbued with a new ideology. It was seen as a retreat or sanctuary, an oasis or refueling station from the "outside" (male) world of commerce and industry. It was a "separate sphere," a private domain which was in many ways a world unto itself (Lerner 109; Cott 64; Humphrey 16; Smith-Rosenberg 311-342; "Sphere of Woman").

Women were the overseers of this domain, and were responsible for its upkeep and wellbeing. In the rhetoric of the day, it was "proper" and "natural" that women fill this role, for they had naturally high moral values and could act as a countervailing force to the evil, exploitative, pecuniary values of the workplace (Cott 68, 84; Green 93; Epstein 81). "It is woman who informs the home with light and life," proclaimed Laura Holloway in her household manual, *The Hearthstone; or Life at Home.* "Her touch is that of a purifying, transforming and beautiful angel" (Holloway 33).[5]

Fancywork was an integral part of woman's mission in the home. Ornamentation was generally positively thought of in the early part of the Victorian era; if an item was plain it was unremarkable, but once decorated and embellished, it became beautiful, elegant, and good. A morally uplifting home needed morally uplifting—i.e., beautiful and elegant—objects; they exerted an ennobling and uplifting influence by their very presence, and benefited residents and visitors alike. Part of woman's task in home-building was to provide these objects, to "beautify the walls and enshrine...the kindly arts within them" (Lichten 119, 192; Green 93-94; Holloway 33).

All ornamented fancywork was beneficial, but instructive objects that manifested qualities of the natural world and brought its edifying lessons into the family parlor were particularly helpful. Fancywork constructed or embellished with shells, fish-scales, moss, pine cones, seaweed and similar materials can be understood as domestic expressions of a Victorian interest in natural history (Green 93-97; Winkler and Moss 49).[6]

A woman who filled her home with tasteful and instructive fancywork could not only ennoble her family but also demonstrate to the world that she herself was noble and virtuous. Many fancy goods were made from available materials—moss from the woods, sprays of lavender from the garden, or most importantly, odds and ends from the scrapbag (Green 100). "We are continually requested by our subscribers to issue designs for small articles...which will cost nothing to make," noted *Godey's* fancywork editor in April, 1867 ("Pincushion" 165).

Womanly virtue was seen not only in the fancywork objects, but also in the very act of doing or making fancywork. *Godey's* expressed the prevailing social norm when it claimed that "the mind of the idle, like the garden of the slothful, will be overgrown with briars and weeds...indolence is a dangerous enemy" (Lichten 170). In *Like and Unlike* novelist Mary Braddon indicated how strongly individual women felt that they must keep—or appear to keep—busy. The protagonist was "not very fond of needlework, but she felt constrained to put on an air of occupation in the long wet afternoons, lest her future mother-in-law take offence [sic] at her idleness" (84). If one wanted to appear to be both busy and genteel, it was especially appropriate to be seen doing ornamental or *fancy* work. "To the early Victorian eye—especially the masculine eye," Frances Lichten asserts, "nothing presented a more appealing picture than a lady working at her embroidery frame." Victorian women "relished" the "little tableaux of elegant leisure [they] created for [their] audiences" (117). Fancywork and related artistic pursuits were acceptable because they were "light" handcrafts rather than serious "fine" art; they were amateur rather than professional pastimes, and were suitable to the home environment, which was not a sphere of professional activity (Green 147).[8]

It would be inaccurate and demeaning to imply that fancywork was not a satisfying creative activity for many women. Periodical features on fancywork, especially earlier in the period, did not typically include precise patterns or instructions, and it was assumed that there would be individual experimentation and variation in many cases. "The forms of all sorts of fancy ornaments may be infinitely varied—we shall merely give examples of the general principles," stated *Godey's* in 1860 (165). It was commendable to be able to work from the illustrated examples. In its description of a dog-shaped penwiper in 1867, *Godey's* concluded, "a lady with clever fingers will no doubt be able to make it up herself" (367). When a woman placed her hand-wrought pieces in her home, then, she might well have been making a statement about her personal creativity as well as her womanly virtues. Fancywork filled the time, and it could be relaxing. "Even a woman of the intellectual prowess of George Sand," exclaimed *The Decorator and Furnisher* magazine in 1889, found it soothing. Sand remarked, "I think [needlework] has a natural attraction for women, an invisible charm which I felt at every period in my life, and which has often tranquilized my strongest agitation" (19).[9]

The personal, positive relationship that at least some women had with fancywork is also related to the fact that fancy objects were given and received as gifts. Even Queen Victoria recorded in her childhood diary giving a pincushion to her governess and a seaweed album to the Queen of Portugal, and receiving a pincushion from her maid (Lichten 8). Adults exchanged gifts as well. "Household Elegancies," an 1877 fancywork instruction supplement to *Harper's Bazar*, for example, was advertised as a source of the "best of Christmas presents to your lady friends" (Jan. 6). In another Christmas issue *Harper's* explained that a woman's advantage in gift giving was that she could give handmade items, "something that breathes of the qualities and tastes of the giver" (Dec. 20, 1879, 806). Smith-Rosenberg has shown that such gifts were an integral part of the Victorian woman's culture and were expressions of the strongly valued friendships between women (Smith-Rosenberg 320). *Harper's Bazar* also spoke of the sentimental value particular pieces of fancywork might hold if they were associated with a particular individual:

> It is not for what they tell of us to outsiders, though, that we want our pretty trifles; they answer a requirement of our own, and give us a gratification that renews itself every time we look at them, . . . given by the . . . precious histories they hold (June 2, 1877, 338-339).

In sum, women found needlework and fancywork both confining or limiting and personally meaningful, sometimes creatively so. This seeming contradiction is echoed on several levels. For example, fancywork was commonly referred to as "useful and ornamental work"—an inherently contradictory phrase. No clear definition of either "useful" or "ornamental" is available, and the words were primarily used together as a pair. The implication is that fancy objects could be used, but were still highly decorative. We might classify items such as tidies and "duster covers" as unnecessary ornaments, but the Victorian woman definitely considered them useful, and considered the time that went into their production well spent. What seem to our eyes to be mismatches of form and function in Victorian fancywork (see Figure 1) can also be understood in this light; if the object had an ostensible purpose of any kind, it was both ornamental *and* useful. Lichten speaks of a particularly American (as opposed to British) conflict between the Puritan work ethic and the new leisure of the Victorian middle classes (170), and the idea seems well illustrated in the "useful and ornamental" epithet.

Fig. 1 This "work case" was to be made of a dried pumpkin (probably a gourd) that was hollowed out and dressed with ribbon and cording. It was featured in *Godey's* in October, 1870.

The very word fancywork is also a contradiction in terms, and another reflection of the ambivalent Victorian attitude about women and work. Women did of course work, but given the strong distinction and separation made at the time between the outside world of work and the inside world of the home, women were by definition not "workers" and their tasks carried other names. The only work that was acknowledged as such was light, ornamental and non-pecuniary—i.e. needlework or fancywork. Fancywork features in the periodicals were called "work sections," "work departments," or "work baskets." Cooking and cleaning advice columns were never referred to this way—they were "household" departments— and since childrearing was considered more a holy mission than a job (a woman was a "benediction" for her children; the home she made for them was an "altar" or a "temple" (Holloway 356), the word "work" did not appear in commentary about mothering either. At mid-century agricultural fairs, "Woman's Work" displays included the familiar cushions, stool covers, needlecases, and ornamental wreaths, and local newspapers printed lists of these objects under the same heading.[10] In

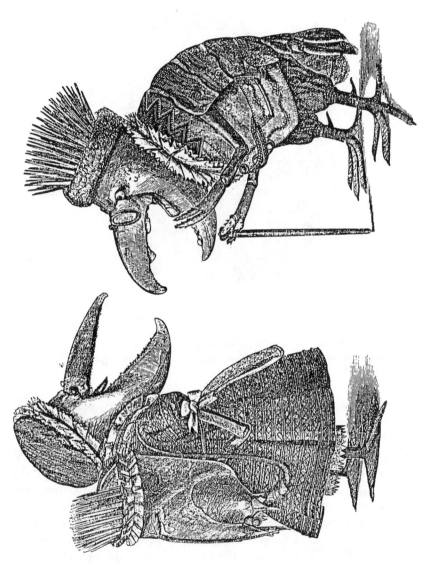

Fig. 2 Bright red lobster shells were dressed in cheerful fabric and designed to hold toothpicks or matches. This design appeared in *Godey's* in May, 1867.

other words, women may have milked the cows or otherwise tended the livestock on display at the fairs, and they may have contributed significantly to the crops, but such outside activities were man's work; woman's work was done inside, with a needle.

The other half of the fancywork term—the fancy part—is also worth examining more closely. *The Oxford English Dictionary* lists several definitions for the word that relate strongly to the underlying meanings of Victorian fancywork. A fancy is, firstly, a fantasy or mental conception, an illusion of the senses or a hallucination; in early use the term was synonymous with the word imagination. It is also defined as a whim or supposition resting on no solid ground; as something that pleases or entertains; as an invention; and as something "bred" or made into a more beautiful form. If something is "fancied" to be like something else, lastly, it is transformed (*Oxford English Dictionary* 60-62).

Nineteenth century epithets such as "airy (or little) nothings," "trifles," "pretty fancies," and "superfluities" imply that fancywork objects were seen as whims—as ephemeral things that did not quite "rest on solid ground." Many objects were made of the most ephemeral of materials: of paper, straw or gauze net, for example, or of egg, lobster or crab shell (Figure 2). Several guidebooks gave instructions for making skeletonized (phantom) leaves—treating leaves to a series of fermentation baths so that the soft tissue would decompose and the vein structure remain intact (Urbino, Jones and Williams, Howe 123, 134-135). This involved a process which was anything but ephemeral, as it was necessary to tend pots full of foul-smelling solutions for long periods of time, but the effect was an other-worldly, fairy-like leaf that seemed to have little substance.

There were also ephemeral motifs. One of the most frequently suggested images for embroidery designs, wall pockets and pincushions was the butterfly (Figure 3). No image could more clearly symbolize flights of fancy and non earth-bound matter.

The miniature cottage suggested in *Godey's* in April, 1867 as a receptacle "for wafers, pins, pens, etc." (462) (Figure 4) was not quite so ethereal as the phantom leaf or the flitting butterfly, but it typified the predilection for fanciful objects and the use of less than solid material. Perforated cardboard (actually about the weight of the paper used for manila file folders) was popular as a ground for woolwork (what would now be called canvaswork or needlepoint), and was typically used for bookmarks and preprinted frameable mottoes. It could also be used for "trifles" like the cottage. The base of the pictured cottage was only two by two and a quarter inches, and the whole piece was approximately four inches high. It was stitched with colored silk, and steel beads were added to the roof to serve as "little stones." There was a trellis on the "little balcony," and trellis, balcony, gallery and chimney could be added

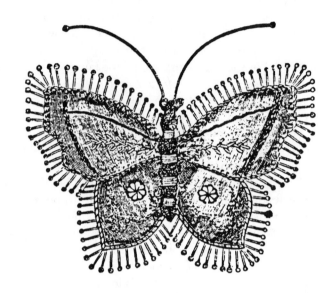

BUTTERFLY PIN-CUSHION.

Fig. 3 Two related designs for butterfly-shaped pincushions—one appeared in *Godey's* and the other in *Peterson's* in 1870. Straight pins were inserted in the edges of the cushion to add to the airy effect.

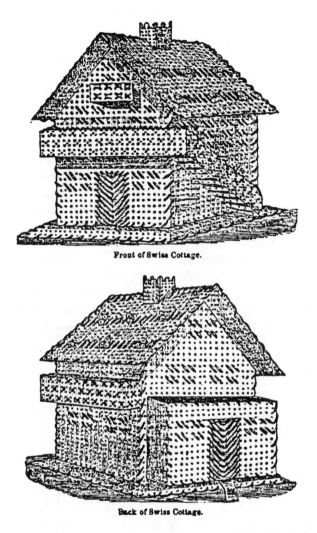

Front of Swiss Cottage.

Back of Swiss Cottage.

Fig. 4 This design for a miniature Swiss cottage was published in *Godey's* in May, 1867. It was to be made of perforated cardboard, silk thread, and beads. Ostensibly, it could hold pins, pens, or wafers.

"according to fancy." The house could be opened by the bottom ribbon loop.

A cottage of this sort is the epitome of a Victorian fancy. A large, solid building has been miniaturized and translated into a material that is totally antithetical to the original, as it is flimsy and literally full of holes. The type of building that is represented is romantic and exotic (it is foreign) as well as cozy (it is a cottage). Particularly romantic detailing—the balcony, the roof stones, the overhanging roof and the trellis—has been retained; other, more practical detailing is left out. The building has been totally tamed and domesticated, in other words; it has been reduced in power as it is now just a "little box,"[11] and it has been "feminized" as it is no longer stone and mortar but paper and silk.[12] It is clearly ornamental, but is ostensibly useful as well.

Other man-made objects were also domesticated as they were translated into fancywork (a suitcase and a shield were worked as needlecases, a bell was softened into a penwiper, and a coffee mill was made as a tape-measure case), and natural phenomena were domesticated as well. Taking a leaf from the forest and transforming it into an airy phantom is a form of domestication, as is taking apart a pine cone or skinning a fish and using the scales to construct a flower ornament.

The "coral" ornaments that appeared in *Peterson's* in the 1870s (in addition to the flower pot case illustrated in Figure 5, a chimney ornament appeared a short time earlier) (Mlle. Roche, Feb. 1861, 167; Mlle. Roche, June 1861, 498) indicate domestication of a slightly different sort. This was not actual, but "fancy" or simulated coral. To a wire base, wax tinted with Chinese vermillion was poured over the framework, and cotton cords were arranged on it in a branching fashion. A second coat of wax was applied, and moss was arranged as a lining inside the wire structure. Nature was used, therefore, primarily as a model or a suggestion; the fancy coral could be "better" than the natural variety—it could be fashioned to the whim of the maker, and behave as she wanted it to. Such coral was truly "fancied," or bred into a "more beautiful" form. An actual natural material, moss, was also used, but it was taken out of its natural context and then used in a totally unnatural manner (moss does not grow where coral does). The flowerpot cover was indeed a flight of fancy or imagination. It, like the paper cottage, was both ornamental and useful.

Many fancywork objects played on the theme of transformation and masquerade. As in the case of the coral, one material was made to appear as another. Wool might be crocheted so as to imitate fur, for example, or sheared so as to imitate moss. *Trompe-l'oeil* was carried quite far. In the case of the imitation moss, a popular effect for table mats in the 1850s and 1860s, the ends of the sheared wool were singed to create the effect of brown-tipped ends. Imitation soda crackers were popular

CORAL CASE FOR FLOWER-POTS.

BY MADEMOISELLE ROCHE.

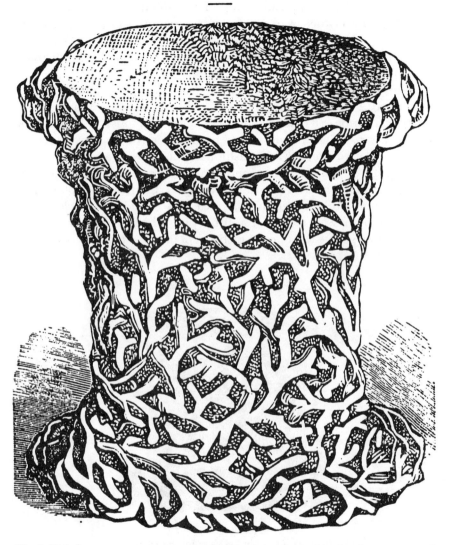

Fig. 5 This flowerpot cover was made of cotton string covered in tinted wax, arranged so as to simulate coral. It appeared in *Peterson's* in June, 1861.

about 1880. These were made of lightly padded white silk, stitched at intervals to imitate the indentations of the cracker, and scorched slightly to imitate the edges browned in the baking process (*Godey's*, Jan. 1870, 84; Howe 158; "Favors for Luncheon," 138; "About the Dressing Table," 286). Wax and leather were molded to simulate flower petals, bulrush pith was carved in imitation of ivory, and plain glass vases were transformed into imitation fine china by the application of glued pictures and paint on the inside.[13]

One object was also made to appear—was disguised or transformed—as another. A penwiper was typically "dressed" as something else, for example; it appeared "in the form of" a rat or mouse, a butterfly, a parasol, a cap, a sheaf of wheat, or a footwarmer. A matchbox appeared in the shape of a drum, and a pincushion masqueraded as a boot, ottoman, brush, beetle or fish (Figures 6-8). Everyday objects were also given new meanings when they were put in new contexts. Lobsters, pumpkins and other kitchen familiars were transformed into "wondrous articles" that had never been seen before. A rolling pin, which according to *The Delineator* magazine was once "a plebeian of the most pronounced type,"

Fig. 6 Many fancy objects were in "fancy dress'— i.e., they were one object in the form of another. The object illustrated here, a matcholder in the shape of a drum (*Godey's*, December, 1876); indicates the playful nature of this transformation.

PARASOL PEN-WIPER.

BY MRS. JANE WEAVER.

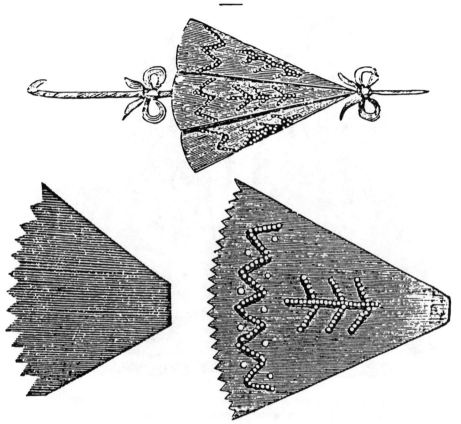

Fig. 7 The penwiper in the shape of a parasol that appeared in *Peterson's* in October, 1865 can be seen as a type of doll accessory.

THE "LITTLE COMPANION."

BY MRS. JANE WEAVER.

Fig. 8 This "little companion" was little more than a dressed doll outfitted as a sewing accessory. It is typical of the "amusing" fancywork that can be understood as toys. The design appeared in *Peterson's* in January, 1865.

was transformed into "a decided aristocrat" in a "satin robe." It had been made into a dressing table ornament from which gloves and shoe buttoners could be hung, and it was almost unrecognizable as a kitchen tool ("About the Dressing Table," 286).

Transformation and masquerade of this type must be understood as an exercise in fantasy, as an amusing theatrical game. Just as masquerade parties or "fancy dress" balls were popular entertainments in the public sphere in the Victorian era (Stevenson and Bennett), "masquerade" fancywork was a popular entertainment in the private, domestic sphere. Masks and costumes allowed partygoers to try on new identities and experiment with different parts of themselves. A "masked" object—an object in fancy dress—did not allow the woman who worked and lived with it to become someone else, but it did reflect her predilection for fantasy and her desire to play with reality and go beyond the confines of what was possible. Fancywork was a symbol and a mirror of the desire for something beyond the mundane and repetitive reality of domestic life.

The element of play was significant. Masquerades and transformations were amusing. Sewing may have been work, but sewing or otherwise fashioning fancy objects was a fanciful and playful type of work—these objects were quite literally amusements. Some were closely akin to toys. A miniature Swiss cottage was like a dollhouse; a penwiper fashioned as a parasol or a sewing emery fashioned as a sailor hat were like doll's accessories. A mouse or dog penwiper was made by simply attaching extra pieces of cloth to a toy stuffed animal.

Actual dolls were incorporated into many fancy objects. Jane Weaver's design for a doll pincushion, featured in *Peterson's* in 1865 (209), and an uncredited design for a fancy penwiper, featured in *Godey's* in 1860 ("Fancy Pen Wiper," 66), were typical in that they incorporated doll parts (Weaver's instructions read: "Get a small china doll [and] break off the legs;" *Godey's* instructions read, "Take the head of a doll...") and "dressed" figures. In 1865 *Peterson's* also featured a sewing accessory doll—a combination pincushion, thread and needle holder, and scissors scabbard—which was expressly titled a "little companion" (Figure 8). This was another of Jane Weaver's designs (79). These items could be given to children, and girls were encouraged to do fancywork,[14] but because the objects were useful and contributed to the proper atmosphere of the home, they were primarily adult toys, and were not thought of as juvenile.

Toys and amusements take on great importance when one is confined, for they help not only to pass the time but, by stimulating the imagination, to transport the player to other times and places. It is significant in this regard that the only time fancywork objects were regularly made by men is when the men were confined also. Ornamental needlework pictures were made in the 19th century by sailors who could not leave their ships for long periods of time. These men also carved fanciful pie crimpers and similar playful gadgets, and workbags and other sewing accessories (Hansen; Flayderman). The *Oxford English Dictionary* specifically referred to fancywork done on whaling voyages in its sentence illustrating usage of the term (62). Male prisoners, especially prisoners of war, also produced fancywork. In *Collecting Georgian and Victorian Antiques* Field notes that the majority of fine straw-work available today was made by prisoners of war (28). Prisoner of war and hospital inmate work was also featured at large scale fancy fairs during the Civil War and World War I (*History of the Northwest Soldiers' Fair* 51; *The Bazaar Daily*, Dec. 16, 1916, 2).

If we move beyond our 20th century viewfinder, we can appreciate the poignancy in fancywork objects. Women, the primary producers of fancywork, were keepers of the home, and for practical purposes in the middle of the 19th century were largely confined to it. Their confinement was seen as a noble one, however, and they were portrayed in their own time as people who could create an oasis and a sanctuary; they were transformative beings. When *The Hearthstone* reminded its readers that woman's touch was transformative, it proclaimed woman could "wave her magic wand like Cinderella's fairy godmother," and the home could be a "true fairy tale" (Holloway 33-34). Fancywork objects of the type illustrated here show us that women did indeed try to wave a magic wand, but much of their transformative effort was directed to the small-scale objects and materials over which they had complete control—objects of the domestic sphere and objects that were accessories to, but not perpetrators of, life's major dramas. If we return to the dressed lobster match holder or the ornamented rolling pin, we see the narrow range in which the transformation was apt to take place.

We must, however, give full credit to the transformative vision. Geoffrey Warren and other contemporary observers may see fancywork as a waste of intelligence and a sign of limited imagination (Warren 16-17), but it can also be understood as a silent testimony to the irrepressibility of humor and play, fantasy, and *un*limited imagination. Fancywork involved long hours of painstaking effort and in many ways epitomized the confinement it was a part of, but it was an inventive form, and represented an escape from confinement. Women who engaged in fancywork were fulfilling or accomodating their obligation to create a moral and edifying home, but at the same time were, at least symbolically, creating a different and less constrained reality. Fancywork must be accepted on its own terms and understood in its 19th century context as an expression of escape and transformation.

Notes

[1]See for example *Godey's Lady's Book, Peterson's Magazine,* and *Harper's Bazar,* especially in the period between 1840 and 1880. See *Ladies Work Table Book,* Florence Hartley, Mrs. Pullan, Levina Urbino, Mrs. C.S. Jones, Henry T. Williams and Annie Frost. See also Beverly Gordon (144-160). Gordon is also working on a book on fundraising fairs which should be published in 1989.

[2]Despite Church's proclamation and the popularity of the term "art needlework," much of the embroidery Church and other proponents of the artistic or Arts and Crafts styles produced was still generally known as fancywork (Church intro.).

[3]Advice or instruction manuals that were consulted are listed in miscellaneous citations. Three periodicals geared to upwardly mobile middle class women, *Godey's Lady's Book, Peterson's Magazine* (the title varied somewhat over the years) and *Harper's Bazar,* were surveyed systematically. The periodical survey consisted of a thorough examination of the "make-it" or "work" sections of an entire year's issues at five year intervals. In the years where all three periodicals were available (*Harper's* only began publication in 1867), therefore, each issue of each magazine from 1860, 1865, 1870, etc., was examined. In a few cases the appropriate volume of *Godey's* or *Peterson's* was unavailable to me (e.g. *Godey's* 1860) but the next possible volume (e.g. *Godey's* 1861) was substituted. Other periodicals such as *Decorator and Furnisher* magazine were also perused on a less systematic basis.

For a discussion of the importance and influences of these magazines in the lives of Victorian women, see Helen Woodward and James Playsted Wood.

I am fully aware of the distinction between proscriptive literature such as that found in the magazines and an accurate assessment of what was actually made. The only way to track the range of fancywork, however, was to systematically follow this literature throughout the period under discussion; if the study were limited to an analysis of selected objects, it would be impossible to know how representative they are. My own research on fancy fairs (in progress) has indicated, furthermore, that there was a close correlation between what was suggested in the women's press and what was actually done in communities across America.

[4]I use the word accessory advisedly. Since "fancy" stitches and decoration could be applied to dresses, jackets and other major elements of dress, and instructions for such needlework were sometimes included, my distinction could be seen to be a false one. Many middle class women had dresses prepared for them by dressmakers, however, and were more likely to work only on accessories and small elements of dress. As the ensuing discussion will make clear, furthermore, the meaning of major articles of clothing and of fancy work was quite different.

[5]See also Catherine Beecher and Harriet Beecher Stowe.

[6]See also C.S. Jones and Henry T. Williams.

[7]See also "Odds & Ends of Fancy Work" (397).

[8]See also Anthea Callen (219) and Rozsika Parker and Griselda Pollock.

[9]Lichten even refers to fancywork as the "occupational therapy of its day" (171). This attitude perpetuates the bias against both fancywork and the validity of such therapy.

[10]See for example "Agricultural Fair Proceedings" (1).

[11]Experimental research on the effect of scale manipulation has indicated that miniaturization increases one's sense of control and alters one's perception of time. See Alton J. DeLong. The butterfly in Figure 3 appeared in *Peterson's,* April, 1870 (261). The coral case in Figure 5 appeared in *Peterson's* June, 1861 (488).

[12]Soft materials were (and still are) thought of as female, and hard materials as male; even today, it is considered extraordinary if a woman is a stone carver or a metal caster. Green captures the idea of this perceived "natural" order when he remarks that in the Victorian home "the female realm of decorative textiles covered and softened the usually wooden [and metal] forms wrought by the male world of machines and commerce" (111). The great majority of fancywork objects discussed in the literature were cases and covers (even a scent bottle was given a "cozy"), and Warren's comment (59) that the Victorians' "need to surround themselves with possessions of this kind was like a shield of protection against the stark realities of the outside world" is congruent with the thesis presented here.

[13]Imitation flowers and fruit appear in nearly every volume of the periodicals and in every instruction manual. Molded leather flowers are discussed at length in Jones and Williams, chap. 6. Pithwork is discussed in Howe (157). See Lichten (172), Howe (157-158) for a discussion of the imitation china work known as potichomanie.

A case can be made for the fact that fancywork was a leveling or democratizing influence. Even relatively poor women could produce "elegancies" for their home when fabric scraps, bulrush pith and the like were all that were needed in the way of materials. Although the display of fancywork is often equated with a display of socioeconomic status because it would seem that only leisured women would have the time to engage in such pursuits (Green 148), it is overly simplistic to make a simple correlation of this sort. Lichten cites an unidentified New England writer of the 1850's who recalls a servant girl in a farm household who worked on potichomanie and similar activities in her spare time (172). By the 1870's "cheap luxury" was a theme discussed at length in the periodicals (Winkler and Moss 51). See the "Economical Home Decorations" column in *Decorator and Furnisher* magazine, (December 1883, 89).

I include this discussion of democratization in a footnote rather than the body of the text because I consider the issue of social class to be almost irrelevant to my thesis. All women were defined according to the same ideology, and fancywork reflected the same fantasy and imaginative escape for all of them.

[14]There were occasional columns for children (girls) in the women's magazines, and some manuals (e.g. Jones and Williams) had special children's sections. Children also ran their own juvenile fancy fairs during this period. See Mary Livermore (152-153); New England Hospital for Women and Children, *Annual Reports* 1876, 1889.

Works Cited

"About the Dressing Table." *The Delineator* (May, 1885).

Agricultural Fair Proceedings," *Northhampton* [Massachusetts] *Courier* 18 Oct. 1845: 1.

The American Heritage Dictionary. New College ed. Boston: Houghton Mifflin, 1976.

The Bazaar Daily 7 (Dec. 16, 1916) [National Allied Bazaar, New York City].

Beecher, Catharine and Stowe, Harriet Beecher. *The American Woman's Home, or, Principles of Domestic Science.* New York: J.B. Ford Co., 1869.

Braddon, Mary Elizabeth. *Like & Unlike.* London: Simpkin and Marshall, 1887.

Callen, Anthea. *Women Artists of the Arts and Crafts Movement 1870-1914.* New York: Pantheon Books, 1979.

Church, Ella Rodman. *Artistic Embroidery.* New York: Adams and Bishop, 1880.

Cott, Nancy F. *The Bonds of Womanhood: Woman's Sphere in New England 1780-1835.* New Haven: Yale University Press, 1977.

Decorator and Furnisher 15 (Oct. 1889).

DeLong, Alton J. "Phenomenological Space-Time: Toward an Experiential Relativity." *Science* 213 (Aug. 1981).

"Fancy Pen Wiper." *Godey's Lady's Book* 60 (July 1860).

"Favors for Luncheon." *Decorator and Furnisher* (July 1884).

Flayderman, Norman E. *Scrimshaw and Scrimshanders, Whales and Whalemen.* New Milford, Ct.: N. Flayderman, 1972.

Frost, Annie. *The Ladies Guide to Needlework, Embroidery, etc. (Being a Complete Guide to All Kinds of Ladies Fancy Work).* New York: Henry T. Williams, 1877.

Godey's Lady's Book 59 (Feb. 1860).

———. 74 (April 1867).

———. 80 (Jan. 1870).

Gordon, Beverly. "Playing at Being Powerless: New England Ladies Fairs, 1830-1930." *Massachusetts Review* 27 (Spring, 1986): 144-160.

Green, Harvey. *The Light of the Home: An Intimate View of the Lives of Women in Victorian America.* New York: Pantheon Books, 1983.

Hansen, Hans Jurgen, ed. *Art and The Seafarer—A Historical Survey of The Arts and Crafts of Sailors and Shipwrights.* Trans. James and Inge Moore. New York: Viking Press, 1968.

Harper's Bazar 10 (Jan. 6, 1877).

———. 12 (Dec. 20, 1879).

———. 10 (June 2, 1877).

Hartley, Florence. *Ladies Handbook of Fancy Work.* Philadelphia: G.G. Evans, 1859.

History of the Northwest Soldiers' Fair. Chicago: Dunlop, Sewell and Spalding, 1864.

Holloway, Laura C. *The Hearthstone; or, Life at Home: A Household Manual.* Chicago and Philadelphia: L.P. Miller, 1888.

Humphrey, Herman. *Domestic Education.* Amherst, Mass.: J.S. and C. Adams, 1840, cited in Barbara Leslie Epstein, *The Politics of Domesticity: Women, Evangelism and Temperance in Nineteenth Century America.* Middletown, Ct.: Wesleyan University Press, 1981.

Jones, C.S. and Williams, Henry T. *Household Elegancies.* New York: Henry T. Williams, 1875.

Ladies' Fancy Work, Hints and Helps to Home Taste and Recreations. New York: Henry T. Williams, 1876.

Ladies Work Table Book. Philadelphia: G.B. Zeiber, 1845.

Lerner, Gerda. "Just a Housewife." *The Female Experience: An American Documentary.* Indianapolis: Bobbs-Merrill, 1977.

Lichten, Frances. *Decorative Art of Victoria's Era.* New York: Charles Scribner's Sons, 1950.

Livermore, Mary. *My Story of the War: A Woman's Narrative of Four Years Personal Experience.* (Hartford: A.D. Worthington, 1888).

Morris, Barbara. *Victorian Embroidery.* New York: Thomas Nelson and Sons, 1962.

The Oxford English Dictionary. 4 vols. 1933. Oxford: Clarendon Press, 1961.

New England Hospital for Women and Children. *Annual Reports* 1876, 1889.

The New York Times Everyday Dictionary. New York: New York Times, 1982.

"Odds & Ends of Fancy Work." Work Department, *Godey's Lady's Book* 111 (Oct. 1885).

Parker, Rozsika and Pollock, Griselda. *Old Mistresses: Women, Art and Ideology.* New York: Pantheon Books, 1981.

"Pincushion." Work Department. *Godey's Lady's Book* 74 (August 1867).

Pullan, Mrs. *The Lady's Manual of Fancy Work*. New York: Dick and Fitzgerald, 1859.

"The Sphere of Woman."*Godey's Lady's Book* 39 (March 1850).

Smith-Rosenberg, Carroll. "The Female World of Love and Ritual: Relations Between Women in Nineteenth Century America." *A Heritage of Her Own: Toward a New Social History of Women*. Ed. Nancy F. Cott and Elizabeth Pleck: New York: Simon and Schuster, 1979.

Stevenson, Sara and Bennett, Helen. *Van Dyck in Check Trousers: Fancy Dress in Art and Life 1700-1900*. Edinburgh: Scottish National Portrait Gallery, 1978.

"Swiss Cottage," *Godey's Lady's Book* 74 (April, 1867).

Urbino, Levina. *Art Recreations*. Boston: J.E. Tilton, 1860.

Warren, Geoffrey. *A Stitch in Time: Victorian and Edwardian Needlecraft*. New York: Taplinger, 1976.

Weaver, Jane. "Doll Pin-cushion." *Peterson's* 48 (Sept. 1865).

———. "The Little Companion." *Peterson's* 47 (Jan. 1865).

Webster's Seventh New Collegiate Dictionary. Springfield, Mass: G. and C. Merriam, 1970.

Winkler, Gail Caskey and Moss, Roger. "Exploring Grandmother's Parlor." *Historic Preservation* (March-April, 1983).

Wood, James Playsted. *Magazines in the United States* New York: Ronald Press, 1949, 1971.

Woodward, Helen. New York: Ivan Obolensky, 1960.

The American Front Porch: Women's Liminal Space

Sue Bridwell Beckham

> *Sitting on the Porch*
> An event, in those days
> for which one freshened up.
> The houses were close to the street
> and to sit on the porch
> meant to be accessible
> to visit, to chat and receive,
> to be public and on display.
> My grandmother did not
> sit on the porch
> before four o'clock
> but sometimes stayed there
> through sweet summer evenings.
> And when I was with her
> I thought of it as
> an occasion. (Easter 15)

Every evening of a summer, after supper dishes were done, my mother-in-law insisted that the whole household gather on the front porch to "cool off." The ritual made good sense before her husband persuaded her to let him install air conditioners in their Mississippi home, but long after the house was kept at a comfortable 70 degrees, Ms. Beckham continued to insist that we all troop out on the porch after supper to cool off. Whenever I tried to beg off because I wished to read a book or watch a television show, the lady was convinced that nothing less than a rift with some family member would keep anybody indoors. And she was equally certain that whatever pique there was would disappear once I occupied a rocker on the front porch and communed with the group. Clearly, her faith in the ministry of the porch went deeper than relief from the heat. The porch for my mother-in-law was, as it was for Mary Easter, author of the poem above, and her grandmother, a ritual space. For those women, it was a space which met certain largely female needs, a space which, like a church, required compliance with certain forms for maximum benefit—and also, like a church, permitted the casting off of other social forms in order to realize a largely hidden self.

While virtually all American porches owe their architectural being to forms developed in other cultures, the American front porch is a peculiarly American institution. The earliest porches in recorded history were ceremonial. Porticoes on Greek temples and on the ceremonial buildings of America's Mississippian Indians alike blurred boundaries between the populace outside and the high priests performing their rituals in the inner sanctum. They were bridges between the sacred and the profane from which the highly revered could speak with the lowly and on which they could perform public rites for untutored—or unsanctified—audiences on the outside. It is far in space and time from Greek temples and pre-Columbian Indians to the porches on American houses and yet, unless the function were somewhat similar, my mother-in-law would not have placed so much faith in her porch and its restorative power. Nor would Mary Easter have recalled the ritual of freshening up at the appropriate time of day for the "occasion" of sitting on the porch.

Those authors, particularly women, who write of the American experience have long been aware that a ritual significance attaches to the front porch; the absence of direct allusion to that significance, however, suggests the realization to have been subconscious. In *The Ballad of the Sad Cafe*, for example, Carson McCullers recounts the peculiar use her protagonist, Miss Amelia Evans, made of her porch. Having lost her mother in early childhood and her father at the vulnerable age of nineteen, Miss Amelia, six feet tall and utterly masculine in build, had not learned—or chosen to acknowledge—the womanly virtues, but implicitly she understood the proprieties of a woman living alone. In the daytime, she admitted men to the store on the ground floor of her house where they bought necessities such as feed, fertilizer and snuff. In the evening, when male visitors inside would have been improper, she sold men her moonshine through the kitchen door—liquor she would never permit to be consumed in her house or her store.

Miss Amelia did, however, permit the men to drink her liquor on her front porch. The porch was Miss Amelia's property, readers are told, but this intensely possessive woman "did not regard [it] as her premises; the premises began at the front door and took in the entire inside of the building" (118). Clearly Miss Amelia understood the porch to be neither her home nor public property. She allowed the men to consume her liquor on the porch and to enjoy a certain amount of social interchange, but all the time she remained standing in the doorway guarding the inner sanctum and presiding over the proceedings. For this woman and for the town in which she lived, the porch was a space "betwixt and between" private and public, and once we consider the special properties attributed to the liquor consumed there, it becomes a place for ritual communion as well:

> For the liquor of Miss Amelia has a special quality of its own. It is clean and sharp on the tongue, but once it is down a man it glows inside him for a long time afterward. And that is not all. It is known that if a message is written with lemon juice on a clean sheet of paper there will be no sign of it. But if the paper is held for a moment to the fire then the letters turn brown and the meaning becomes clear. Imagine that the whisky is the fire and that the message is that which is known only in the soul of a man—then the worth of Miss Amelia's liquor can be understood. (107)

It was night on the front porch when, after consuming the liquor of self knowledge, Miss Amelia first encountered love and did the most ill advised and spiritually significant act of her life: She shared the liquor with a total stranger and *invited him into her house.* The fictional Miss Amelia and her creator Carson McCullers clearly sensed the front porch as a space of ritual significance. So did Russell Baker. In his autobiography, *Growing Up*, Baker's grandmother Ida Rebecca, had a very different ritual use for her porch.

In the 1920s, women of rural towns were generally proscribed from the exercise of public power. Despite feminist movements that thrived in the cities, the heady power of getting the vote waned, and the reprieve from domesticity provided by World War I was history. The majority of women were once again housebound, and their accepted authority was only over furniture and children. Women, however, found socially acceptable ways to circumvent their public limitations. Whatever the mores of her time, Ida Rebecca, mother of twelve strapping sons and one daughter, was the acknowledged head of "a sprawling empire" and the unacknowledged ruler of the small Virginia town of Morrisonville. Baker's earliest and most vivid memories of his grandmother reveal her "sitting in state in the front porch rocker that served as her throne." Whether she was waiting for a son to bring home a prospective bride, presiding over the mandatory Sunday family gatherings, or surveying her domain, Baker recalls her sitting in that rocker, on that porch situated on a rise that put her at one end of and a few feet above the rest of Morrisonville. And in Morrisonville, "everybody said, 'It's her way or *no* way' " (28-32).

Whether or not Ida Rebecca thought of her porch as a mystic space from which she as high priest would preside, that is certainly the way it impressed young Russell and the citizens of Morrisonville. And why not? Forbidden by her motherhood to run for public office or to engage in business enterprises as Miss Amelia did, forbidden by custom and, as we have recently learned, by fearful male clergy, to seek the ministry, forbidden then to have an official office or temple, Ida Rebecca devised her own space from which to rule, and if we are to believe her grandson, she did it with aplomb. For Ida Rebecca, then, the front porch must have been a space betwixt and between the dwelling to which she had been condemned and the public arena in which she was forbidden to function, between the sanctity of the home and the profanity of the marketplace.

The porch for Miss Amelia and Ida Rebecca—and for millions of women from the mid-nineteenth century to the mid-twentieth—was a sort of "liminal space." Anthropologist Victor Turner speaks of a "liminal state" which occurs in those more primitive cultures studied by anthropologists—a time when the participants in a ritual are "betwixt and between" two cultural states—neither completely inside the culture nor yet outside it since their position is a transitional one.[1] Among those Turner describes as liminal are stone age peoples undergoing puberty rituals and medieval squires practicing the rites preparatory to knighthood. Two comparatively modern female liminal states are experienced by women who have declared their availability for marriage but who have not yet been claimed (debutantes, for example) and engaged women—both betwixt and between the protection of their parents and that of their husbands.

During their liminal period, such people are neither children nor adults, neither aspiring nor fully achieving. Using Turner's model, the front porch becomes a liminal space—neither sanctified as the hearth nor public as the road. One must be *invited* to sit on the porch, but, on the other hand, one has the right to *expect* that invitation because a person sitting on the porch has declared herself "to be accessible/to visit, to chat and receive/to be public and on display." Occupants of a porch are betwixt and between because they are neither fully sheltered from the elements nor fully exposed to them—neither fully a part of the workings of the public sphere nor fully excluded from them.

Although every structural feature of the porch is borrowed from another culture, the domestic front porch is an American institution —owing its origin to the Southeastern climate and gradually spreading into the fabric of American life in all geographic regions. While it was English settlers and African slaves who conceived of and built the first American front porches early in the seventeenth century, they borrowed concepts from the Indian bungalow, the Haitian "shotgun" house, and the French side and back "galleries."[2] Later, wealthier English stock tempered the practical porch with majestic columns and ornate porticoes borrowed from the ancient Greeks. While those formal porches testify to the architectural genius of such men as George Washington and Thomas Jefferson, and even the more humble porches of the common people were usually conceived and built by men, one suspects that women had something to do with their proliferation and their pervasiveness by the mid-nineteenth century.

The widespread use of the domestic front porch in the United States came at a time when the functions of male heads of households and of their female counterparts were being redefined. Late in the eighteenth century and early in the nineteenth, the Industrial Revolution for the first time made working away from home the order of the day for great numbers of people. Before that, soldiers and adventurers left home for months on end, hunters for shorter periods. Wealthy Europeans, perhaps, maintained multiple dwellings and moved freely among them as they do today. But the masses of the earth's people lived and worked together in exceedingly small geographic areas. While their chores were often delineated by sex, both men and women were involved in work in or near the dwelling—even when, as with nomads, home itself moved seasonally. Families and groups of families could count on social intercourse and highly valued work. In the western world of the nineteenth century, however, all that would change. Particularly in the United States, the Industrial Revolution and unbridled capitalism brought about for all classes a departure from traditional ways of life. And it brought about corresponding changes in domestic architecture. One historian of American domestic architecture characterizes the new culture of the American mid nineteenth century this way:

> The dynamics of this entire era was nothing less than the industrialization of America.... Life itself was harder and more cynical. The old Jeffersonian vision of an agrarian democracy, of independent men, rooted in the security of their own land or their own handicraft skills, had become more dream than actuality. The ruptures, dislocations, and insecurities of wage work and absentee ownership were increasingly the realities of American life.
>
> But with these miseries came also the optimism that was part of a period of phenomenal growth. It was the opening of an age of untrammeled *laizzez-faire* capitalism, of rugged individualism, of unparalleled opportunity.... America felt herself to be the inheritor of all the riches of the historic past and scientific present, claiming furthermore an inalienable right to do with her inheritance exactly as she wished. This was true no less in architecture than in the mining, lumbering, and marketing conquest of a continent. (Foley 163)

American men may certainly have enjoyed that sense of unparalleled opportunity and the inalienable right to do with their political inheritance exactly as they wished. Women, however, are notably absent from that female writer's concept—and with good reason. With the industrial revolution and the rise of the middle class in European and American societies, it became possible for large numbers of families to "enjoy the luxury" of sending their men out to earn a living while the women stayed home and "enjoyed" the pleasures of domestic life. Wealthy women, of course, still could employ servants to handle domestic chores and carriages to to move about in society. At the other end of the spectrum, every able bodied member of less fortunate families was required to work for wages just to keep food on the table.

But increasingly, the class which could neither afford servants nor needed the proceeds of every member's work to survive became the dominant class. What developed was a caste of women whose roles kept them largely indoors and solitary during the day. These women were to engineer domestic bliss, "influence" the children in Christian virtue, and act as moral guides to their men. Much has been written about the stress and frustration women suffered in this period because of their isolation and the gradual devaluation of their work. And much has already been written about ways they devised to deal with it. But one strategy women used to maintain contact with the community remains unconsidered.

The author of the quote above who celebrated the unparalleled opportunity for American men and the accompanying effervescence in domestic architecture of the period includes in her book dozens of drawings of representative American houses built between 1860 and 1941. And virtually every one of those examples has a front porch of some sort. And yet, like the women of the period she celebrates, the porches seem to be invisible. As in most other histories of American architecture, porches are virtually unmentioned in this book and, while architecture is seen as indicative of the consciousness which spawned it, no quarter is given to implications of ubiquitous porches.

It is probably impossible to prove that women had any direct influence on the porch mania that swept America from this period through the early 1940s. But it is a notable coincidence that, in the era in which the house became woman's domain and man exited to the market place, porches blossomed with an unprecedented abandon and pervasiveness. Before that time, American porches were confined to the Southeast where climate demanded the indoor-outdoor space. Beginning in the 1850s, however, virtually every domestic structure was built with a porch. And to those whose builders failed to catch on to the trend soon enough, porches were sure to be added. A careful look at older residential sections of almost any American community reveals a healthy sprinkling of appended porches among the more common houses on which the porches are integral.

Whether or not women were responsible for the explosion of porches spanning three generations, there can be no doubt that indoor/outdoor living space became for them a way of countering domestic isolation, at least during the warm months. For women, kept at home by children in need of care and the labor necessary to keep a household going, the porch functioned as a social place—their own space—at home yet not inside—a space simultaneously work place and salon—where they could visit, keep track of neighborhood activities and exchange news flashes with passers by while they watched their children and performed their more portable and sedentary chores. Middle class women could—and did—sit on the porch swing to prepare vegetables and fruits for cooking, even for preservation. Shelling peas, peeling apples and peaches, snapping beans, shucking corn—all were acceptable porch activities. So were hand sewing, endless mending, knitting in preparation for the colder indoor months and the more leisurely "fancy work." And while women performed those chores, they could keep an eye on the children—those middle aged people who today remember the porch as partially sheltered playground.

The more fortunate women who had a back porch as well could do their more strenuous and less presentable chores in the back. Their poorer sisters, however, often actually canned those peeled apples and shelled peas on the front porch. The cramped kitchen would have been just too hot. The porch also served as summer laundry room. Today, adults from the South especially recall playing the familiar automobile game of "counting washing machines on the front porch" in the late thirties, the forties and into the fifties. Those washing machines had replaced earlier boilers and washtubs.

Porches did make heavy chores more pleasant in hot weather, and they did offer the opportunity to take quieter tasks into the semi-public, but the most liberating use women found for the porch, one imagines, was social. On the porch, the casual visitor, the maid separated from the family by class and caste, the family itself experienced "communitas." One characteristic Turner ascribes to people in a liminal state is "Communitas"—the temporary but vital attachment that only people caught between cultural states can establish. Communitas, according to Turner, is "undirected, equalitarian, direct, nonrational, existential." Thus behavior in the liminal space is "spontaneous, immediate, concrete." The rules that apply to relationships and behavior in the structured environment on either side of the liminal space do not apply within it. So it is with the porch. There, betwixt and between absolute private and absolute public, relationships that would be impossible elsewhere can flourish for however brief a time—and they can be spontaneous. Thus, bashful and protected youth in the first flush of intimacy are free to experiment with new relationships; thus, caste and class can be suspended and commonality explored; thus the boundary between friend and stranger breaks down; thus, the powerless are empowered; and thus, established relationships are freed from the constraints and tensions of business on the outside and busy-ness indoors to commune and, if my mother-in-law is to be taken seriously, to heal.

The communitas established on the porch has contributed to the transmission of culture from generation to generation. In the evening, when whole families gathered on porches, family lore was passed in the guise of stories of old times. On my grandfather's porch, in the long televisionless summer evenings, I learned family history—and family legend. But in the day, with my grandmother, I learned my proper place. The turn of the century girl child in the illustration learns from a female family retainer how to sweep a porch—and the importance of keeping it swept. At the turn of the century, at the height of Jim Crow, she also learned that it was sometimes socially acceptable for blacks to sit with whites—at least with white children—on porches, but never in living rooms. On some porches white female employers could indulge the friendships they formed with black employees without public censorship. It was my mother-in-law's custom to invite her maid for a mid morning Coke on the screened part of the front porch—and again in the mid afternoon. Ida Rebecca Baker's realm was more strict. Her black maid and lifelong friend Annie was permitted the sanctity of a porch rocker only in times of sickness or death and then only, like the woman in the illustration, in the company of children. (Baker 42) It was a reward for service rendered.

The porch also provided a setting within which blacks could maintain social relationships with whites. A white woman who would never have entered her black friend's living room unless it was to impart some matriarchal service could sit on the black woman's porch with impunity. When he filmed *The Color Purple*, Stephen Spielberg retained Alice Walker to advise him on cultural mores with which he was unfamiliar. In the film he illustrated proper decorum for whites visiting blacks. When Sophia's white employer brought Sophia to spend the day with her relatives, she could not start the car to return home. One of Sophia's sisters, eager not to have her celebratory dinner interrupted while her menfolks ministered to the white woman's car, offered to fix her a plate of food and serve it on the porch. While the white woman refused the proffered gift, it is clear that eating "colored" food on the porch was permissible. The liminal porch was clearly a place where the color barrier could be weakened if not destroyed.

The sex barrier was also weakened on the front porch. In literature and the popular arts, as in life, the porch was the place for innocent courting. Young men have always been more or less able to come and go as they please. Not so young women. Traditionally, they must wait for men to come along, men to make the first move toward courtship, men to suggest marriage.

Most of us know that while women did often initiate acceleration of a relationship, the myth of the male initiator was a charade that had to be maintained, and it was maintained with the help of the porch. Since it was inappropriate for women to go into the public arena in search of potential mates, they needed a way to shop and to sample before making a selection—while all the time seeming to acquiesce in a male decision. Thus the porch, betwixt indoors and out, between public and private, became a sexual market place where the woman seemed to be on display but where she actually sampled wares presented before her.

The nineteenth century was a time, it must be remembered, when peddlers sold house to house, when dressmakers brought their bolts and patterns to the consumer, when fruits and vegetables were delivered to the back door. So it was with men. While Amanda Wingfield in Tennessee Williams' semi-autobiographical *The Glass Menagerie* does not mention her front porch, we are rather certain her living room would not have contained the seventeen gentlemen callers who visited her one fateful Sunday afternoon. And both Margaret Mitchell and David O. Selznik opened *Gone With the Wind* with Scarlet surveying masculine wares on the front veranda. Incidentally, Selznik was at least subconsciously aware of the ritual significance of a porch. While Scarlet is at her feminine best, the veranda is intact. When she returns to Tara to take over the man's job of running the place and even working in the fields, the porch is gone. We are led to believe that Yankees destroyed it, but the subtext is that a gritty female farmer has no use for the accoutrements of a girl whose only responsibility was to snare a husband.

It was for good reason that the porch was the place to entertain gentlemen callers. Inside the rules of propriety and chaperonage were restrictive. On the porch, neither in the parents' parlor nor in the forbidden public arena, certain rules could be broken. A girl on her mother's porch was properly chaperoned, but so long as her mother was inside, she could steal a touch or even a kiss and, in the cover of night, she could talk of subjects inappropriate indoors.

Conversely, while the porch offered relative freedom for the protected young lady, for unchaperoned women it was itself protection from men who thought *they* were doing the shopping. In the movie *Judge Priest*, set sometime around 1910, the principal female character was an orphan condemned to live alone in her inherited house. While she could never invite gentlemen callers indoors, this young woman could entertain the occasional male guest on her porch secure in the knowledge that, were he to get out of line—and one did—she was in the hearing of Judge Priest next door. And she could hardly have become the subject of gossip when she entertained in full view of the street.

Not only had women the right to expect such protection from male neighbors—their virtue was the responsibility of such neighbors. An incident that Amory, Mississippi, residents would almost as soon forget illustrates the extremes to which that obligation extended. Early one sweltering summer eve in the 1920s, dentist and respected Amory citizen Dr. I.W. Beauchamp (pronounced Bee-chum) sat on the porch of his ornate Victorian house on Amory's Fifth Street with his wife and his

Fig. 1 The house at 104 S. Fifth Street in Amory, Mississippi. From this porch—still in use today and still well furnished—Dr. Beauchamp, his wife, and his virginal nieces witnessed the disrobing at 105 S. Fifth Street. Photograph by Richard H. Beckham, 1985.

two visiting and virginal nieces. Dr. Beauchamp was secure in the knowledge that his young charges would witness nothing unseemly from the sanctity of his porch, but that particular steamy evening as the women and the man sat decorously fanning, chatting, and observing events on Fifth Street—usually few and commonplace—the unspeakable and the anti-social happened. Across the street in the less stately home at 105 S. Fifth Street lived the Frashes, a large family with several adult unmarried sons. All of Frash boys including one "Billy" known to be "not quite right" and his brother "Jim" worked for the Frisco Railroad maintaining engines.

Having guests the Beauchamps probably sat on the porch later than usual. On the other hand the working men across the street had to be up with the sun and opted for an early bedtime. Billy went to his room to prepare for bed as usual—except this time he veered from the norm. He forgot to lower the shade over the large front window to his bedroom! The japonica that now provides a degree of privacy even for forgetful people had not yet reached window level. The result was the virginal nieces learned more about male anatomy than was ever customary before marriage. The nieces may have secretly been delighted, but Dr. Beauchamp was enraged. He was entitled to entertain female guests in his outdoor

Fig. 2 Here, at the turn of the century, Everetta learns the arts that will define her adult life at the feet of her mother, Ada, doing needlework and probably hoping for chance visitors on their front porch. Photograph courtesy of the State Historical Society of Wisconsin.

Fig. 3 The dogtrot house provided deep southerners breezes indoors as well as outdoor living space for mothers fortunate enough not to have to work in the fields and their children. Farm Security Administration Photograph by Walker Evans, 1935.

Fig. 4 This migratory worker has not the luxury of a washing machine on her front porch, but thanks to a New Deal housing project she does have the convenience of running water for her laundry—and a porch was the right of all. Farm Security Administration Photograph by Jack Delano, 1940.

Fig. 5 These women and children were probably enjoying a carefree social interlude but when the male FSA photographer came along, the porch became a "front place." Farm Security Administration photograph by Jack Delano, 1941.

Fig. 6 The elderly, single owner of this porch seems to cry out for the community the porch once provided. She has decorated her porch with plastic animals, live plants, wind chimes, empty wine bottles, among other things in a mute effort to communicate with whoever walks by while she remains cool in the air conditioned indoors. Photograph by Richard H. Beckham in Cynthiana, Kentucky, 1986.

Fig. 7 This woman, old enough to remember grand porches sporting swings and hammocks, steals a moment of porch community from her "mean little house." The carport full of her large status conferring car, she has only the eve to use as outdoor living space. Photograph by author, Okolona, Mississippi, 1984.

sitting room confident that their innocence would not be violated. The willing compromise to privacy one accepts by sitting on the porch in full view of the street does not extend to being forced to witness indecent exposure.

In the humid dawn of the next day, after what was probably a night of trying in vain to sleep on sticky sheets in a ninety degree plus bedroom, Dr. Beauchamp made his angry way to the roundhouse in search of his neighbors. Unfortunately, the first Frash he came upon was Jim—entirely innocent of all wrong doing. Equally unfortunately, Jim bore a strong family resemblance to his forgetful brother. Thinking he had found his man, Dr. Beauchamp collared his prey, threw him against the wall and shot Jim—not Billy—dead. And he was never brought to trial![3]

The incident makes a good story—amusing, shocking and tragic, even gothic—but its real significance is what it reveals about the culture of porches. Nobody today remembers much about the legal proceedings following the shooting. What they know, however, is what Dr. Beauchamp and the Mississippi legal system knew then—that young women had the right to sit on porches and expect the community to protect their virtue. That right, in fact, was so sacred that men were

justified in going to any extreme to assure that it was maintained—
even to the point of shooting the wrong man.

While Dr. Beauchamp could avenge his nieces' loss of innocence
if he could not protect them from it, the dead parents of the protagonist
in Bobbie Ann Mason's short story "Residents and Transients" were
entirely helpless to protect her from her own instincts. Mason creates
an entirely 1980s version of the liminal nature of porch entertaining
when Mary Sue, left at loose ends while her husband is away on extended
business obligations, relies on her inherited porch, and perhaps the spirits
of her parents, to protect her from her own darker desires. Bored and
confused about her place in her culture and her marriage, Mary Ann
is surprised one afternoon when her dentist seeing her on her porch,
stops for a friendly chat. Nothing unseemly in that—except that the
porch is the back porch! Since hers is a farmhouse, the back porch faces
the road and functions as front porches usually do, but for Mason the
fact that it is a back porch offers the chance for ambiguous messages.
While no taboos forbid men to visit women on front porches, back porches,
with their suggestion of privacy and even secrecy, are something else
again. Thus, the character herself is in the ambiguous position of not
knowing whether she is being unfaithful or merely friendly.

The dentist's first visit grows into a custom with which Mary Sue
can live—so long as they are visible from the road, the couple have
not done anything technically anti-social. The crucial step in the
relationship is not taken until the dentist crosses the threshold into the
inner sanctum of the house. Then, just as when Miss Amelia took the
stranger into her house after dark, an irreversible and fateful step has
been taken. It is Mason's custom not to make reading her stories easy
for the reader by resolving them, but the reader knows that once the
visitor is inside, Mary Sue can no longer refrain from confronting her
own ambiguities.

Mary Sue's dilemma is definitely a twentieth century problem with
well articulated options once she interprets her own feelings. In earlier
decades women confused about their place in the world had no clearly
delineated choices. But they did have porches, understood—
subconsciously at least—as places where rules could be suspended. In
The Awakening, when Kate Chopin's protagonist, Edna Pontellier begins
to awaken to the limiting nature of her role as a Creole wife, much
of the action takes place on the porch of her summer cabin. Vacations
are suggested by Turner to be liminal periods when the vacationers
temporarily move outside the expectations of their culture. Resorts then,
must be themselves liminal spaces. Thus Edna, summering at a vacation
spot where many of her daily routines are suspended, is outside her culture
enough to examine her lifestyle. And she doesn't like what she sees.

Edna's culture, however, has not taught her fulfilling alternatives. Even so, timidly at first, she begins to experiment. One experiment she tries is flirtation. At the resort, that is entirely acceptable. When she entertains her chosen gentleman friend on her own porch, her husband remarks how pleased he is that she has the young man to keep her amused while he is away during the week attending to business. It is only when, back in the city in colder weather, Edna invites her guests *indoors* in her husband's absence that family and friends perceive something untoward in her search for self.

But receiving gentleman callers is not the most significant indication that Edna—and Chopin—perceive the front porch to be a liminal space. On the night that Edna first awakens to her intense dissatisfaction with her life, the night that she begins a long campaign to declare her independence, she does it on the porch. Edna is accustomed to honoring her husband's every nighttime whim whether it be for a sexual encounter or to leave her bed to check on children who are obviously sleeping peacefully. On this particular night, however, she refuses to come in from the porch when her spouse announces it is time for bed. Throughout the night, she continues to reject any ruses her husband devises to attract her indoors where his rule is supreme. Subconsciously, at least, she realizes that, on the porch, she is subject neither to the rules that govern her performance in her husband's house and nor to those of the public domain.

Edna, of course, becomes acutely aware that her life thus far has been a series of command performances. In *The Presentation of Self in Everyday Life*, Erving Goffman outlined his now classic contention that in their everyday lives virtually all people present themselves to others in full fledged performances that include costume, setting and, most of all, acting. Thus, the place where people act becomes a stage and the witnesses an audience. Preparation for such a performance, of course, demands a backstage. In his chapter on "Regions and Regional Behavior," Goffman discusses "front places" and "back places" (106-140). A front place is where performances are staged. A back place, on the other hand, is not only where the actor prepares for performance, but where she can be herself. For women and their porches, a strange reversal of back and front sometimes occurs. We have already seen that for Edna Pontellier, the front porch in full view of friends and neighbors— the audience—is where she feels most free to try being herself. Indoors, in the bedroom, one of the most back places for Goffman, with only her husband for audience, Edna must act the role of perfect wife and mother.

In *Their Eyes Were Watching God*, Zora Neale Hurston suggests a variation on the reversal theme when her protagonist Janie tries to free herself from the restrictions of her role as wife. In earlier times, before the advent of air conditioning, businesses were often equipped with porches, but these public porches were gathering places for men. Women were unwelcome. So it was with the store Janie ran with her husband. Janie was expected to mind the store for the occasional customer when groups of men—and sometimes unattached women—gathered on the store porch. To Janie, excluded in the dark store—merely a spectator to the camaraderie in front,

When the people sat around on the porch and passed around the pictures of their thoughts for the others to look at and see, it was nice. The fact that the thought pictures were always crayon enlargements of life made it even nicer to listen to. (81)

When Janie moved to join the tempting revelry on the porch, her husband told her in no uncertain terms that her place was inside, and when finally, in defiance, she engaged her husband in a game of insults on the porch, it was an act of rebellion that was to destroy the marriage. A wife sharing his porch with him was not part of the role Janie's husband wanted to play. That happened in the middle of Janie's story. After taking the reader with Janie on a strenuous journey into genuine love and self knowledge, Hurston involves her protagonist and the reader in another porch scene. Having learned that she need not conform to society's artificial rules for her, Janie exchanges pictures of her spiritual journey with her bosom friend on the porch of her own house. The porch for Janie was symbolic of both her limitations and her freedom. While the store porch was a front place for Janie's husband, for her it had been a back place from which she was excluded. In the store, she acted the role of dutiful wife; on the porch she broke the rules and learned something about herself. And on the house porch, another back place located on the front, Janie experienced communitas with her female friend.

Goffman, writing in the 1950s, had an interesting view of women— a view possible only in a patriarchy. While in his examples, drawn primarily from the workplace, women have roles every bit as important as men, he sees the places where women get together alone as "back places"—no concept that they might perform for each other since he seems to consider women alone as "back people." With some accuracy he cites Simone de Beauvoir to bolster his position. What both he and de Beauvoir miss is that in the same chapter from which he quotes, de Beauvoir mentions situations in which women present themselves for women.[4] Surely when women decorated their houses, collected china, glassware and other paraphernalia for entertaining, they did not do it to impress men. And surely, when they decorate their porches they do it neither purely for personal satisfaction nor to impress some all male world.

Nineteenth and early twentieth century women seem to have been more free to be themselves on porches than any place else. They could enjoy the communion of passers by and chance visitors on the porch while they watched children and did some of their more portable chores. And they could keep up with community news via casual exchanges with people on the street. As a matter of fact those people on the street were very important in building a porch culture. The porch served a dual role as stage and orchestra for Goffmanesque performances. As Mary Easter indicates, sitting on the porch at certain times of day, was "an occasion." People planned it; people freshened up for it. Women retired to their porches after demands of the protestant work ethic had been met to see and be seen. From their perch above the street, they could look down on passers by, wave, greet, and, after the passer had gone, comment. Each new event on the street was occasion for new stories or for dragging out old ones. And at the same time, those who walked by were audience for the performance on the porch.

Except at resorts and vacation cottages, the stage function of the porch seems to have been the only part of women's porch culture to survive into the 1980s. True, people do still sit on porches—when they have them—in the spring and fall, but it seems usually to be a sentimental harkening to days gone by. When it gets really hot, they huddle indoors with their air conditioning. Women, equipped with cars and telephones, no longer need to sit outdoors to maintain social contact. Television supplies continuous undemanding entertainment for those who are bored. And most women of the eighties are too busy performing the superwoman roles today's society has assigned them to have time to sit outdoors to greet and be greeted. In our frenetic society, a new need for "privacy" demands that what serious outdoor activity remains be relegated to decks at the rear of newer homes. And houses are seldom built with porches any more.

At the end of *The Ballad of the Sad Cafe*, Miss Amelia, bereft of the love who appeared one night on her front porch, waits three years on the same porch for his return, but no longer is there any communion on that porch, and finally she shuts herself inside—away from all society. So it seems in the American summertime as row upon row of tightly shut up air conditioned houses suggest that communion is unwelcome, that the pedestrian is an intruder. Many of the porches that remain have been enclosed to provide indoor living space. Like Miss Amelia, female residents in these houses have shut themselves inside away from communion with their neighbors. And the porches that remain outdoors have often been partially enclosed with unsightly screens—allowing occupants to be indoors and outdoors at the same time but denying access to passers by. Traces of the porch as stage remain, however, to show that women reluctantly relinquish the liminality of the porch.

In the South, where porches provided indoor/outdoor living space for most of the year, new houses are built with rudimentary vestiges of the once grand veranda. With spindly columns and scarcely three feet of width, these so called porches are furnished as carefully as the living room within, but not as if to be used. Women spend hours scouting to find the correct antique mammy's bench, wickerwork cradle or hand caned rocker to suggest that any minute now a woman in hoop skirts, baby in hand, will come out to sip iced tea and wave at the neighbors. Untold thousands are spent on wrought iron furniture never intended for the derriere to suggest gracious living in a time just past. Blossoming plants tended as the babies once were extend the garden a little closer to the seldom used front door—people today enter through the attached garage, never seeing the outdoors as they emerge from their air conditioned cars. Those fortunate enough to own older homes, north and south, furnish their porches with comfortable traditional swings and rocking chairs, but often they reveal the merely decorative nature of the furniture by placing them so close to the walls that rocking or swinging would be disastrous.

Those remembrances of community past are amusing and often even attractive. Other porches, however, seem almost tragic in the longing they reveal for a time of greater neighborliness. Women deprived of self actualization, not by today's mores but by their age and the era in which they grew, sometimes decorate their porches as if they were their last mute contact with other people. It is not unusual to find a single porch sporting wind chimes, all season wreaths, plastic flora and fauna, concrete plant urns and, in the case of the illustration, even a wine bottle or two. Even more heart rending for me, however, are the houses with no porch at all.

Once air conditioning made porches expendable, people for whom home ownership itself must have been a dream come true put the money that might once have gone for a porch into window units. The result was what I call a "mean little house"—mean in the sense of stingy, giving only what must be given, begrudging even that. These unadorned dwellings seem often to occupy lots with few or no trees, and equally often they seem to house older people—people who were once part of porch culture. And in front of or beside these houses, older women can often be seen huddled under the eave on a kitchen chair, or in the car port, knowing, regardless of an air cooled interior, the need to "cool off" on the porch just as my mother-in-law did.

Last summer I visited my home town in Kentucky to show my children where I grew up and, incidentally, to photograph porches. As we strolled by one of the grandest houses from my day—the house of the federal judge—I was telling my children how excited I had been when the judge's granddaughter invited me to play with paper dolls on that very porch when we noticed in the corner of that great front porch, a tiny, shriveled up woman. Her live-in companion confirmed that the woman on the porch was the judge's wife and grandmother of my childhood friend and invited me to speak with her, warning me she wouldn't know me. True, she did not recognize me, but she would never forget the ritual of the porch. Strapped in her chair so that she wouldn't fall, bereft of most of the knowledge she had accumulated in ninety odd years, she greeted me as she had hundreds of other visitors to her porch over all those years—as if it were once again 1951, and she had yet to have a car of her own, the only air conditioning was to be found in movie houses, televiewing was relegated to those who had a stomach for professional wrestling, and the ritual of the porch had never ended. She had freshened up to sit on the porch, she was "assessable, receiving," and I was a neighbor who passed on the street and stopped to chat.

Women of her era, often foggy about the present, have no difficulty recalling the porch's meaning for women for over a century of American history. For her, for me, and for countless other women the front porch will remain an artifactual testimony to the isolation women once experienced and the resourcefulness with which they overcame it.

Notes

[1]All information on Turner's liminality and communitas is drawn from Victor Turner, *Dramas, Fields and Metaphors: Symbolic Action in Human Society*, Chapters 1 and 7, although he has written of the concepts in many of his writings.

[2]Material on the actual history of porches is difficult to find, and most of what is available is impressionistic—as is this article. The most serious scholarship on the front porch as significant domestic architecture to date is a mere two pages by John Michael Vlach. In *The Afro-American Tradition in Decorative Arts*, Vlach has carefully documenting the African and Caribbean origins of the traditional American front porch (136-138). In "The North Carolina Porch: A Climactic and Cultural Buffer," Ruth Little-Stokes reported the same origins but her essay is primarily interpretive. Davida Rochlin's essay, "The Front Porch," reports the social significance of American porches but eschews history. In his classic history of architecture, Sir Bannister Fletcher acknowledges the ancient European origins of the "grand porticoes" and galleries of the early American Southeast, but porches *per se* are beneath his concern. Other sources have undoubtedly mentioned perfunctorily the appendages on American houses, but the architectural history of porches is most significant for its invisibility.

[3]This story, very difficult if not impossible to track down through newspapers of the day was related by T. H. Beckham, 86 year old lifetime resident of Amory and Beauchamp's neighbor after 1940 when he bought and moved into the house at 105 S. Fifth Street.

[4]Goffman quotes de Beauvoir when he quite accurately demonstrates that women alone are often freed from the restraints of social performance (125). In *The Second Sex*, a startling new book when Goffman wrote *The Presentation of Self in Everyday Life*, Simone de Beauvoir also shows that women perform for other women as well as for men although she appears unaware that she is describing performers when she describes women's behavior among themselves (528-545).

Works Cited

Baker, Russell. *Growing Up*. New York: Congdon and Weed, 1982.

de Beauvoir, Simone, *The Second Sex*. New York: Alfred A. Knopf, 1953.

Easter, Mary, "Sitting on the Porch." *Absorb the Colors: Poems by Northfield Women Poets*. Ed. Beverly Voldseth and Karen Herseth Wee. Northfield, Minnesota: privately published, 1986.

Fletcher, Sir Bannister. *A History of Architecture*. 17th ed. New York: Charles Scribner's Sons, 1983.

Foley, Mary Mix. *The American House*. New York: Harper and Row, 1980.

Goffman, Erving. *The Presentation of Self in Everyday Life*. Garden City, NY: Doubleday, 1959.

Hurston, Zora Neale. *Their Eyes Were Watching God*. 1937. Urbana, Illinois, University of Illinois Press, 1980.

Little-Stokes, Ruth. "The North Carolina Porch: A Climactic and Cultural Buffer." *Carolina Dwelling*. Ed. Douglas Swaim.

Mason, Bobbie Ann. "Residents and Transients." *Shiloh and Other Stories*. New York: Harper, 1983. 121-131.

McCullers, Carson. *The Ballad of the Sad Cafe*. *Seven Contemporary Short Novels*. 3rd ed. Ed. Charles Clerc and Louis Leiter. Glenview, Illinois: Scott, Foresman and Company, 1982.

Rochlin, Davida. "The Front Porch." *Home Sweet Home: American Domestic Vernacular Architecture*. New York: Rizzoli, 1983.

Turner, Victor. *Dramas, Fields and Metaphors: Symbolic Action in Human Society*. Ithaca: Cornell University Press, 1974.

Vlach, John Michael. *The Afro-American Tradition in Decorative Arts*. Cleveland, Ohio: The Cleveland Museum of Art, 1978.

"Making the Best of Circumstances": The American Woman's Back Yard Garden

Beverly Seaton

The American garden, regardless of its scale, has always been the province of the woman of the house. Whether this situation was caused by the difficulties of settling the frontier or by social differences between pioneer America and Europe, the American male's interest in growing plants has been largely agricultural or commercial. The housewife was expected to care for both the flower garden and the vegetable garden, and, while there are of course numerous exceptions, especially among Italian and middle-European immigrants of the early twentieth century, this pattern has held true until our own times. Today, vegetable gardening is perhaps becoming a common pastime of male Americans—a last vestige of agricultural America—but male flower growers are still few and far between, at least until retirement, when non-traditional male activities of all sorts are countenanced. Thus, between 1840 and 1940, the American woman was the principal creator and sustainer of the gardens around her home; the average American homeowner did not hire a landscape architect or a gardener. Garden historians have begun documenting many of America's large and elaborate gardens, and the plans of landscape architects and photographs of the gardens they made are beginning to be preserved and studied. It is equally important, though, to write the history of those gardens made by average Americans, even those gardens relegated to the back yard.

To begin, we can distinguish back yard gardens from front yard gardens very simply: the front garden presents the home's social face, being the outdoor equivalent of the parlor. The back yard garden, then, is the outdoor extension of the kitchen, the laundry room, and the playroom—the home's private, domestic aspect. While the front yard garden was also the woman's province, in this paper I want to concentrate on the back yard garden and its role in the lives of average American women. Wealthy Americans did not have "back yards," of course, but extensive kitchen gardens, hothouses, and whatever, not always directly behind the house. But the average American home plot, throughout our history, has been organized into front garden (public), back yard (private), and side plantings (usually complementing the front garden). This pattern was observed in city and suburb, country town and rural neighborhood, regardless of the size or style of the house. Perhaps the "front garden" was merely the strip of flowers along the front of the log cabin, or the vegetable garden a row of tomatoes along a chain-link fence in a post-war housing development—whatever the circumstances of the plot, the back yard is distinguished from the front yard in appearance and function.

In farm homes, the fact that visitors always come to the back door does not change the dominance of the pattern. Countless heroines in novels with a rural setting apologize for the back porch with its gourd or bean vines, while the author means us to see that setting as the very one to set off the heroine's charms to perfection. My own home, an old farmhouse in rural Ohio, is planted this way, I have suddenly realized; although the front porch and yard are only seen by the family, sitting on the porch or cutting the grass, I have planted it with perennial flowers and shrubs, while the entrance everyone uses, at the back of the house, displays the vegetable garden, mops drying in the sun, garbage pails.

The functions of the back yard have been many. It is of course the place for the vegetable garden and some of the flower gardens, usually the homelier flowers and those intended for cutting. In rural areas, animals are raised there—chickens, always the province of the woman and children, along with bees, perhaps, or a few hutches of rabbits. The back yard is the children's playground, from sandbox to plastic pool. On washdays clothes are hung in the back yard, and in past years all summer long a shady spot under a tree or grape arbor formed an outdoor workroom where the housewife shelled peas, peeled potatoes, or sewed. At some periods, it has been the site of teas on the lawn; at others, backyard barbecues.

Naturally the back yard gardens had to suit themselves to conditions, to "make the best of circumstances" in Eben Rexford's words (see illustration 1). Many American families have not had room for all of the functions listed in the previous paragraph, but Rexford's photograph showing a work place near the house and a plank walk with gardens on both sides suggests the ways in which even the smallest back yard was made useful. While the traditional vegetable garden is rectangular in shape, many back yard gardeners have placed their growing beds along the side fences of the property, and a common sight in city neighborhoods is the screen of shrubs or flower beds along the back of the property, where the garbage cans sit next to the alley. But there are all sorts of

Fig. 1 Making the Best of Circumstances
Eben Rexford, *Four Seasons in the Garden*

different ways to organize the back yard living space to accommodate the needs of the family.

The Vegetable Garden

The very earliest American vegetable gardens were matters of greatest necessity, of course, and included herbs as well as vegetables (Leighton). The colonial housewife raised seasonings, medical remedies, and other useful plants in her gardens along with ordinary food plants. By the nineteenth century, it was the pioneer wife who had responsibilities similar to those of the colonial wife, for in the settled parts of the country folks were not so dependent on their own efforts. Pioneer sagas, both fictional and autobiographical, often recount the planting of the precious vegetable seeds on the homestead, the care of the plants by the women and children of the family, and first harvests. Sometimes these seeds and plants represented their old homesteads and the families they had left behind, especially such sentiment-laden plants as rose-bushes and apple trees. The vegetable harvests do not rank in importance with those crops harvested from the fields by the men of the family, the cash crops, especially in the autobiographical narratives; they received about the same respect given the heavy kitchen work done by the women in pioneer farm homes. Males did not consider the raising of "garden sass" much of an accomplishment—it was women's work, or possibly something grandfather could work at when he was too old for other farm work.

In nineteenth-century town back yards, a vegetable garden was a normal part of life along with chickens and other mildly agricultural pursuits. Again, though, it was usually the woman's domain as the man went off to business. Sometimes the women and children grew enough surplus to sell, a circumstance which figured in many contemporary domestic narratives. Popular writer Anna Warner grew enough to feed her family—sister Susan, father, aunt, and other dependents—and sometimes enough to sell to neighboring hotels, from her garden on Constitution Island in the Hudson River opposite West Point. She fictionalized her experience in a short self-help book, *Miss Tiller's Vegetable Garden and the Money She Made By It* (1873), in which a single woman with dependents turns her entire back yard into a vegetable garden so that she can keep her home (Seaton, "Idylls of Agriculture").

By the turn of this century, suburban living began to change the nature of the typical American back yard. In the nineteenth century, only the wealthiest people disdained their own vegetable garden and related pursuits. Even when there were servants kept in the town home, there was usually some sort of a kitchen garden. But suburban life, since it was associated with upward mobility, began to play down the role of the woman of the house as domestic manager, and emphasize her role as her husband's social equivalent rather than a working partner.

While suburban dwellers were a small group at first, they had enormous influence on the attitudes of American women in the first half of the century. An excellent portrayal of this class of woman can be found in Mabel Osgood Wright's *The Garden of a Commuter's Wife* (1901), a mildly autobiographical work in which the wife gardens in Connecticut while her husband commutes to New York. The first gardening books for these women emphasized growing flowers, not vegetables, and flower gardening became one of the expected activities of the suburban wife, really more a front yard matter, socially speaking.

As the influence of the suburban lifestyle began to grow, American women in non-rural areas changed the "outdoor kitchen" image of the back yard. Thus, the twentieth-century back yard became, except in times of economic hardship or war, a place for flower growing, playtime activities, and family gatherings in good weather. The dominant back yard image of the century is a "good times" image, one suggesting that the wife is not obliged to supplement family means by agricultural pursuits.

There was a mild flurry of interest in returning to more practical use of the back yard during the depression years centering around 1907, when writers like Kate St. Maur (*A Self-Supporting Home*, 1906; *Earth's Bounty*, 1909; and *Making Home Profitable*, 1912) were popular, but this was a minor strain. World War I was a greater influence on the home back yard, for a short time turning many flower gardens into "War Gardens," growing vegetables to help with the war effort. The Depression years saw another mild "back to the land" movement in the back yard garden, since expansion of the back yard functions was something a woman could do to help out in difficult financial times. And finally, with the Victory Gardens of World War II, a large number of average American women put their back yards to good use, growing food for their families (see illustration 2), sometimes even plowing up the *front* yard. These activities were encouraged by the government and propagandized widely in the popular press, giving the homemaker her own shot at being as important for the war effort as Rosie the Riveter. Throughout this century, vegetable gardening and related practical back yard activities have been seen as a response to troubled times, rather than a normal way of life. This was illustrated very soundly in the late seventies and early eighties when, with high unemployment and high inflation, Americans returned to vegetable gardening in such numbers that the major mail-order seed sellers such as the W.A. Burpee Company had serious difficulties handling the volume of orders.

The Flower Garden

While the front yard flowers and shrubs have been mainly decorative

Fig. 2 *The Home Garden* March 1943

in intent, the flowers grown in the back yard, besides being pleasant to look at, have often been functional. Their major use was to be cut for home or church decoration, for presentation as gifts, or for ceremonial use such as in weddings and funerals. There is a major distinction here between the nineteenth century back yard and that of the twentieth century, just as there was in the aspect of food production. The florist business, in its infancy in 1840, is now a feature of normal American life. Flowers for ceremonies are supplied by the industry, as are gifts on all sorts of occasions (many of them created by the industry itself). While affluent homes may have flowers from florists decorating the house, the average American home still relies on home-grown flowers for this function. But flower arrangements are no longer so important a feature of home decoration anyway, their place taken by house plants, especially the popular hanging basket.

The history of popular flowers is interesting. Flowers go in and out of fashion just like anything else, and American women have been interested in the varieties of floral fashions although there has not been so much concern for having the right flowers in one's borders as in having the right sleeves on one's dresses or the latest in bonnet shapes. A story in *Vick's Monthly Magazine* for September 1885, "Miss Muffet's Dahlias," tells of a girl just home from boarding school who, in gloves and a sunbonnet, sets out to dig up her mother's dahlias (old-fashioned and ugly) and replace them with more fashionable flowers. She is stopped by an old family friend who explains the personal history of the dahlias (282-85). The flowers and proper dress are equated in this story, which sets fashion against kindness and decency.

In colonial America the woman of the house depended on perennial flowers and annuals which seeded themselves or which offered easy seed storage. In the nineteenth century many new varieties were developed, and the successful seed sellers like James Vick of Rochester or Peter Henderson of New York prided themselves on offering new colors and shapes every year. As greenhouse technology advanced it became cheaper for growers to produce bedding plants, so many women were able to buy, either in person or by mail, annual plants such as petunias, geraniums, or verbenas rather than growing them from seed.

This new technology went along with a major change in garden design, a subject far beyond my topic in this paper, but one that must be mentioned. The old perennial gardens were redesigned into gardens which displayed annual plants in a bright and intense show for only a few months of the year. This style is called bedding-out, and it produced specialized types such as carpet-bedding, in which bright-colored plants, often those with colored leaves such as coleus, are planted very thickly and clipped low so as to form patterns like an oriental carpet, or ribbon-gardening, in which colorful annuals are planted in strips by height. Very elaborate examples of carpet-bedding and ribbon gardening required more money and time than the average American woman could find, but she imitated these styles in her own garden, often creating small circular flower beds patterned in concentric rings. These styles were front-yard matters, of course, but they also entered the back yard domain. Garden walks were edged with ribbons of annual plants, and fashionable annuals took the place of older plants such as peonies or lilies. The lady gardeners thus had to become involved with growing more annuals, or ordering them from the catalogs, or buying them locally, and many women subscribed to garden periodicals such as *The Ladies' Floral Cabinet* (1871-1886).

"Old-fashioned" gardens came back into style in America by the end of the century, and perennial plants and many flowers popular in colonial times were once again planted. All of these garden fashions were part of the average woman's home duties. The suburban wife who wanted to have a proper garden read Mrs. Ely and Mrs. King to help her cope with her responsibilities (Seaton, "Gardening Books for the Commuter's Wife"), while the less affluent woman read about new fashions in her newspapers or her magazines.

When I first began reading late nineteenth-century popular novels written by and for women, I was often puzzled by the amount of time the lady of the house spent arranging flowers, while the more basic housework was done by servants. But when I read articles in women's magazines of the time, and Annie Hassard's *Floral Decorations for Dwelling Houses* (1876), and saw the complexity of the floral decorations considered tasteful at the time, I understood. The typical lady of the house would gather and arrange her flowers daily, with special attention to dinner parties. A dinner table might display a fountain of flowers coming up through the middle of the table, or hanging over it in a sort of canopy; flowers might be strewn the entire length of the table, with smaller arrangements at every place. Here is Mabel Osgood Wright's description of her duties:

I spent several hours every day now in arranging my flowers, for outdoor roses are blooms of a day that need frequent renewal. I have a special shelf in the pantry for this work, the tool house being overcrowded. I am also now realizing the benefits of a large supply of flower holders of various shapes and sizes. Not only have I inherited a whole family of blue and white bowls, the most fascinating receptacles for short-stemmed garden roses, and two darling India jars that belonged to father's mother, as well as some pieces of fine cut glass; but friends knew my foible, and my wedding gifts ran to vases, instead of coffee spoons and pie knives; while Evan has given me half a dozen inexpensive jars of a fine shade of dull green glass for holding heavy, long-stemmed flowers, like peonies, hollyhocks, and lilies, (262)

Fig. 3 The Trowel, The Label, and Various Baskets
Mrs. Francis King, *The Well-Considered Garden*. N.Y. Scribner, 1915.

This kind of women's work remained current through the early years of the twentieth century, when it became a matter for garden club competitions (the American Garden Clubs were founded and run by women) and displays at state and county fairs. Illustration 3, from Mrs. King's *The Well-Considered Garden* (1915), shows a grouping of baskets suitable for the lady gardener's flower-gathering expeditions. Women also needed to own a variety of vases and flower containers, and nineteenth-century women's magazines often featured directions for decorating a more humble utensil to serve as a vase. Such containers can still be seen, often at garage sales or thrift shops, for the idea has been a lasting one.

Wealthy Americans employed gardeners to do the real work in their gardens, of course, and so did many upper middle-class families in the late nineteenth and early twentieth centuries. Average women did their own garden work, however, with the exception of some spading or plowing by "one of those useful articles called men," as Anna Warner called them in her book on how a woman can manage a garden, *Gardening by Myself* (1872). Many books on gardening for women stressed its healthful aspects, picturing gardening as a genteel and useful way to exercise in the open air. Women were not expected to dig borders or plant trees, but all the physical work of gardening thought to be within her scope—most of the garden work, in fact—was seen to be suitable for women, especially weeding. Long before there were women landscape architects or "farmerettes," there were women who worked, professionally one might say, as weeders in the large gardens of wealthy Europeans. Just as the servants disappeared from middle class homes in our century, so did the gardener or outdoor man, one result of which has been the stress laid on minimum maintenance gardens in our time, with its emphasis on ground cover, low-care plants, and functional garden design. Gardening is still no doubt healthful, but women now swim, bike, jog, and lift weights when they want to exercise. A workout with Jane Fonda has replaced the brisk cultivation of the onions, it seems.

Gardening clothes for women were naturally a matter of comment in those days before jeans and shorts. "Stout shoes" were often recommended—one of the famous paintings associated with gardening, in fact, is of Gertrude Jekyll's shoes. Sunbonnets were suggested by Helena Rutherfurd Ely in 1903, long after they had passed out of fashion for the average woman: "With its poke before and cape behind, protecting the neck, one really cannot become sunburned, and pink ones are not so bad" (199). Mrs. Ely also pointed out that the busy housewife cannot hear others calling her in from the garden when she wears a sunbonnet, or at least she can give that as an excuse. Gloves were necessary, another protective measure; Mrs. Ely recommended suede. Of course women of those days were not expected to wear trousers, but blue denim does make an appearance, in the gardening outfit designed (and modelled) by Ida Bennett in her *The Flower Garden* (1903). Miss Bennett's gardening costume was a blue denim skirt, high-necked calico blouse worn with a necktie, and checked apron. Although this sounds quite unsuitable to a modern woman, I wonder what it was like to dig, rake, and hoe wearing corsets, petticoats, a heavy dress, and stockings.

The buying and growing of plants has become much easier, also, in this era of garden centers offering "paks" of flowering annuals and vegetable plants, large perennial plants in plastic tubs, and roses in fiber containers. Earlier American women had to grow their own plants from seed or buy small plants by mail unless they could dig some from other people's gardens. Nineteenth-century women started seeds in wooden boxes filled with soil which they had treated with hot water, setting the boxes in kitchen windows. Depression-era women used tin cans for the same function, while today there are all sorts of seed-starting kits sold in the discount stores and garden centers, from plastic trays to peat pots. While the modern woman often lacks access to an "animated shovel," unless she can picture her husband or other male family member in the role, she has many advantages in her flower gardening over her earlier sisters.

But the modern woman does not depend on her flowers. While the home interiors featured in the *New York Times* home sections almost always show flowers, usually a lily or exotic obviously bought at a city flower stand, average American homes no longer feature cut flowers, nor are they a matter of great importance in most American churches. Flowers are often welcome gifts to home-bound or hospital patients, but these days the flowers most admired are jammed into a theme planter of some sort by a professional florist. A small bouquet can be picked up at the larger supermarkets. And, while flowers are still used at funerals, these are almost exclusively prepared by florists. Furthermore, American women no longer need flowers for the laying out of the dead.

Garden Furnishings

Buildings, furniture, garden art, and other garden features exist in great variety, quite beyond the scope of this paper. But they are part of women's material surroundings in the back yard. Illustration 4 shows a very out-of-scale paved arbor used to join the kitchen to the clothes yard, and many homes in the nineteenth and early twentieth centuries had such arbors, although on a much smaller scale. Grapes were usually grown on them, although ornamental vines were also common.

Another shady spot in the back yard might have been the garden house or gazebo. My grandfather built such a little shelter, which we all called "the summer house." It had wood floors and benches around the walls, and it was open on all sides, much like park shelter houses

Fig. 4 A shaded walk from the kitchen to the vegetable-garden. Manning, *Joyous Art of Gardening* (1917)

Fig. 5 The Homely Back Yard.
A.M. Earle, *Old-Time Gardens*. N.Y. Macmillan, 1901

today. It was planted round with trillium dug from the woods, something frowned on today (and even in my childhood, when the sacredness of the trillium was impressed on me during wildflower walks). These summer houses were used as outdoor work stations or as picnic houses; some were screened. Just as in the nineteenth century such heating activities as soap and maple sugar making were done out of doors, some country homes had "summer kitchens" in the back yard near the house, sometimes attached to it. These were used for cooking during hot summers to allow the regular kitchen to be cool enough for work and dining, a necessity in those days of large wood-burning ranges. But twentieth-century technology removed the reasons for these summer kitchens, and summer houses were much more common late in the century and in our own times.

Garden furniture has been an almost constant feature of American back yards, wrought iron benches giving way to rustic wooden furniture of Victorian times and wood deck chairs of the twenties giving way to today's aluminum and webbing styles. As in all things relating to furnishing the home, these were the business of the American housewife, and I have noticed that painting the lawn furniture (in those days when it was needed of course) is often used by writers to symbolize one of those often put-off, undervalued jobs which make one feel very efficient to have accomplished. Art in the garden is especially related in the public mind to class and taste. Gardens with statues in them instantly symbolize wealth, while the pink flamingo or the garden gnome brand the homeowner as hopelessly lower middle-class, with poor taste at that. Much garden art is a front yard matter—the blue globe sitting on the bird bath in the housing development front yard—but bird baths, sundials, and even gnomes were (and are) frequently purchased as back yard decorations by American housewives. This is perhaps the aspect of back yards most removed from the work function, but just as back yard flower borders parallel the row of blooming geraniums in the kitchen window, so does the donkey and cart which stands near the gate in the chain link fence parallel the ceramic donkey and cart which sits in the middle of the kitchen table, bearing silk flowers from Thailand. American women like to decorate their quarters, indoor or outdoor, whether or not they are "work stations." Those startlingly functional, efficient, impersonal kitchens so often featured in home magazines early in this century have never been popular, except perhaps in homes with servants.

Conclusions

The American back yard can be read as an economic indicator and as a symbol of social status, but mainly it parallels the status of the woman of the house. It is an extension of her domestic duties, whether they be raising vegetables and chickens, making soap, and milking cows, or gathering fresh flowers to arrange for the house. The husband who farmed or the husband who commuted to New York both were the main providers, while the wife who was allowed to keep her egg money and the wife who studied flower arranging with others in her garden club were both seen as dependents. Throughout this century, as American women have moved out of the homes into the working world, the back yard has reflected their situation.

The material artifacts of the American back yard are various and deserve study, for they reveal the tastes and ideas of the times as well as the technology. But whether the subject be garden furniture, art objects, tools, outbuildings, cooking equipment, or paving styles, the American woman is at the heart of the story.

Works Cited

Bennett, Ida. *The Flower Garden*. New York: McClure, Phillips, 1903.

Ely, Helena Rutherfurd. *A Woman's Hardy Garden*. New York: Macmillan, 1903.

Hassard, Annie. *Floral Decorations for Dwelling Houses*. London: Macmillan, 1876.

Leighton, Ann. *Early American Gardens*. Boston: Houghton Mifflin, 1970.

Seaton, Beverly. "Gardening Books for the Commuter's Wife, 1900-1937." *Landscape* 28 (No. 2, 1985): 41-47.

———. "Idylls of Agriculture; or, Nineteenth-Century Success Stories of Farming and Gardening." *Agricultural History* 55 (No. 1, 1981): 21-30.

Warner, Anna. *Gardening By Myself*. New York: Anson Randolph, 1872.

———. *Miss Tiller's Vegetable Garden and the Money She Made By It*. New York: Anson Randolph, 1873.

Wright, Mabel Osgood. *The Garden of a Commuter's Wife*. New York: Grosset & Dunlap, 1901.

Interior Decorating Advice as Popular Culture: Women's Views Concerning Wall and Window Treatments, 1870-1920

Jean Gordon and Jan McArthur

Traditionally, interior decorating advice when investigated historically has been treated as high culture. Attention has centered on the stylistic explanations and pronunciamentos of leading design innovators—men like William Morris and Frank Lloyd Wright. Yet the rooms of most houses are the work of the people who live in them and can be described as popular culture. Similarly, the average person when engaged in a decorating project does not read the writings of major design innovators. If he or she consults anything at all it is usually the domestic advice disseminated in popular magazines and books. Consequently most decorating advice can be thought of as popular rather than high culture.[1]

This genre of writing, at least until recently, has been dominated by women's magazines and women authors. Its origins go back to the household handbooks of the antebellum years and to such early women's magazines as *Godey's Lady's Book*. At first women were content to offer a few suggestions in single chapters in household advice books or in short magazine articles. But by the 1870s they were writing entire monographs on the subject.[2]

Several factors account for this proliferation of decorating advice in the decade of the seventies. One was the emerging consensus that women were the sex primarily responsible for the home. Another was the flood of manufactured goods which deluged American markets after the Civil War. The exhibits of the Philadelphia Centennial of 1876 overwhelmed visitors with an incredible cornucopia of readily available household furnishings. Unfortunately most of the women (and men) who were expected to create tasteful domestic interiors from this abundance lacked the background to do so. One reason was the chaotic

Reprinted from Vol. 9, No. 3 of the *Journal of American Culture*. Reprinted with permission.

state of the decorative arts. The architect, Henry Van Brunt, complained that designers were "embarrassed by the unbounded range and variety of precedent" at their command. Furniture and decorative objects drew on the Greek, the Japanese, the Gothic, the Renaissance and the Queen Anne, not to mention "the inexhaustible East." Another problem was the fact that many Americans whose new wealth permitted them to live fashionably came from rural or small town backgrounds and thus had little experience with matters of taste. To make matters more complicated the Puritan beliefs of many of these people held personal display to be potentially sinful.[3]

In this situation the doctrines of the English Arts and Crafts Movement, as popularized by Charles Eastlake, came as a godsend. According to the "Gospel of Eastlake," the new furnishings, available to the new rich, could be justified as morally superior. During a period when the aristocratic French rococo styles of the 1850s had become somewhat passe and family heirlooms were not yet popular, everyone, even families of old wealth, might choose to get rid of their Chippendale and Louis Seize furniture and redecorate in the Eastlake-Gothic style. For the less affluent, newly fashionable, "do-it-yourself" decorating projects could be embraced as a revival of traditional handcraft skills. No wonder Harriet Spofford described Eastlake's *Hints on Household Taste* as meeting "a great want." "Not a young marrying couple who read English were to be found without [it]...in their hands" she wrote, "and all its dicta were accepted as gospel truths."[4]

This article concerns the evolution of the decorating advice of American women writers from 1870 to 1920. Its object is to identify the kinds of women who published in this genre and to characterize the personal and social context in which their thinking was imbedded. The focus is the overall mind-set of the authors rather than a comprehensive analysis of their writing. However, to get a sense of the different schools of interior decoration with which they were associated it is helpful to comment on some of their specific decorating recommendations. To do this we have selected examples concerning wall and window treatments. Walls, as writers on interior decoration frequently point out, give the key to the whole room; thus a discussion of wall treatments suggests, by implication, the attributes of an entire stylistic outlook.

Concentrating on women's advice concerning wall treatments also makes it possible to emphasize the particular circumstances of American women with regard to domestic interiors. In Europe the most elaborate wall treatments were reserved for gala assembly rooms where, on special occasions, elaborately dressed people gathered for formal entertainments. Painted frescoes and carved moldings formed the primary decoration. But in nineteenth-century America, even the grandest houses were usually conceived as an enlarged *maison bourgeoisie*. In such houses comfortable furnishings were the main consideration. Walls tended to be comparatively simple.

Another difference between Europe and America was that European writers on interior decoration assumed control over the design of the house itself. So did such American nineteenth-century male experts as the architect, Hudson Holly. Women, not being architects and having very little say concerning the building of houses, were left with the task of making do with what existed. As Lydia Maria Child, the early nineteenth-century abolitionist, observed, the " 'patching business' is women's proper sphere." The consequence for decorating advice was that women writers gave endless advice on how to make high ceilings look lower, dark rooms seem lighter and small rooms appear bigger. (In fact, making do with what you have was, and still is, the single most important theme in women's magazines.)[5]

The first group of women to publish discussions of interior decoration grew up in families that were firmly rooted in rural and small town early nineteenth-century America. Although they wrote for money they did not, with the exception of Harriet Spofford, consider themselves professional writers. Rather, they were women who took advantage of the greater opportunities for education and self-improvement available in the second half of the nineteenth century to reach out, through publication, to a wider audience than their immediate circle of family and friends. Interior decoration was not the primary concern of any of these women except Candace Wheeler. It was partly a matter of personal interest, each woman taking up the topic in middle age after having had children and a home of her own. It was also an opportunistic publishing response to a popular subject.

In recent studies of the history of American interiors the writing of these authors is often quoted as indicative of the taste of their times. Yet even though one may wonder just how influential it really was, the writing is, nonetheless, of value to the historian of popular culture. It represents an important early effort by a group of women to come to terms with and proselytize a self-conscious view of interior decoration. Before this time matters of interior decoration had been left to specialists— architects and upholsterers who, on behalf of wealthy clients, selected and arranged household furnishings. Women writing on interior decoration for women readers implied something quite different. This was that tasteful home decoration was now considered an important attribute of the cultivated women. For such women taste, like virtue, was considered to be innate. Although income might be limited, it was assumed that the housewife would make her home an expression of the highest values of her family. In the complex world of consumption of the 1870s this required a sophisticated ability to strike a balance between expensive goods of intrinsic value and improvised decorating stratagems which created a pleasing effect. It also required balancing the dictates of aesthetic authorities with individual family tastes and possessions.[6]

Things had been much simpler for the housewife of an earlier generation. A contributor to *Scribner's* magazine reporting on Candace Wheeler's Decorative Arts Society directed attention to this fact by contrasting the first decades of the nineteenth-century with the 1880s. The earlier period, the author recalled, was a time when "the household art ideal...was the notion of neatness allied with industry." "Having things ship-shape," was more important than "having pretty things." Decorations, if they existed at all, were made by the housewife herself. If she had the time and the skill, the best room or chamber might display as its primary ornament "a framed worsted representation of 'Samuel Anointing Saul'."[7]

The rooms remembered by the *Scribner's* contributor belong to the period of the grandmothers and, in some cases, the mothers of the women who would later popularize the ideas of Eastlake and William Morris. These women's earliest recollections were of similar rural and small town houses. Such homes, as domestic environments, represented collective family space. Furnishing had been acquired piecemeal over long periods of time and their disposition in various rooms conformed to the usages of many people, not just one person with a self-conscious aesthetic point of view. "Decorating" was something that took place on special occasions—like Christmas or weddings. For such events rooms were filled with flowers and greenery superimposed on the traditional arrangement of household furnishings.[8]

Throughout the nineteenth century, flowers constituted a major source of aesthetic pleasure for most American women. Even sophisticated city dwellers remained fiercely loyal to the house plants and flowers they had learned to love as children. Henry Ward Beecher, writing in *Good Housekeeping* in the 1880's, referred affectionately to the "charming infliction" of "floral insanity suffered by American women." This was certainly true of his sisters, Catharine and Harriet. Their *American Woman's Home* (1869) gives complete information on how to decorate windows with growing things. This could be done by training vines around the window to form a kind of natural curtain. Catharine advised filling the window with potted plants or placing before it a type of oversized terrarium known as a Ward box.[9]

In making these recommendations the Beecher sisters were not suggesting anything new but merely describing a common practice. There are a number of surviving 19th century photographs showing vines trained around windows and Seymour Guy's painting of an upper middle-class New York dining room includes a Ward box in the window.[10]

Helen Hunt Jackson in a short story of the 1870s reveals the lengths to which "floral insanity" might go. She described a parlor which evoked the "decorative style of the Berkshire hills," embellished by flowers and vines in "all possible and impossible places." Among the "impossible places" were the frames of the pictures which covered the walls. As Jackson elaborated, "Yellow wall-flowers waved above the picture of the Norway pines; great scarlet thistles branched out each side of the Venetian palace; cool maiden-hair ferns seemed to be growing all around the glowing crimson and yellow picture of the Arabs in the Desert." "Afterward," Jackson concluded, "I learned the secret of this beautiful effect; large, flat, wide-mouthed bottles, filled with water, were hung on the backs of the picture frames, and in these the vines and flowers were growing; only a worshiper of flowers would have devised this simple method of at once enshrining them, and adorning the pictures."[11]

Jackson's example was admittedly extreme but most nineteenth-century women who wrote on interior decoration included plants in ways that male writers never would have considered. It was only one of a number of ways in which women writers tempered the more formal design recommendations of the experts with concerns that were more traditional and familiar.

To turn to specific decorating advice, three women were important propagandists of the ideas of Eastlake in the 1870s and 80s. Harriet Spofford (b. 1835) is best known today as a writer of realistic New England stories enlivened by rhapsodical evocations of nature. She spent the first fourteen years of her life in Calais, Maine, a small river town on the Canadian border, upstream from the Bay of Fundy. Later her family moved to Newburyport, Massachusetts, a town like its neighbor Salem, noted for its quietly elegant Federal houses. The cultural focus of Spofford's early career was Boston and the *Atlantic Monthly*. Her venture into interior decoration consisted of a series of articles which appeared anonymously in the New York magazine *Harper's Bazaar*. They were published in book form as *Art Decoration Applied to Furniture*.[12]

Mary Elizabeth Wilson Sherwood (b. 1826) spent her first years as the eldest of seven children in Keene, New Hampshire. When, as a teenager she was sent to a boarding school in Boston she was painfully aware of her rustic dress and manners. It was an experience which she would later fictionalize in a novel about a raw western girl who was transformed into an acceptable member of New York society. Sherwood herself was "transformed" by her marriage to a New York lawyer. She plunged into New York society with enthusiasm and remained, in the recollection of her grandson, the playwright Robert E. Sherwood, "a very gaudy old lady until the end."[13]

Biographical data is less readily available for the third early writer, Ella McIllvane Church. She was born in 1831. She married a Mr. Church and published popular fiction as well as books on topics dealing with nature and small town concerns. Both she and Mary Elizabeth Sherwood wrote articles on New York interiors for the magazine, *The Art Journal*. Subsequently Church's essays were expanded into the book, *How to Furnish a Home*.[14]

Of the three women Mrs. Sherwood was the most superficial and socially self-conscious. Her contribution to the *Art Journal* consisted of a group of articles describing some of New York's most up-to-date, and opulent houses. At the beginning of the series she hailed the Pre-Raphaelite wave "which, amidst much valuable flotsam and jetsam, threw up to us Eastlake's books, Morris' wall-papers, Doulton's pottery, tiles, fireplaces, and jugs; [and] which taught us properly to appreciate the sincerity and purpose of true Art." Sherwood used Eastlake's terminology to commend the home of W. H. De Forest for its "conscientious" library. Then shifting over to the language of Whistler she praised the way the tiles had achieved "symphonies in red and blue," "nocturnes in white," and "overtures in the fashionable peacock green." What Mrs. Sherwood communicated by these descriptions was an excited enthusiasm for the possibilities of interior decoration. She did not however give any concrete advice.[15]

Harriet Spofford and Ella Rodman Church, in contrast, were all advice. Approaching the house room by room, they explained wall treatments both theoretically and practically. Walls, they pointed out were analogous to columns—the base was similar to the dado, the space above, or fill, the column, and the frieze the capital. In making this distinction they were embracing Eastlake's division of walls into three parts—something which departed from an earlier practice of treating the wall as one big expanse of paint or wall paper. They also advocated Eastlake's range of colors. The light colored walls and white woodwork of the neoclassic period were out. "Nothing can be done with dead-white walls," Church protested. Even if one covered them with pictures the "interspaces" would "stand out in harsh and ghastly contrasts." As for white ceilings and white woodwork, they were hard to manage and "put a room out of tone."[16] Colors were to be chosen depending on the function of the room and its exposure. Southern rooms required cool colors and northern ones warm, reddish or yellowish shades.[17]

Although Church and Spofford distinguished between walls that were intended as a background for pictures and those that were decorative in their own right, the consequence of dividing the wall up into three distinct segments—each with its own pattern had the effect of making the background of the room more complicated. Furthermore, Eastlake was interpreted as recommending that wooden doors be taken down and replaced by decorative curtains known as portieres. These tended to give rooms a somewhat oriental look. If wooden doors were preserved their panels might be decorated with painted pictures of birds and flowers. Windows were shrouded with lace curtains surmounted by heavy drapes. Walls, with their tripartite division were further embellished with pictures, hanging shelves and racks of plates. And finally there were the plants and flowers. Harriet Spofford, in one example, suggested placing branches of fall leaves over the windows of a formal parlor. Needless to say the total effect of all of this was overwhelming complexity; an ironic result when one considers that the goal of Eastlake's doctrines was to achieve simplicity.[18]

At the same time that Spofford, Church and Sherwood were writing about interiors another middle-aged matron, Candace Wheeler, was setting about becoming a professional decorator. If anything, Wheeler's background was even more old fashioned than that of the other women. She was born on a farm in 1827 in the Catskill mountain region of New York. Her father's household was one which she described as being a hundred years behind the times. Her mother taught her all the traditional domestic skills, including spinning and weaving—the latter being particularly important since Wheeler's abolitionist father required that all his children protest slavery by wearing only homespun. It is a tribute to the rigor of Wheeler's Puritan upbringing that she was able to marry a New York businessman and enter into cultivated New York society on perfectly equal terms.

As a young matron Wheeler and her husband became closely associated with New York's artist-studio set. Prominent among them were the painters of the Hudson River School who had immortalized the Catskill mountain region where Wheeler had grown up. From these artist-friends, Wheeler learned how to paint, her favorite subject being, not surprisingly flowers. Wheeler was almost fifty, an age when most women of her generation were settling into the role of grandmother, when she took up the new profession of decorative arts.[19] Her motivation was not artistic, but philanthropic. Grieving over the sudden death of her eldest daughter, Wheeler determined to do something positive for other women. A practical person, she focused on the obvious need of single or widowed genteel women to earn their own living.

Many years before, as a girl in upstate New York, Wheeler had observed that the only kind of employment available to educated women was teaching. Doing productive work for pay caused a woman to lose caste. Consequently, it was with a great deal of excitement that Wheeler visited the exhibits of the English Kensington School of Art Needlework at the 1876 Philadelphia Centennial. This school had been established with the specific object of giving work to "decayed gentlewomen." Wheeler at once saw a possibility for the kind of project she had in mind. She set about to establish the Society of Decorative Art. However, her organizational model was quite different from the Kensington School. During the Civil War American women had earned large sums of money for the Union Army by selling their handiwork at Sanitary Fairs. Attracted by the financial success of these Fairs Wheeler asked Mrs. David Lane, who had raised a million dollars through the New York Sanitary Commission, to be the co-head of her Decorative Arts Society.

Just as the organizational precedents for the Society of Decorative Art were different from those of the English Kensington School, so the American women participants differed from England's "decayed gentlewomen." American ladies were not interested in the tediously repetitive Kensington apprenticeship. They were determined to plunge directly into the most advanced projects, learning the necessary skills as they worked. Furthermore, many of the society's members were not needy at all but were affluent middle-class matrons looking for a fulfilling avocation. They embraced household art with the same kind of enthusiasm with which similar women took up the new women's club movement.[20] Constance Harrison, a middle-aged matron from Virginia and semi-professional novelist, contributed her bit to Wheeler's endeavor by writing a series of articles on household art for the Decorative Arts Society's organ, *Art Interchange*. "Everywhere throughout our broad land," Harrison enthused, "there is a stir, a chirping, a meeting together as of birds in early spring-time, while feminine schemes are projected for the embellishment of the home." The most serious "ladies put themselves under the yoke of one of those delightful modern institutions, an advisory artist."[21]

Although the members of the Society of Decorative Arts studied with professional artists the great majority, including Wheeler herself, were amateurs. In her autobiography Constance Harrison described how she and her friends met at different houses to study stitches and fabrics and how they "committed to unoffending burlap and coarse crash marvels of crewel-work, to be ultimately consigned to the depths of cedar chests or given away to servants contemplating matrimony." The do-it-yourself aspect of the Decorative Arts Society reinforced women's traditional association with household crafts. Only in this case the necessary skills were learned in formal classes as opposed to the earlier practice of learning from other women.

The whole undertaking underscored the assumption of contemporary magazine writers that the test of a truly cultivated woman was decorative improvisation. If a housewife did not have the money to buy expensive things she could create a tasteful effect through the work of her own hands. There was no excuse for an ugly home.[22]

Providing an artistic avocation for privileged women was not, however, why Wheeler had founded the society. As she admitted, philanthropy and art were not natural sisters. Therefore she moved to separate the two. For philanthropy she organized the Women's Exchange to sell women's handiwork. For art she joined Louis Comfort Tiffany, Samuel Colman and Lockwood de Forest to form the Associated Artists (1879-1883), a pioneering decorating firm.[23]

Wheeler's role in the Associated Artists was to design textiles and wallpaper. She and her daughter Dora organized a group of young women artists to help with the work. Some were students from the Cooper Union and the Artist Artisans. Others were talented amateurs who had taken up design through the earlier Society of Decorative Arts. Such was the success of the women that when Wheeler and her associates entered a wallpaper contest sponsored by the firm of Warren and Fuller their group won all four prizes. Candace took first place and her daughter Dora, second.[24]

Wheeler's major interest however, was not wallpaper but textiles conceived as wall decoration. Contradicting Eric Erickson's theory of women's preference for enclosures, Wheeler believed that walls should give the illusion of limitlessness. In an article published in 1895 she observed that although walls are necessary for privacy, "limitation of space, confinement within given limits, is, on the whole, repugnant to either the natural or the civilized man, and for this reason we are constantly tempted to disguise the limit and to cover the wall in such a way as shall interest and make us forget our bounds." "Tapestries" she claimed, "for the most part, offer us a semblance of nature, and cheat us with a sense of unlimited horizon."[25] Putting her theories into practice Wheeler patented a method of making needle woven tapestries or embroidered pictures. She and Dora made the designs and women in their employ did the actual embroidery.[26]

Obviously such wall treatments were only for the rich—people like the younger Cornelius Vanderbilt who ordered an entire tapestry series. The average person had to be content with wallpaper. Wheeler took time out in 1895 to advise such people what to buy. The most successful wallpaper, she wrote, "makes the wall almost disappear from one's sight or consciousness in a pleasant vision of color." However, nothing could be worse than badly designed wallpaper. "It is to wallpaper that we owe most of the disturbing and mistaken decoration of our walls," she declared. "Bunches of flowers seem to start out from every plane of surface, making it impossible to dodge them; or zigzag forms writhe in platoons along the walls, until the unhappy occupant might almost as well be struggling with a nightmare." To avoid this she recommended a new kind of ingrain paper which followed the "impressionist" method of painting by mixing two differently colored pulps closely together so that they seemed to form one tint.[27]

With observations like these it was clear that by the 1890s American homes were, decoratively speaking, becoming simpler. At the same time women were addressing other than purely aesthetic matters when dealing with wall treatments. One concern was the efficient use of space. Catharine Beecher was a pioneer in this area. Twenty years earlier in the *American Woman's Home* she had designed movable storage walls for both middle-class and lower-class homes. Although her proposals were essentially utopian (in the manner of Orson Fowler's octagon house) her concern for easy housekeeping anticipated turn-of-the-century strategies to simplify housekeeping.[28]

While Beecher tried to save steps and space, other women were worried about the healthfulness of walls. Housing reformers wanted to forbid the use of wallpaper in tenements because of its tendency to harbor vermin.[29] Ellen Swallow Richards, the MIT chemist, tested wallpapers to make sure the colors were not poisonous.[30] Jane Addams, on the other hand, was interested in the educational potential of walls. Clients of Hull House could borrow reproductions of French cathedrals or Raphael madonnas to hang in their rooms. It was hoped that by doing this they would be weaned from an insistence on garish, unhealthy wallpaper and uplifted by living in the presence of great art.[31]

Jane Addams was not alone in thinking that middle-class women had an obligation to use domestic space to help the disadvantaged. Both Wheeler and Church in writing on interior decoration made a special effort to include the needs of servants. The walls of the kitchen were to be finished in cheerful easily washable materials. One recommendation was oil cloth glued to the wall and embellished with pictures of interest to the cook. Servants' bedrooms were to be carefully decorated as well— with special emphasis on simplicity and cleanliness. As Wheeler reminded her readers, the maid may have come into your home directly from a tenement, "therefore everything in the room should be able to sustain very radical treatment in the way of scrubbing and cleaning."[32]

The self-taught, practical approach to interior decoration of Spofford, Sherwood, Church and Wheeler is a far cry from the magisterial advice of Edith Wharton who, in 1902, published the *Decoration of Houses*. What had seemed the latest in urban sophistication to the generation of Sherwood, and Church, struck Wharton as stuffy New York provincialism. In contrast to the earlier writers whose taste had been formed by the superimposition of city life on a rural or small town background, Wharton's values were the product of the juxtaposition of New York and Europe. With rather touching naiveté she presented American readers with photographs of the rooms of Europe's great palaces assuring them that the principles underlying these rooms could just as easily apply to a modest American home. To the extent that the rooms were based on classical proportions she was right, however, to translate these proportions to an American domestic scale would have required far more explanation than Wharton was willing or able to give.[33]

There are other important differences between Wharton and the earlier writers. Candace Wheeler had spent much time talking about surface effects that could create the illusion of improvement—how to make a high ceiling look lower, a dark room sunny or a cold room warm. One section of her book, *Principles of Home Decoration* was frankly called "Expedients." Wharton was not interested in "make do." She blandly recommended that if the architectural relationships of door and fireplace in a room were wrong, to change them.[34] Obviously her book was not for the average homeowner. If it did influence middle-class readers it was probably to encourage them to make their rooms lighter in color and more simple in their furnishings. In Wharton's illustrations, walls are usually paneled and painted white and furniture sparse to the point of making the room seem unfurnished.[35]

Edith Wharton was, of course, primarily a novelist and the *Decoration of Houses* an isolated literary venture. It remained for Elsie de Wolfe to adapt eighteenth-century French decoration to the middle-class American home. The fact that Elsie's family connections were less socially correct than Edith's, was, if anything, an advantage in this undertaking. In spite of her high-class clientele de Wolfe's decorative advice tended to be practical and her style of writing unassumingly chatty.

In many ways Elsie de Wolfe was like Edith Wharton's heroine, Lily Bart. Like Bart, Elsie was a woman who loved luxury but, lacking an inherited fortune, had to choose between marrying for money or sharing in the glamour of wealth by making herself useful to the rich. De Wolfe, like Lily Bart, chose to do the latter. She attracted attention first as an amateur actress and ultimately as a professional decorator. Yet in terms of intellectual perception Elsie was a far cry from Wharton's sensitive heroine. Her books and articles drip with the gushy superficiality of the magazine writer. Nevertheless, she really did have a feel for interiors which she preferred to literature, music or any other aspect of culture.[36]

Like Edith Wharton, de Wolfe became sensitive to the New York homes of her youth through an experience of revulsion. Acutely aware of her own plainness she was equally upset by the ugliness of her environment. The first chapter of her autobiography is titled "A Rebel in an Ugly World" and opens with a story of how as a little girl in a linsey-woolsey frock, she returned one afternoon to the family house on West Thirty-fourth street in New York to find that the drawing-room had been repapered in a Morris design of gray palm-leaves and splotches of bright red and green on a background of dull tan. "Something terrible that cut like a knife came up inside her," de Wolfe wrote. She "threw herself on the floor, kicking with stiffened legs, as she beat her hands on the carpet." When finally able to speak she jumped up and down crying over and over. "It's so ugly, it's so ugly!" De Wolfe concluded from this experience she was "an ugly child" living "in an ugly age." "From the moment I was conscious of ugliness and its relation to myself and my surroundings" she wrote, "my one preoccupation was to find my way out of it. In my escape I came to the meaning of beauty.[37]

It was all very dramatic and very superficial. De Wolfe wasn't worried about the plight of unemployed women as Candace Wheeler had been or depressed by the vacuous lives of the privileged like Edith Wharton. She was cross because she wasn't pretty. Yet shallow though it may be, this kind of narcissism was just the tone for the popular magazine culture of the 1920s. Women wanted to feel it was all right to spend time and effort to be pretty and to create pretty homes. After all this was what they were told daily in hundreds of magazine advertisements.[38]

De Wolfe's first experience of a satisfying interior was in 1881 when, as a sixteen year old, her father took her on a trip to visit his family home in Wolfville, Nova Scotia. The house itself was built in 1779 in the Federal style which Elsie found a vast improvement over the Eastlakean clutter of her New York home. When looked at with historical hindsight her reaction is indicative that taste had come full circle. To Elsie the only bearable interiors were in the neoclassic style which the first generation of women writers on interior decoration had grown up with and left.[39]

However, by the early twentieth century when de Wolfe became a practicing decorator her models were more eighteenth-century French than eighteenth-century American. To her way of thinking the French had perfected interiors. All Americans had to do was combine French style with modern convenience. Once this was achieved interior decoration was set for all time to come. In a series of articles for the magazine *The Delineator* which were later published as the *The House in Good Taste*, de Wolfe proclaimed "I believe in plenty of optimism and white paint." Walls were to be plain, either paneled or painted a flat light color, preferably cream. Less affluent persons could make their walls appear to be paneled by nailing strips of narrow molding on the walls. Another much recommended stratagem was the use of mirrors attached to the wall without frames. Not only did it make the rooms look bigger it gave a lovely reflected image of the lady of the house and her guests. Elsie's preferred textile was chintz in light, bright colors. Chintz was both elegant, washable, and came in endless patterns.[40]

When the *The House in Good Taste* was published in 1913 American women's magazines had been showing colonial revival houses with light painted woodwork, plain light colored walls and chintz or cretonne for over a decade.[41] De Wolfe merely gave the American colonial revival a French accent. By the 1920s her decorating solutions had become almost a cliché. Even Sinclair Lewis made Babbitt follow the precepts of de Wolfe in decorating the family living room. As Lewis described it: "The gray walls were divided into artificial paneling by strips of white enamel pine.... A blue velvet davenport faced the fireplace, and behind it was a cherrywood table and a tall piano lamp with a shade of golden silk. Among the pictures, hung in the exact center of each gray panel, were a red and black imitation English hunting print, an anaemic imitation boudoir print with a French caption of whose morality Babbitt had always been rather suspicious, and a 'hand-colored' photograph of a colonial room. Though there was nothing in the room that was interesting, there was nothing that was offensive. It was as neat and as negative as a block of artificial ice."[42]

Elsie de Wolfe's emphasis on the French was not as we have already indicated, the whole story in America's popular interior decorating advice. The other component was the American colonial revival and neo-classicism. By the 1920s educated women, inspired by articles in women's magazines, were out scouring old houses and attics for Queen Anne, Chippendale and Federal furniture. Sometimes they would find other treasures like rolls of hand blocked scenic wallpaper which they could have hung in their modern rooms.[43]

Louise Andrews Kent, who wrote for the *Ladies Home Journal* under the pseudonym of Mrs. Appledore, was a leading celebrator of the enthusiasm for colonial and early nineteenth century American decorative arts. In a novel published in the thirties called *The Terrace*, she recreated in fiction the antique craze of the preceding decade. The first person narrator is a young woman from an old family in a small New England town very much like Salem, Massachusetts, who capitalizes on her art training and her family connections to create (along with her best friend) an interior decorating and antique business. In one episode the heroine describes how she and her friend did over a bedroom in the Federal-style home of a crippled young veteran of the First World War. An earlier owner of the house, the veteran's great uncle, Old Ezekial, had made so much money after the Civil War that he had refurnished it in horsehair, black walnut, and marble. The object of the decorators was to restore the nephew's room back to its original eighteenth century look. They rescued the old pine wainscoating from under its mustard-colored paint; they put a gay piece of hand-loomed carpet on the floor; they found a "wonderful" red-and-white coverlet for the bed and hung an old English chintz at the window. They brought in the best bannister-back chairs, and a comfortable sofa, and filled the shelves with books, set off with "beautifully polished tankards and copper bowls of chrysanthemums." Yet although the object was restoration, the young women admitted that the room probably never looked in the least as it did when they finished with it. "But," the heroine observed, "decorators learn to shut their minds resolutely to such subversive ideas."[44]

With the American colonial revival, modified by forays into French and English eighteenth-century styles, American popular interior decorating advice was set. Since then the eighteenth-century revival has outlasted attacks from the international style, minimalism, high tech, and post modernism. As any glance at a popular home magazine will confirm, it is still going strong today. In terms of what had been most durable in American popular taste, Elsie de Wolfe was right when she said that, decoratively speaking, the eighteenth century had said all there was to say.

Notes

[1]Nikolaus Pevsner in his much cited *Pioneers of Modern Design* (New York: Museum of Modern Art, 1949) treats interior design as high culture. David Handlin in *The American Home* (Boston: Little, Brown and Co., 1979) and Gwendolyn Wright in *Building the Dream* (New York: Pantheon Books, 1981) include much advice from popular books and magazines; however they do not make a distinction between "high" and "popular" culture.

[2]Laura C. Holloway Langford, *The Hearthstone; Or Life at Home. A Household Manual* (Beloit, Wisc., The Inter-State Publishing House, 1883) and Almon Varney, *Our Homes and their Adornments* (J.C. Chilton & Co., 1882) are examples of the more old-fashioned, encyclopedic type of advice books. Harriet Spofford, *Art Decoration Applied to Furniture* (New York: Harper & Brothers, 1878) is an example of the newer, more aesthetic, historical treatment of interior decoration. Spofford's approach is similar to that of such male authorities as H. Hudson Holly, *Modern Dwellings in Town and Country* (New York: Harper Brothers, 1878) and Clarence Cook, *House Beautiful* (New York: Scribner Armstrong & Co., 1878).

[3]Henry Van Brunt, "Growth of Conscience in the Decorative Arts," The *Atlantic Monthly*, 42 (August, 1878), pp. 204-215.

[4]Harriet Spofford, *Art Decoration Applied to Furniture*, p. 222.

[5]Edith Wharton, *The Decoration of Houses* (New York: W.W. Norton, 1978 reprint ed., originally published in 1902), pp. 122-133. Child quoted in Nancy Woloch, *Women and the American Experience*, (New York: Alfred Knopf, 1984), p. 171.

[6]Herbert Croly wrote, "the very best promise of American decorative improvement lies in the increased interest which the American woman will take in her own house...", *Stately Homes in America* (New York: D. Appleton & Co., 1903), p. 468. Harriet Spofford, Ella Rodman Church, Elizabeth Sherwood and Candace Wheeler are quoted in Peter Thornton, *Authentic Decor (New York: Viking, 1984)* and *Catherine Lynn, Wallpaper in America* (New York: W.W. Norton, 1980) to cite two recent studies.

[7]"The Society of Decorative Art," *Scribner's* 22 (Sept. 1881) pp. 697-709.

[8]Jean Gordon and Jan McArthur, "Living Patterns in Antebellum Rural America as Depicted by Nineteenth-Century Women Writers," *Winterthur Portfolio*, 19 (Summer/Autumn, 1984), pp. 177-192. Harriet Spofford revealed her New England upbringing when she observed that the "notable housewives" of her youth considered

as "trash and trumpery" the kinds of bric-a-brac which adorned homes in the 1870s and 80s. *Art Decoration Applied to Furniture*, p. 224.

[9]"Practical Window Gardening," *Good Housekeeping*, 9 (Oct. 12, 1889), p. 274. Catharine Beecher and Harriet Beecher Stowe, *The American Woman's Home*, (Hartford, Conn., Stowe-Day Foundation, 1975 reprint ed., originally published in 1869), pp. 94-103.

[10]Peter Thornton, *Authentic Decor*, p. 303 and 306.

[11]Helen Hunt Jackson, "The One-Legged Dancers," *Saxe Holm's Stories* (New York: Scribner's, 1874), pp. 217-218.

[12]Elizabeth Halbeisen, *Harriet Prescott Spofford: A Romantic Survival* (Philadelphia: University of Pennsylvania Press, 1935).

[13]Barbara E. Welter, "Mary Elizabeth Wilson Sherwood," in Edward T. James and Janet Wilson James, *Notable American Women*. 3 (Cambridge: Harvard University Press, 1971), pp. 284-285.

[14]Ella Rodman Church, "The Dining Room," *Art Journal*, 5 (1879), pp. 282-285 and Ella Rodman Church, *How to Furnish a Home* (New York: D. Appleton, 1881).

[15]M.E.W.S. "Some New York Interiors," *Art Journal*, 3 (1877), pp. 329-334.

[16]Church, *How to Furnish a Home*, p. 48.

[17]*Ibid.*, p. 81.

[18]Harriet Spofford, *Art Decoration Applied to Furniture* (New York: Harpers, 1878).

[19]Madeleine B. Stern, "Candace T. Wheeler," in *Notable American Women*, 3 (Cambridge: Harvard University Press, 1971), pp. 574-576.

[20]Candace Wheeler, *Yesterdays in a Busy Life* (New York, 1918), pp. 209-229.

[21]Constance Cary Harrison, *Woman's Handiwork in Modern Homes* (New York: Charles Scribner;s Sons, 1881), pp. 133-134.

[22]Constance Harrison, *Recollections Grave and Gay*. (New York: Charles Scribner's Sons, 1911), p. 309 and Spofford, *Art Decoration*. pp. 232-233.

[23]Constance Harrison, "Some Work of the Associated Artists," Harper's Magazine, 69 (August, 1884), pp. 343-350.

[24]Wheeler, *Yesterdays*, pp. 231-241.

[25]Candace Wheeler, "Decoration of Walls," *The Outlook*, 52 (Nov. 2, 1895), pp. 705-706.

[26]Wheeler, *Yesterdays*, pp. 257-259 and Madeleine B. Stern, *We the Women* (New York: Schulte Publishing Co.), pp. 291-296.

[27]Wheeler, "Decoration of Wells," p. 706.

[28]Catharine Beecher, *American Woman's Home*, pp. 25-29 and 441-445.

[29]Anthony Jackson, *A Place Called Home* (Cambridge, Mass., MIT Press, 1976), pp. 98-99. One reason why the poor used wall paper was that it was cheaper than painted walls.

[30]Janet James, "Ellen Swallow Richards," in *Notable American Women*, 3, pp. 143-146.

[31]Jane Addams, "Art work," *Eighty Years at Hull-House*, eds. Allen F. Davis and Mary Lynn McCree (Chicago: Quadrangle Books, 1969), pp. 50-52.

[32]Candace Wheeler, *Principles of Home Decoration* (New York: Doubleday, Page & Co., 1908), p. 46.

[33]Edith Wharton, *The Decoration of Houses.*

[34]Wharton, *The Decoration of Houses*, pp. 19-20.

[35]See for example her photographs of rooms of the Palace of Fontainebleau in Chapter X.

[36]Jane Smith, *Elsie de Wolfe, A Life in the High Style* (New York: Atheneum, 1982).

[37]Elsie de Wolfe, *After All* (New York: Harpers, 1935), pp. 1-3.

[38]Stephen Fox. *The Mirror Makers: A History of American Advertising and its Creators* (New York: William Morrow & Co., 1984).

[39]Jane S. Smith, *Elsie de Wolfe*, p. 10.

[40]Elsie de Wolfe, *The House in Good Taste* (New York: The Century Co., 1915).

[41]See issues of *House Beautiful*, 1900-1910.

[42]Sinclair Lewis, *Babbitt*, New York: Harcourt, Brace, 1922) p. 92.

[43]Margaret H. Pratt, "The History of a $10,000 Wall-Paper," *House Beautiful*, 30 (Oct., 1911), pp. 140-141.

[44]Louise Andrews Kent, *The Terrace* (Boston: Houghton Mifflin, 1934), pp. 66-67.

"Fine Arts and Fine People": The Japanese Taste in the American Home, 1876-1916

Jane Converse Brown

The Japanese Taste was a late-nineteenth and early-twentieth-century style of home decoration with important philosophical, moral, and educational elements, strongly allied with contemporary values. In addition to many popular motifs that became almost cliches, the Japanese Taste included distinctive arrangements of those motifs. Some of the most charming and frequently copied motifs and arrangements were displayed in the recent (1986-1987) exhibit on the Aesthetic movement in America at the Metropolitan Museum of Art in New York City, *In Search of Beauty* (Burke, et.al 18, 172, 201, 206, 207, 269, 273). Magazine writers told American women that Japanese art and design could enhance their homes not only decoratively but also in many other respects. The home, a significant element of late-nineteenth-century society, provided physical shelter, as well as a suitable environment for Christian nurture and the artistic and general education of the whole family. Its decoration, therefore, was emblematic of the family's morality, taste, and culture and was something the aware visitor could "read".

Information about Japanese art and design came from two sources. One was the Aesthetic movement in England, which provided examples of integrating Japanese art with other historic forms to create a new style. The other was Japan itself. The opening of Japan by the American, Commodore Matthew C. Perry, in 1853 had awakened the public's curiosity. Some information appeared in magazines like *The Atlantic Monthly* and *Harper's New Monthly Magazine* even while the Civil War preoccupied the public. In the mid-1870s magazines began publishing a variety of articles such as Noah Brooks' "Some Pictures from Japan," in *Scribner's Monthly* (1875), one of the first to describe both the art and the artists of the nation (177-193). Japan's participation at the Centennial Exhibition in 1876 created a sensation. Dallas Finn writes that in addition to women, whose "husbands deplored the time and money...spent in the Japanese Bazaar," "aesthetes, carpenters, pottery manufacturers, gardeners, and architects flocked to the Japanese exhibit" (33).

After the centennial, magazines continued to publish more about Japan, its people, customs, and arts. In the late 1870s and early 1880s, during the "decorative craze" or the height of Aestheticism, there were articles on Japanese cloissoné, rock crystal, fans, and prints, with suggestions for using these "important" items in the American home. Travel articles abounded, with several outstanding illustrated series in the 1890s by the artists John La Farge, Robert Blum, and Alfred Parsons. Thus in the last quarter of the nineteenth century Americans could become quite knowledgeable about Japan and understand why Japanese bric-à-brac was a suitable addition to the moral home.

Physical Attributes of the Style

The "Japanese Taste" is a modern term referring to the use of Japanese motifs and objects in the Western home. Japanese motifs, such as cherry blossoms, swallows, butterflies, bamboo, crescent and full moons, and wisteria, were embroidered, painted, stenciled, or burned (in "pyrography") upon textiles, ceramics, plaster plaques, and leather and wooden objects. Motifs were usually arranged asymmetrically, appearing as in nature, and truncated by the edge of a frame or the object itself. Common formats were attenuated rectangles, modeled on screen panels, and circles. Objects such as fans, parasols, porcelains, paper and stone lanterns, folding and flat screens, ivory and wood carvings, bronzes, textiles, and fretwork could be found singly or in combinations in every room of the house. As *Arts and Decoration* said in 1911, "many of the [artistic Oriental products] are applicable to the decoration of ordinary homes, even though there may not be an Oriental scheme" ("Oriental" 316).

The Japanese Taste was used in a variety of ways and degrees. At the minimum, a fan might be placed on the mantel or a Japanese flower embellish a set of doilies. Embroidering long-stemmed flowers on a screen or a stork border on a portiere were bigger projects. "So popular has this...embroidery work become that stamped designs and the materials for working them may be purchased at most fancy-work stores" (Griffin 31). China-painting patterns appeared in the magazines as frequently as embroidery patterns, even though the former required more equipment. The patterns were designed for sets of dishes: twelve oyster plates with marine motifs or six fruit bowls with appropriate blossoms. Other larger-scale projects included Japanese bric-à-brac stands and bamboo furniture. The ultimate expression of the style was a full-blown Japanese room, with special treatments of the floor, walls, woodwork, and ceiling and appropriate furniture and bric-à-brac, or a summer house.

Philosophic Aspects of the Japanese Taste

Acceptance of the Japanese style by the late-nineteenth-century American middle class was based on philosophical considerations as well as aesthetic ones. What the objects and their motifs symbolized was important. Perhaps because Japanese art was thought to be wholly foreign, perhaps because the Japanese themselves were non-Christian "heathens," or even "barbarians," those who promoted the style justified it elaborately, stressing the philosophy of the Japanese and their arts. Since the objects themselves were found to embody ideals similar to those of the West, they would enhance a Christian home. Important philosophical elements in the acceptance of the Japanese art were the attitude of the worker, the degree of craftsmanship involved, and the resulting "sincerity" of the object. Beauty and its effects in the home were also a consideration. Only "first-class" objects would create a "proper" home environment.

Many writers described the sincerity and high quality of Japanese work. Japanese workers toiled for honor on account of their enthusiasm for the beautiful and their love for their profession (Griffis 135). As a result, they "threw their souls into their work," creating sincere, well-made objects which would be important elements in the Christian home (Carpenter 436). According to Lafcadio Hearn, the "Japanese...recognize that the truth of beauty belongs to the inner being....," and "they recognize moral beauty as greater than intellectual beauty" (Hearn "A Trip." 623; "The Genius" 475). These attributes, combined with the fact that the craftsman strove after beauty, not money, made for sincere objects. The objects also answered Emerson's prescription that "beauty must come back to the useful arts, and the distinction between the fine and the useful arts be forgotten." Furthermore, the objects reflected the "relationship between the people, religion, and history," a configuration of the integrated society which the popular philosopher, John Ruskin, idealized ("Review." 524). He and his apostle, William Morris, also publicized the notion that well-crafted, sincere products can be made only by workers who enjoy their work. Obviously Japanese objects fulfilled this requirement.

The desire for good craftsmanship had a number of roots. Some must be attributed to a desire for "old-fashioned" standards and a nostalgia for the past, a reaction to the industrial revolution. Another was Ruskinian, the desire to avoid the negative influence of poorly-made objects and badly-crafted art works. Sincerity was thought to be an important attribute of good craftsmanship; it is a Christian virtue, an aspect of fundamental honesty. Traditional hand-crafted works were described as "sincere" because of their makers' attitude and the unpretentious use of raw materials. The objects were in contrast to the more shoddy industrial products, whose workers took no joy in their labor and whose materials often masqueraded as more expensive ones.

To create a sincere environment at home a woman needed to avoid all "sham:" furniture with inexpensive woods veneered or painted to imitate marble, all cheap reproductions, and pretentiously decorated objects. Honest pieces would reinforce the moral ideas she established. Ruskin's American follower, Clarence Cook, wrote extensively about the effect of the properly decorated home upon its inhabitants. Cook had very specific ideas about how to achieve a beneficial atmosphere and discussed them at length in his series of ten essays, "Beds and Tables, Stools and Candlesticks" (published first in *Scribner's Monthly Magazine* from 1875-1877 and reprinted as *The House Beautiful* in 1878). The introduction strikes a warning note:

I look upon this ideal living-room of mine as an important agent in the education of life; it will make a great difference to the children who grow up in it, and to all whose experience is associated with it, whether it be a beautiful and cheerful room, or only homely and bare one, or a merely formal and conventional one.... But it has a real vital relation to life, and plays an important part in education, and deserves to be thought about a great deal more than it is. It is therefore no trifling matter whether we hang poor pictures on our walls or good ones, whether we select a fine cast or a second-rate one. We might almost as well say it makes no difference whether the people we live with are first-rate or second-rate. ("Beds II" 174)

Other writers reinforce Cook's point of view. There was great insistence upon the necessity for the best and most sincere in both furniture and bric-à-brac.

Japanese art, according to the painter John La Farge, is a sincere expression of tradition, a laudable condition, in Ruskinian terms. In his travel articles, La Farge describes viewing Japanese art as a religious experience: it is "to live again in the oneness of mind and feeling which is to open to us the doors of the kingdom." He saw "the simplicity of attitude in which we were once children," a New Testament attribute praised in the late nineteenth century as a utopian contrast to the complications of modern life (429). He also discovered echoes of the ancient Greeks, touchstones for modern artists. La Farge felt that the combination of Greek or eternal qualities with Christian or sincere ones gave Japanese art a special value and beauty.

Beauty was not just an aesthetic quality, and creating beauty in the household had philosophic overtones. In 1880, *Harper's Bazar* told women that "a love of the beautiful is a refining influence, one that raises the mind to a higher level, and opens to it an ever-widening field of intellectual enjoyment" ("Painting" 790). Love of beauty was, in fact, the sign of a "refined mind" (Dewson 89). Women who wanted to choose elevating bric-à-brac were reminded that "all objects are artistic in Japan"

(P.I. 146). Thus a woman could fulfill her duty to educate her family directly and indirectly by decorating her home with beautiful, sincere Japanese objects, capable of improving their viewers.

Morality and Japanese Art

Justification for using the artistic products and ideas from a "heathen" nation in a "Christian" home was a fairly complicated process, but one writers approached with an almost missionary zeal. Finding morality in any style presented to the middle class was a necessity since the effect of the moral home upon its inhabitants was a central preoccupation of the period.

Goodness, beauty, and truth

Thanks to the popular writings and lectures of Ralph Waldo Emerson and John Ruskin, Americans had learned that art could be an effective vehicle to introduce religion and its images into the home. Emerson's essay "Art," published in 1841, equates beauty with an expression of the good in nature, itself part of the oversoul. Art singles out "one object from the embarrassing variety" of nature, thus "educat[ing] the perception of beauty." The best art is "universally intelligible," evokes "the simplest states of mind," and is "religious." The universal language of great art is "a confession of moral nature, of purity, love, and hope" (307-309).

Art, therefore, had a purpose—a distinctly missionary aspect. Ruskin and his first American disciple, James Jackson Jarves, believed that "beauty could help men perform their moral duties; art could inspire morality and high ideals and thereby insure the nation's prosperity and adherence to the path set by God who had implanted the laws of art with the laws of nature" (Saisselin 94). Jarves found Japanese art important because it was "a *spiritual* rendering of the realisms and naturalisms of the daily life...," "as much the outgrowths of political and religious sentiments as of the more material interests of a people" (Jarves 22-23, 29). Its spiritual aspect, therefore, made Japanese the kind of art that Emerson could have endorsed.

Art was promoted to the new middle class as a benefit to themselves and their children, since it could teach lessons, elevate the moral atmosphere, and cultivate the aesthetic senses. Art created an environment which had an elevating effect upon its inhabitants, a particularly critical quality for children in their formative years. Japanese was just as "useful" as Western art in creating the proper home.

Christian Nurture

Isolated from the wickedness and temptations of the world, the home had a special role in producing properly functioning Christians and future citizens. Horace Bushnell, a Congregational minister in New

Haven, Connecticut, first raised the idea of home as an agent of "Christian Nurture" in sermons and pamphlets in the 1830s and 1840s. Opposed to early-nineteenth-century revival movements, Bushnell was convinced "that the child is to grow up a Christian," not suddenly convert. Domestic "Christian atmosphere" would unconsciously shape him, as well as dignify home life. "The house...should become the church of childhood, the table and hearth a holy rite...." "Christian nurture," integral to the home, would create the right "atmosphere," "better than teaching," for the process (6, 8, 13).

Establishing a home was in itself a moral act. According to an anonymous writer in *The Art Amateur*, purchasing a house was the beginning of a religious process.

Every improvement in the house is an improvement in morality.... The efforts to acquire, to maintain, and to improve it are a daily, life-long schooling in morality. Industry, forethought, and self-denial are then the natural growths of this condition. And in the train of these virtues, and akin to them, comes the sense of the beautiful.... And in this way is quickened within [the householder] the germ, also, of the fine arts ("Morality" 80).

The Art Amateur's comment suggests that a home with some fine arts was a more effective spiritual shelter than one that was overly plain. Since "decorations, like words, have a meaning imparted to them by the associations which cluster about them," what better assistant in creating a religious atmosphere than the carefully chosen bric-à-brac of one's own house ("Editor's" 307)?

Some authorities, however, felt that one could work with whatever was available and still achieve satisfactory results. Writing in *The Art Amateur* in 1888, an anonymous "Architect" states that "good effects" can be obtained with "everyday" articles, a fortunate situation since "we must live amid such surroundings daily; and the moral influence that they exert, whether for good or bad, is an established fact which cannot be ignored by the intelligent householder" ("Hints" 136). The American woman must, therefore, choose or arrange objects to create the right moral influence. As Williams and Jones stated in the introduction to *Beautiful Homes or Hints on House Furnishings*, an inexpensive domestic manual, "she is a wise woman who surrounds those she loves with objects of beauty; for she may safely rely on the influences (so intangible) which the beautiful (both in nature and art) ever exerts in a moral, intellectual, spiritual and social point of view" (3).

Nature

Nature was seen in the nineteenth century as being strongly evocative of religion and the deity, ideas established by the English Romantic poets and elaborated by Emerson. The late-nineteenth-century woman, having read Ruskin's version of Emerson's ideas, was likely to use images and elements that evoked nature to create a sincere, religious atmosphere in her home. These natural motifs could be a part of the architectural fabric of the house, applied to any of its decorative elements, or be plants, flowers or other natural objects. A Japanese object with a beautifully and realistically drawn motif was an easy way to suggest the natural world indoors, imbuing the house with a natural sanctity, producing a harmonious, sincere home, the proper environment for "Christian Nurture." Japanese art was a sure way to bring nature to the home because nature and natural laws were its base (Hearn "About Faces" 226; Hicks, "Talks": IV 119). The "innate love of nature [is] caused by [the people's] close acquaintances with it...." (Hicks, "Talks: Historic," 158), a condition the urban Western world had lost. Furthermore, unlike American factory workers, the Japanese were "trained by nature," which created an intuitive good taste (Griffis 562). According to *Peterson's*, "nothing is more noticeable than the close observation of nature conspicuous in [the art], and the sympathetic feeling shown by the artists in their treatment of natural subjects" (Meredith 150).

Various travel articles describe the union of the Japanese with nature and the resulting positive effects upon their art and morality. The Japanese themselves were considered "child-like" and "natural," attributes of inherent sincerity. The art works were, therefore, emblems of positive virtue (Bisland 174). Nature being a reflection of the deity and his power, the woman who wished to create a feeling of natural religion in her home could use Japanese art without hesitation. Although it came from a "heathen" country, the spirituality of its creators and the subject matter of the pieces themselves combined to make art that elevated the spirit. "Children of nature" created sincere works that reflected a "national love of beauty" (Brooks 191). Since the pieces had "characteristic good taste" and fine craftsmanship, they would reinforce all the moral lessons taught by the woman of the house.

Japanese art, therefore, belonged in the heart of the home. Within the living room, writers singled out the fireplace area for special emphasis, perhaps following Bushnell's description of the hearth as a "holy rite" (13). Illustrations of the hearth and mantelpiece, the family's shrine, often have Japanese bric-à-brac. Cook includes two in his second essay. The first merely has a shelf topped with three pieces of porcelain. The second illustration, however, is very Japanese: a design by the English architect E.W. Godwin, a well-known admirer of Japanese design. Its two shelves contain a flat fan and five assorted pieces of porcelain, in a strongly asymmetrical arrangement (342-343). Mantels in *The Decorator and Furnisher*, *The Art Amateur*, and *The Art Interchange* also are decorated with Japanese porcelains, fans, and fabrics. Fire screens and lambrequins were other areas in which moral and sincere Japanese motifs could be painted or embroidered for the family shrine.

General Education and Culture

In their zeal to educate themselves and their families, late Victorian women could turn their homes into small museums, full of evocative objects and emblems of culture. These were important tools in both the direct instruction and the unconscious shaping of the children. Naturally the bric-à-brac needed to be the best possible quality.

Most writers agree that the enormous task of child rearing would be aided by the proper physical surroundings. In 1884 *Godey's* editor states that "the home influence that is daily exerted will be the main arbiter of the extent of what that light [of intelligence] in the family and its children shall be" (298). Women needed to create an environment which would educate their families. Tillinghast's "Talks on Home Decoration," in *The Art Interchange* in 1896, includes the assumption that the "human mind is more sensitive to surroundings than we are in the habit of believing..." (IV 88) and that "our homes express the strongest influence upon our characters and lives." Thus, for the sake of "our moral and aesthetic education, and the development of ourselves and our children,...the home should show the highest standard of art that our means and condition will permit." She concludes that children brought up in such an environment would obtain an "unconscious education," "the best and most lasting" type, by being always surrounded by the beauty chosen by their mother (I 14-15).

An anonymous editorial in *Scribner's Magazine* (1901) reiterated the idea that "unconscious aesthetic education" aids the development of "the elements of moral character" ("The Unconscious" 252). The "germ" of the appreciation and "perception of beauty" would only be "vital" if it were subconsciously instilled in the child by a well-planned environment. The conscientious mother must exercise care in arranging a suitable home for all the family. Writers were in agreement that beauty was an important element in the moral Christian home. Choosing specific beautiful elements that would combine into an aura redolent of "Christian Nurture" was the housewife's greatest problem.

But one method of making certain that one's home contained aesthetically pleasing objects was to use Japanese pieces. Women were told that rather than paint plaques or pottery badly themselves, they should "get things that are decorative in themselves. Of these are Japanese, Chinese, and India goods" [sic] (M.L.E. 468). As previously noted, all objects were well-crafted, since artisans took more pride in creating a superior object in the traditional methods, respecting their materials, than in making a large profit (Van Ingen 128). The novelist Harriet Prescott Spofford also recommended Japanese art within the home. The combination of the inherent beauty or quaintness of the objects with their fine craftsmanship was important in developing aesthetic appreciation in young children. Developing imagination was another skill not to be ignored. Thus she recommended "a Japanese scroll or two to take the young fancy travelling...." (Spofford 200).

Another method to heighten the educational qualities of the home was to collect "evocative" objects. These might be carvings, bronzes, other art objects, or natural items found by family members. An evocative object, in addition to having aesthetic or decorative qualities, told a story or taught a lesson. The variety of illustration found on fans caused one writer to remark that "take it all in all, Japanese fans are a liberal education in a condensed form" ("The Japanese" 87). Porcelains and carvings were also good sources for discussions with children. The late-nineteenth-century love of didacticism could, therefore, be fulfilled with Japanese objects.

Japanese art could also be used to teach family members about craftsmanship and nature. Cook felt that Japanese *netsukes*, or ivory carvings, were particularly useful in teaching children about skill, observation of life, and the attitude of the artist toward his work (IV 819). The fact that Japanese motifs are based on natural forms was also important: they were lessons about nature, a subject rich with moral and religious overtones. In fact, Keats' "Ode to a Grecian Urn" could just as well be about a Japanese vase. If "goodness" is defined in utilitarian terms, with references to efficiency and standards of craftsmanship, Japanese objects would readily measure up. Thus Japanese art had a role in the general education of the household. It could be used to evoke lessons in geography and natural history. More importantly, it was a model of excellent, sincere craftsmanship, and, therefore, a natural element in the Christian home.

Japanese art could play an important part in the aesthetic education in the home. In addition to its moral qualities, it could teach Westerners about design and the use of nature in art. Several writers had noticed that Japanese art was also a good source of art education. In 1875, Cook had written:

It is almost inevitable that we should be thrown upon the Japanese for our first hints and instructions; their art is so perfect as decoration, their methods so varied, and their materials suited to every subject and belonging to our own time, and we so rich in its productions (III 494).

Frederic Vors, in *The Art Amateur*, praises "its subtleness and its truth". His statement, "as for truth, especially in decorative art, the Japanese have taught us many a lesson..." is a convoluted reference to Western adaption of Japanese arrangements, particularly asymmetrical, naturalistic ones. Vors admired the Japanese practice of allowing a motif to "grow" around an object (53).

The late nineteenth century was the beginning of the period in which art activities at home seem to have been most popular. The Centennial Exhibition of 1876 was the beginning of an active interest in all the arts by the American public, an "important social development" according to a review in *Scribner's Monthly Magazine* (McLaughlin 897). Critics in general felt that exposure to ideas about the arts, whether new or revived, was a good thing.

Japan was instrumental in awakening American interest in art. For example, "art embroidery" began, according to the anonymous author of "The Society of Decorative Art," in the late 1870's "when, then, people in general began to hear about 'the South Kensington stitch,' and to see the Walter Crane books, and to learn of the existence of Japan, they naturally—being Americans—became interested in a novelty so interesting" (700). Once the interest was awakened, Americans continued to look to Japan for advice and inspiration. Candace Wheeler, designer, writer, and member of Associated Artists, praised Japanese motifs and arrangements as models for American decorative artists and amateurs. Her major reason is the Japanese love of nature, combined with successfully conveyed natural forms. Clarence Cook also found Japanese art a good resource: "the young people can be asked to look at nature, or—if they can't get into the country—to take the next best thing, and study the Japanese decoration on books and trays and tea-pots..." (II 345).

Women of the late-nineteenth and early-twentieth century had many sources to which they could turn for Japanese motifs. Periodicals, books, and Japanese books and objects themselves all might provide inspiration. Other important lessons came from the Japanese "neat workmanship and exquisite ornamentation" ("World's" 106). Japan and its objects were, therefore, an "influence in the direction of good design" (Hornel 183-184). Making decorative objects for one's own home was an important activity in the late-nineteenth century. The process involved "sacrifice," an important Christian virtue, as well as a demonstration of sincerity and skill. It was the domestically-made decorations which made a home in which "the real life of the family is felt, and wherein the sweetest associations are brought together to make this always and forever the most pleasant spot the world contains" (Williams and Jones 138-139). According to David Swing, writing in *Cosmopolitan* in 1886, being creative and enjoying the fine arts is a way of bringing youth out of "barbarism," thus creating "fine people" (276). If family members, especially the wife, decorated the house, creating and collecting the bric-a-brac, expression of family feeling was sure to be established. Thus the moral home was enhanced by its inhabitants' sincere artistic efforts (Poole 112).

Another area in which Japan was a model was the use of color. The Japanese seemed to have a "natural feeling for [color]" (Alsop 44-45), according to *The Art Amateur*; their color schemes were compared to Medieval stained glass, as being "remarkable for excellence" ("Editorial Chit-Chat" 84). Another writer asserts that "the knowledge of harmony in color seems to be intuitive. The commonest designs of the Japanese artist or even artisan show how rarely the judgement of the workman is at fault in this regard. With us Americans it is different" ("Harmony" 10). However, most believed that Americans could eventually learn to use those "touches" of "brilliant color which are so distinctly associated in our minds with Japan" ("Chicago" 143). Study of even the smallest Japanese product, therefore, could be beneficial to a woman wishing to improve her use of color.

Thus, throughout the period under consideration, Americans were frequently assured that art was "good for" them. They could also read about the inherent worth of Japanese art in choice of motif, craftsmanship, sincerity, and color. Japanese art, it appeared, was naturally uplifting and educational. As such, it and objects modeled after it belonged in the Christian home.

Presentation of Family

It was in the presentation of the family to its public that Japanese art seems to have played one of its strongest roles. Women used it to demonstrate that they were properly carrying out their duties in the home. The positive effects of Japanese art in rearing children and bringing sincerity and morality to the home made it an emblem of a woman's intentions. The presence of Japanese art in the interior decoration of a home demonstrated that family life was well developed. Using the home as a presentational object is an old American tradition. In one of the early books about the theory and practice of house building, *The Architecture of Country Houses* (1850), A.J. Downing wrote that "the character of every man may be read in his house" (25). By the last quarter of the century, women had taken over the decorating of their contractor-built houses, making the statement read: the character of every woman may be read in her parlor.

In presenting the family to the public, women needed to decorate their homes to demonstrate the education, culture, taste, individuality, and economic position of the family. Magazines helped set standards by publishing pictures of the homes of the famous, wealthy, and artistic. Readers interested in the Japanese taste could model their efforts on Tiffany's Japanese library, Dr. William Hammond's Japanese bedroom, or Vanderbilt's Japanese sitting room, all of which were illustrated in

The Decorator and Furnisher. But they were warned that imitations of others' decorating schemes were considered "artistic sins," as well as being insincere ("Home Decorating" 38-39).

Economy

The economical qualities of Japanese art allowed middle-class housewives to create their own "uplifting" art galleries, using inexpensive carvings, bronzes, porcelains, and prints. Fans could be used lavishly to create wall arrangements or friezes, since they were sold for as little as three cents and sometimes even given away. "Japan sends us a lot of material that is as beautiful as it is cheap" one reviewer wrote bluntly (Hubert 42). Another comment was that the art is "economical and recommends itself immediately to lovers of soft artistic effects..." (P.I. 105). Of "moderate cost and considerable attraction" came from *House and Garden* ("Christmas Gifts" 358). Furthermore, Japanese art work was right for those "on a moderate income" (Pattison 22). An ad for Morse's *Japanese Homes and Their Surroundings,* a manual of decorating ideas based on Japanese models, quotes a favorable review in *Scientific American*: "for cultivated people of small means, having tastes...to beautify home." The book itself was "brimful of suggestion...." *(American Architect* n.p.). Thus women who aspired to a home that demonstrated their love of beauty and knowledge of the sincere could, thanks to Japanese art, fulfill their wishes. "Fewer mistakes are made where Oriental pottery is employed than where modern European wares are used" wrote Caryl Coleman in 1899. But he also added that it is "better to have a few good pieces than many second-rate ones...."(82). All the bric-à-brac necessary to "transform a modern house into an earthly paradise" could be purchased economically at the nearest Japanese store (Kaye 132).

Economical decorating could even be done in good taste. According to Cook, "many of the best things in house decorating and furnishing are those that cost the least" (II 346). Choosing rightly was critical; taste was more important than money. All agreed that good taste in the home created an elevating environment for the entire family, and Japanese bric-à-brac allowed even a woman with a limited decorating budget to adorn her home tastefully (Tillinghast 14).

Expressing Individuality

In an age of urbanization and industrialization, when the individual often seemed to be lost in the mass, one important way a woman could reinforce and express her family's uniqueness was through her home. Every detail and object was telling. Nineteenth-century theorists felt that unusual, strange, and "queer" things contributed to an unusual room that expressed its owner's unique personality. Women were urged to "make [the room] unconventional and pretty;" "quaint" was a frequently used word. A unique room could be achieved at the same cost as some "ugly conventional style" (M.L. E. 468). In *Art Decoration Applied to Furniture* (1878), the novelist Harriet Prescott Spofford tells her readers that something out of the ordinary was necessary in a room "since what is slightly peculiar and quaint, without being fantastic, gives vivacity, and is of more worth than uniform and mechanical dulness" (236). Such devices would attract the occupant's attention and interest. The "artistic craze," a pejorative term for Aestheticism, was praised as leading to rooms expressing their owners' tastes and personalities (Sherwood 684). Cook urged each reader to "make her house delightful by simply allowing it to reflect her own accomplished individuality..." (II 351).

Since each Japanese object was unique and handmade, its owner could, merely by her choice, express her individuality. And she could be certain that any object chosen would be in good taste, since "all objects are artistic in Japan," according to *The Art Interchange* (P.I. "A Letter" 146). As a result, where the objects were put became important. The arrangement of bric-à-brac was critical in creating a sincere room. As might be expected, the critics had much to say upon the subject. Since the fireplace was the center of family life, "mantel ornaments were the key to the whole," according to Cook. The objects should be grouped because "things, which, beautiful or handsome or curious in themselves, lose something of their value by isolation...." His nine fireplace illustrations show idealized and artistic set pieces: an eclectic mix of antiques, oriental items, natural objects, modern "art" objects, and homemade works. Theoretically these objects should exemplify the family: its interests, education, travels, and accomplishments. The taste and culture of the family, therefore, were to be displayed upon the family shrine (II 351, 353).

Good Taste

Displaying one's possessions and decorating one's home in good taste were important cultural activities. According to George Parsons Lathrop (1893), the "influence [of decoration] is of the best, also because it carries fine art into the resorts of every day...." "The things done...are frequently excellent, and the general result is not a lowering of art, but a gradual lifting up of the popular taste" (74). A note in *Harper's New Monthly Magazine* mentioned the relationship between house decoration and improvement of taste:

the desire for artistic decoration (not always rightly guided), for the adornment of houses,...has penetrated through all classes; that the homes of the merchant, the tradesman, the city clerk, and even the artisan, all make some pretense and manifest some desire toward the raising of their tastes... ("Work" 385).

The anonymous reviewer suggests that any sort of improvement in the home and its decor will lead to progress in the realm of good taste. Decorating one's house itself is, therefore, an essential vehicle for this desirable process. Decorating it correctly was, however, the ultimate goal.

Good taste was an important concern because the late-nineteenth-century commercial boom had created a marketplace abundant with choice. The general growth of middle-class prosperity allowed women to respond to increased advertising in newspapers and magazines and commercial innovations like the department store with its special sales. Displaying one's purchases at home was only natural. Magazine illustrations of ideal homes showed shelves and tables covered with bric-à-brac. (Articles about artists in their studios include illustrations of equally bric-à-brac filled interiors.) Consumer objects are emblems of the acquisitiveness that came with new economic power. Instead of collecting directly from Europe, as did the very rich whose houses were described in the periodicals, the middle class collected from the department stores and the local bazaars. The effect was, however, the same: a massive display of material wealth.

Good taste included moral considerations: when purchasing and using objects one must avoid vulgarity. American women needed to be cognizant of the fine line between a substantial look that indicated well-deserved prosperity and an insincere ostentation that suggested vulgar riches. In 1880, *Harper's Bazaar* advised that "to show a beautiful thing because it is beautiful, there is no vulgarity in that; but to show anything, whether beautiful or ugly, for the sake of show, this is vulgar" ("Domestic" 12). Japanese art and the Japanese style were suggested as an antedote. The pieces were beautiful because "the Japanese never mistake *bigness* for *greatness*, nor *ostentation* for *splendor*, and throughout their designs exhibit that exquisite refinement and reserve which contribute so much to the beauty of the 'white ideas' of Greece," according to architect C.T. Mathews (392). W.E. Griffis wrote in *The Craftsman Magazine* in 1905 that "we Americans need a little of the Japanesque to tone down our tendency to over display" (311). Reformers urged that simplicity was not only beautiful but also "restful," an important consideration in an industrialized society.

Education and Culture

Not only did Japanese art and design produce an effective and economical display of individuality and good taste, but they also gave their owners an "intellectual pleasure." "The wonderful skill exhibited in Japanese decoration appeals to the educated and artistic taste, on account of its novelty, and a touch of freedom that prevents tame uniformity and sameness, so frequent in ordinary productions of pottery, metal, etc." (Kaye 132). Women who wanted to demonstrate that their families were artistic, intellectual, and knowledgeable could not go wrong choosing Japanese objects for their bric-à-brac shelves.

But, in addition to displaying the proper art works, one needed to be certain that they were the "real thing." Connoisseurship of the arts became a more general activity, especially for women, during this period. It can be seen as part of a general campaign for competence, efficiency, and uniform standards during the rise of professionalism in the early Progressive period. Within the household women tried to develop their own form of professionalism. They needed, for example, the knowledge to choose the "right things" for their homes and for the edification of their families. The columns in many of the "art" magazines were designed specifically with this aim. Even more general women's magazines instructed their readers on the subject. *Peterson's*, for example, had an article on the painter Hokusai. But since Japanese objects were readily available and generally inexpensive, consumers usually didn't need to worry about dealing with fakes. The object of the connoisseurship education in the magazines seems to have been to allow women to become aware of the fine points of the objects that they purchased and discuss them appropriately with their children and friends.

Producing Art at Home

Finally, it was in the production of art works in the Japanese style that women could integrate all aspects of their role. Doing embroidery and painting china was educational, both for themselves and as an example to their children; it was also an indication that the family could afford to have them spend their time in artistic pursuits. But the results, especially if utilizing a natural motif, would influence the children's characters and evoke religious thoughts in all. If the woman truly put herself into her work, the finished piece would be sincere, reinforcing her teaching and example. Displaying the piece in the more public rooms of the house would allow her to demonstrate her culture, knowledge, and skill.

Magazines offered women an ample number of ideas for these projects, including many ready-to-use patterns and inspirational sketches. Designs were published throughout the period, suggesting continued reader interest. The greatest concentration of items on needlework occurred between 1885 and 1889, with 47 examples in 1887 alone. China painting patterns followed a similar trend. One reason probably was that Japanese designs were considered easy to execute, as well as being dramatic and beautiful. For example, an embroidery design for Japanese goldwork was printed with the recommendation that it was "effective, comparatively cheap," and could be executed with "little labor." Obviously if one could easily and inexpensively demonstrate her good taste, sincerity, and accomplishments, one should ("Christmas Display" 8).

Thus the "true woman," eager to do the best for her family and home, would find Japanese art helpful in accomplishing her task. Since mankind was to be uplifted by the "gentle, persevering, incalculable force of woman's influence," women themselves should seize upon all the aid that periodicals could give them in accomplishing this important task (Editorial, *Godey's* 298). Japanese art and design, they were assured, was one of the best tools at hand. Goodness, truth, and beauty would enter the house with Japanese art and home production of pieces in that style. The family's life would be improved in all areas from education to general moral tone. And, seeing the pieces in the living room or on the mantel, the family's public would know that this was a home in which education, aesthetics, and morality were combined.

Summary

The Japanese style involves more than just a listing of the particular motifs used by designers and craftsmen. There was a strong moral and educational value associated with things Japanese. The use of the Japanese aesthetic was further justified on the grounds that it was not only artistic, decorative, and cheerful, but also involved excellent craftsmanship, making for sincere pieces. The design had classical references, with similarities to the art of ancient Greece, the root of Western art. It was also true to nature, thus able to suggest religious and moral lessons.

Nineteenth-century America developed some forms into cliches: drooping branches with a flight of birds, combinations of birds or butterflies with floral forms, and a full moon behind trees and branches. Floral forms were overwhelmingly the most popular, but magazines urged women to create their own combinations, too. One of the strongest Japanese influences is on the arrangement of forms. Asymmetry, truncated forms, and long, narrow formats are among the ideas intimately associated with the Japanese influence.

Japanese forms were used in a variety of ways, ranging in scope from a small embroidery or painted plate to whole rooms. Magazines printed suggestions, with varying degrees of sophistication, on how to embroider curtains, paint plates, construct furniture, embellish mantel areas and cozy corners, and organize whole rooms and summer houses. Even parties and church bazaars could be in the Japanese style. That the style might be overused is attested in various humorous comments and cartoons. But in general, the Japanese taste was felt to be a force for positive change. Displaying Japanese art in one's home presented the family as moral, educated, cultured, and having good taste. Home, the complete shelter from the hostile external world, could be demonstrably enhanced by the Japanese taste. Thus the true woman used Japanese art to decorate her home in such a way that it would further her goals for the family and reinforce what she taught.

Works Cited

Alsop, Adelaide. "Chinese and Japanese Plates" *The Art Amateur* 40 (1893), 44-45.

American Architect and Building News. 20 (1886). n.p. (ad. sect.)

Bisland, Elizabeth. "A Flying Trip around the World." *Cosmopolitan* 9 (1890), 173-184.

Brooks, Noah. "Some Pictures from Japan." *Scribner's Monthly* 11 (1875), 177-193.

Burke, et. al., *In Pursuit of Beauty: Americans and the Aesthetic Movement.* New York: The Metropolitan Museum of Art/Rizzoli, 1986.

Bushnell, Horace. *Views of Christian Nurture and of Subjects Adjacent Thereto.* Delmar, N.Y.: Scholars' Facsimiles and Reprints, 1975.

Carpenter, Frank G. "The Two Capitals of Japan." *Cosmopolitan* 7 (1889). 425-440.

"Chicago Column: Interior of Hooden." *American Architect and Building News* 41 (1893), 143.

"Christmas Display at the London Art-Needle Societies." *The Art Interchange* 10 (1883), 8.

"Christmas Gifts That Furnish the House." *House and Garden* 22 (1912), 357-359.

Coleman, Caryl. "Bric-a-Brac—or What You Will." *House Beautiful* 5 (1899), 80-84.

Cook, Clarence. "Beds and Tables, Stools and Candlesticks-II." *Scribner's Monthly Magazine* 11 (1875), 342-357.

———. "Beds and Tables, Stools and Candlesticks-III." *Scribner's Monthly Magazine* 11 (1875), 488-503.

———. "Beds and Tables, Stools and Candlesticks IV." *Scribner's Monthly Magazine* 11 (1875), 809-822.

Dewson, Edward. "Estheticism." *The Decorator and Furnisher* 3 (1883), 89.

"Domestic Art." *Harper's Bazar* 13 (1880), 12-14.

Downing, Andrew Jackson. *The Architecture of Country Houses*, 1850. New York: Dover, 1969.

Editorial. *Godey's Ladies' Book and Magazine* 108 (1884), 298.

Editorial Chit-Chat: "Why Japanese Art Is Superior." *Peterson's* 84 (1883), 84.

"Editor's Literary Record." Editorial. *Harper's New Monthly Magazine* 56 (1878), 307.

Emerson, Ralph Waldo. *The Selected Writings of Emerson.* Ed. Brooks Atkinson. New York: The Modern Library, 1950.

Finn, Dallas. "Japan at the Centennial." *Nineteenth Century* 2 No. 3-4 (1976), 33-40.

Griffin, L.B. "Japanese and Chinese Embroidery for Girls." *Ladies' Home Journal* (June 1903), 31.

Griffis, William Elliot. "The Craftsman's Life and Lot in Japan." *The Craftsman Magazine*, 8 (1905), 293-311.

———. "The Japanese Artisan at Home." *Frank Leslie's Popular Monthly* 10 (1883), 561-569.

"The Harmony of Colors." *The Art Amateur* 1 (1879), 10.

Hearn, Lafcadio, "About Faces in Japanese Art." *The Atlantic Monthly* 78 (1896), 219-226.

———. "The Genius of Japanese Civilization." *The Atlantic Monthly* 76 (1895), 449-458.

———. "A Trip to Kyoto." *The Atlantic Monthly* 77 (1896), 613-624.

Hicks, A.M. "Talks on Designing: Historic Ornament in Its Relation to the Practical Designer." *The Art Interchange* 34 (1895), 158.

———. "Talks on Designing: IV Practical Aid to be Found in Japanese Art." *The Art Interchange* 35 (1895), 119.

"Hints for Home Decorating and Furnishing." *The Art Amateur* 18 (1888), 136-138.

"Home Decorating and Furnishing." *The Art Amateur* 20 (1889), 38-9.

Hornel, E.A. "Japanese Studies." *The Decorator and Furnisher*, 30 (1897), 183-84.

Hubert, Philip G. Jr. "House Decoration as a Business for Women." (p. 42) *The Art Interchange* 34 (1895), 42.

I., P. "Decorative Notes." *The Art Interchange* 29 (1892), 142-3, 146.

I., P. "A Letter from Japan—with Decorative Hints." *The Art Interchange* 28 (1892), 142-3, 146.

"The Japanese Fan: Its Fashions and Fancies, Queer Uses and Quaint Pictures." *Harper's Bazar* 13 (1881), 86-87.

Jarves, James J. *A Glimpse at the Art of Japan.* 1876. Rutland, Vt.: Charles E. Tuttle Co., 1984.

Kaye, Emma T. "Moorish and Japanese Interiors." *The Decorator and Furnisher* 23 (1894), 130-132.

LaFarge, John. "Bric-a-Brac." *Century* 46/24 (1893), 419-429.

Lathrop, George Parsons. "Progress of Art in New York." *Harper's New Monthly Magazine* 86 (1893), 740-752.

M.L.E. "Two Kinds of Decoration." *Scribner's Monthly Magazine* 19 (1879), 466-468.

Mathews, C.T. "Japanese Architecture." *Architectural Record* 5 (1895-1896), 382-392.

McLaughlin, Louise. Rev. of *China Painting. Scribner's Monthly Magazine* 15 (1878), 897.

Meredith, Jackson. "A Japanese Painter and His School." *Peterson's* 100 (1891), 149-154.

"Morality of Home Decorating." *The Art Amateur* 5 (1881), 80.

"Oriental Hangings." *Arts and Decoration* 1 (1911), 316.

"Painting on Silk." *Harper's Bazar* 13 (1880), 789-790.

Pattison, James William. "Art for the Home—What to Buy on a Moderate Income." *House Beautiful* (1906), 21-22.

Poole, Hester M. "House Decoration." *The Decorator and Furnisher* 7 (1885), 110, 112.

"Review: Japanese Art—Its Past and Present—What Will Its Future Be?" *Arts and Decoration* 1 (1910), 52, 54.

Saisselin, Remy G. *The Bourgeoise and the Bibelot.* New Brunswick, New Jersey: Rutgers University Press, 1984. Sherwood, M.E.W. "Certain New York Houses." *Harper's New Monthly Magazines* 65 (1882), 680-690.

"The Society of Decorative Arts." *Scribner's Monthly Magazine* 22 (1881), 697-709.

Spofford, Harriet Prescott. *Art Decoration Applied to Furniture*. New York: Harper and Brothers, 1878.

Swing, David. "Fine Arts and Fine People." *Cosmopolitan* 1 (1886), 274-276.

Tillinghast, Mary E. "Talks on Home Decoration-I." *The Art Interchange* 36 (1896), 14-15.

_____ "Talks on Home Decoration-IV." *The Art Interchange* 36 (1896), 88.

Van Ingen, W.B. "Two Beautiful Rooms in Japan." *Scribner's Magazine* 29 (1901), 125-128.

Vors, Frederic. "House Japanese Decoration." *The Art Amateur* 1 (1879), 53-55.

Williams, Henry T., and Jones, Mrs. C.S. *Beautiful Homes or Hints on House Furnishings*. New York: Henry T. Williams, 1878.

"Work of John Ruskin." *Harper's New Monthly Magazine* 78 (1888), 385.

"World's Fair: Architecture, Buildings." *The Art Amateur* 29 (1893), 106.

Elmey Sammis Trimmer: Tailoress and Weaver

Patricia Cunningham

Researchers of material culture recognize that the uniqueness of their studies lies in looking through objects for related historical meaning. They believe that artifacts may have particular kinds of information not available from written sources.[1] Therefore, upon discovery of the account book of a tailoress and weaver, Elmey Sammis Trimmer, the subject of this paper, my immediate reaction was to uncover extant garments and textiles produced by her to discover their special meaning. The efforts, however, were in vain for no documented materials have come to light. Of necessity, then, this paper deals with a material culture subject but does not use artifacts as evidence. Indeed, the crucial source is the account book of Elmey Sammis Trimmer dating between 1836 and 1876.

In light of the ends of artifact study—"to discover history"—what does this mean? What particular kinds of information are lost by not having artifacts to examine, and what unique historical meaning can be gained by examining and analyzing the account book? First, it must be recognized that the account book is rare. For while many American women engaged in the textile arts, there are few extant account books kept by women and fewer still of nineteenth-century pioneers in Ohio. The information found in the book has potential to give us cultural-historical meaning that may not be available through artifact study. If we had only artifacts to examine it is highly unlikely that we would have a representative variety or number to study. The account book on the other hand lists a substantial quantity of garments and other textile products and presents us with dates and names of patrons as well as the prices Elmey Sammis Trimmer charged for her work. From her use of common nineteenth-century textile terminology, we have an indication of the types of materials she produced. And from our knowledge of extant clothing and fabrics with similar descriptive names we have a fair indication of what these products looked like.[2] This information can be taken with related documents and written materials to reconstruct

140

a small segment of American history and life in the Firelands area of north central Ohio, on the shore of Lake Erie.

But what is missing? By not examining the artifacts made by Elmey Sammis Trimmer we cannot discover those affective or sensory qualities which many material culture scholars believe are essential. (Schlereth 12-13) That is, we do not have a sense of Elmey Sammis Trimmer's aesthetics, her choice of designs or colors; we do not know her technical skills or the quality of materials she used to create clothing and textile products. We are missing a kind of subjective and highly individual history only available through artifacts or personal accounts found in diaries. In comparing the two types of sources, it is clear that the artifacts would tell us one story and the account book another. Of course, the ideal would be to have both. However, since the account book is a more rare discovery than undocumented artifacts, by having Elmey Sammis Trimmer's own words we may be better off than if we had only a few artifacts.

Elmey Sammis Trimmer began keeping her account book in 1836, when she was single and living in Cayuga County, New York. In a small leather-bound notebook, she recorded her tailoring, dressmaking and weaving productivity. The bulk of entries date between January 1, 1836, and October 30, 1856, with two entries in 1866 and a final entry in 1876. Elmey included such items as recipes for dyes and liniment and a cure for cholera, as well as personal and family information. More importantly she recorded names of her patrons, what she made for them and the prices. In her own writing inside the cover is the inscription: "Elmey Sammis's Book Jan 1: 1836." The record keeping was business-like but not professional. When an account was paid up Elmey crossed it out with a large X. [See Fig. 1] Yet since Elmey recorded personal and family events such as illnesses, births, deaths and a barn raising, the small volume could be viewed as a type of diary. While there are few personal comments or opinions in the book, a highly personal note does appear in her hand on a scrap of paper tucked into the account book. It suggests Elmey's sense of value and pride in her skills:

"I have no book of fancy work except that book of patterns and those are too small for [ ] splashes & c. I have my tabbe scarf it is very pretty but it ought to be for it cost me about eight dollars beside my own work."

Entries in the account book reveals that barter was a customary form of payment for service. Elmey accepted a variety of items as credit: cheese, butter, lard, tallow, buckwheat, corn, pig corn, salt, wheat, apples, cider, hens, wool and peaches. She also accepted cash. Her records likewise reveal that she sold similar farm products: wheat, turkeys, hogs, corn, pork, butter and oak trees. The account was kept in dollars and cents. However, she frequently gave the price in shillings and pence.[3] The

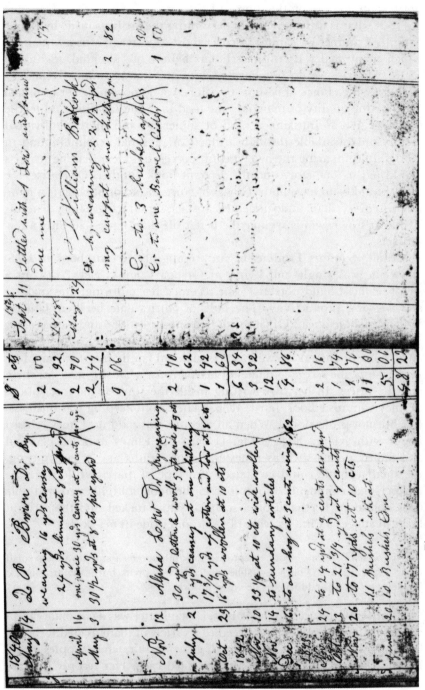

Fig. 1 Page from Elmey Sammis Trimmer's account book with large Xs presumably used to show a completed transaction.

total income registered in her book from clothing and textiles was $945.65 (See Table 1).

Table One

**Amount Earned in New York and Ohio for
Clothing and Textile Products**

New York Year	Clothing	Textiles	Total
1836	57.75	104.10	161.85
1837	55.97	97.19	153.16
1838	27.57	115.94	143.51
1839	——	13.29	13.29
New York Totals	141.29	330.52	471.81
Ohio			
1839	——	2.50	2.50
1840	——	66.11	66.11
1841	——	30.69	30.69
1842	1.64	26.40	28.04
1843	1.32	52.06	53.58
1844	.50	34.35	34.85
1845	——	24.96	24.96
1846	——	23.12	23.12
1847	——	57.66	57.66
1848	.75	53.11	53.86
1849	.25	37.92	38.17
1850	——	10.32	10.32
1851	——	14.56	14.56
1852	——	12.80	12.80
1853	——	4.45	4.45
1854	——	3.50	3.50
1855	——	2.62	2.62
1856	——	7.25	7.25
1866	——	5.00	5.00
Ohio Totals	4.46	469.38	473.84
New York and Ohio Totals	$145.75	$799.90	$945.65

Elmey Sammis was born in Huntington, Westneck, New York, on April 9, 1800. Her family moved to Genoa in Cayuga County, New York, for she recorded that she lived there on December 6, 1820 although in 1818 she was still living in Huntington. The account book suggests that as a single woman, who may have lived with her parents or other relatives, Elmey helped to support the family with the home manufacture of clothing and textile items. At the age of 38 she married Isaac Trimmer in Genoa on February 3, 1839. Mr. Trimmer's first wife had died in 1837, leaving him a daughter, Elizabeth. During the fall of 1839, in a pattern established by many New Yorkers, the Trimmers migrated to Ohio, settling in Townsend Township, Huron County, located in the Firelands area in north central Ohio. A daughter, Sarah, was born in 1842. In moving to Ohio the Trimmers were following the lead of White Sammis, Elmey's brother, who migrated from Cayuga, New York, to Huron County in 1837. The Trimmers settled on property adjacent to Elmey's brother. After a productive life as a weaver and tailoress Elmey Sammis Trimmer died on August 15, 1880, at the age of seventy-nine.[4]

Genoa, New York: January 1836 - September 1839
Elmey's most productive years, as revealed in the account book, were those recorded while she was living in Genoa, Cayuga County, New York. Much of her work during this period centered on sewing, that is, making clothing for men, women and children. The total amount earned from tailoring and sewing was $145.75, $141.29 of which she gained in her New York years. Her efforts earned her $57.75 in 1836, $55.97 in 1837, $27.57 in 1838. She did no sewing for profit in 1839. Thus, sewing and tailoring in New York amounted to 14.9% of the total recorded earnings from tailoring and weaving between 1836 and 1876.

The types of clothing she produced while living in New York included the following:

Type of Garment	Number Made	Price Range
Men:		
Box coat	1	$2.50
Coats	27	$1.50-$3.00
Coat, pants	2	$1.12-$3.00
Coat, vest	2	$2.50-$3.25
Coat, vest, pants	2	$3.25-$4.00
Overcoat	2	$2.25-$3.00
Pantaloons	20	.50-.87
Vest	9	.62-$2.50
Suit	1	$2.00
Socks	1	$1.75

Type of Garment	Number Made	Price Range
Women:		
Bonnet	1	.50
Cloak	3	$1.00-$1.50
Coat	2	$1.50
Dress and capes	1	$1.25
Dress and pantaloons	1	$2.25
Children:		
Round jacket	2	.62-.87
Dress	2	.37-.50
Coat	2	.50-$2.00
Coat and vest	1	$2.25
Cloak	2	.75-$1.00
Stock coat	1	.50

The discrepancy in price may relate to the style and difficulty in construction of particular garments. There is no reference to the type of fabrics used or whether it was supplied by Elmey or the customer. The bulk of her sewing was in men's wear. However, it is not known if Elmey was simply sewing the garments previously cut out by a tailor or if she was tailoring them, that is providing patterns, cutting out the fabric and sewing and fitting the garments. It was not uncommon for families to take cloth to a tailor to be cut out and then to a sewing woman for fitting and construction.

The prices and types of textiles woven by Elmey in her New York years between 1836 and 1839 included the following:

Textile Item	Price* (Per yard unless stated otherwise)
Coverlid	$1.50 each (61 cents extra for dying yarns)
Carpeting	14 p; 18 cents yd.
Rug Carpet	1 shilling
Cearsey	1 shilling
Diaper	1 and 4 pence; 16 cents
Woolen Cloth	8 cents/9 cents or 9 pence/10
Blanket	$1.00 each
Cotton and Linnen	1 shilling
Mix	9 cents
Woolen and cotton	8 cents; 1 shilling
Plane Linen	8 p
Cearsey Linen	1 shilling
Wool Mix	9 cents, 10 cents
Cearsey blankets made from 11 yds. of fabric	$1.00 each
Cearsey Woolen	1 shilling
Horse Blankets	50 cents each
Linen	8 cents

146 **Making the American Home**

Textile Item	Price*
Weaving (nondesignated type)	8 cents, 9 cents, 10 cents, 1 shilling

*One shilling equals 12.5 cents; there are 12 pence in one shilling.

The difference in prices suggests that Elmey's charges may have been dictated by the complexity of the construction. For instance, a distinction is made between "plane linnen" and "cearsey linnen." Cearsey, a more complicated structure, was more expensive (1 shilling or 12 1/2 cents per yard) than "plane" linen (8 cents per yard). Elmey's price for "weaving" without a designation for type of cloth or fiber ranged between 8 cents and 1 shilling. Certain distinctive types of textiles were more costly. For diaper, a cloth that requires a more complicated tie-up on the loom, Elmey charged about 16 cents per yard and for carpeting, which also could be a patterned textile, she charged 14 p and 18 cents per yard. During her New York years she charged 1 shilling per yard for rug carpet. The cost of a woven coverlid (coverlet) generally was $1.50 with extra charges made for dyeing yarns.

It is quite likely that these fabrics had different uses depending on fiber content and weave. The blankets, rag carpeting and coverlids had obvious uses. Woolen, flannel or wool mixed with cotton or linen are found in extant clothing from the period. Linen is found in household textiles (sheets, towels, etc.), and in clothing (shirts and nightgowns), especially clothing worn in a warm climate.

At some point, on a scrap of paper, Elmey totalled her earnings from weaving for the year 1836. This amounted to $104.10. In 1837 she earned $97.19 and in 1838 $115.94. The year she moved to Ohio, 1839, she earned only $13.29 from weaving. The total earned from weaving in her New York years was $330.52, 34.95% of her total earnings for weaving and sewing.

Elmey's customers in her New York years included 80 individuals. Several appeared to be regular customers. Elmey wove and sewed a number of garments for families with the name of Fenner, Goodyear, Shaw, Mow and King. E.P. King was, in fact, the husband of Elmey's younger sister, Charry. It is quite likely that many of these customers were, indeed, related in some way to Elmey or were her neighbors in Genoa, New York.[5]

Townsend, Ohio: September 1839 - August 1880
Pioneer Life

Townsend, the township in the Ohio Firelands district where the Trimmers settled, takes its name from the Connecticut merchant, Kneeland Townsend, who owned the greater part of the land in the first period of settlement. Pioneering in this section of Ohio, often called "New Connecticut," would not have been an easy task for the land was wet and heavily timbered. The heavy forest meant the land had to be cleared for farming. From the first settlement in 1811 and for many years afterward the manufacture of oak staves ("Townsend Wheat") was an important industry (Baughman 270-274).

After 1825 a second wave of settlement occurred which added greatly to the still sparse population. It was during this second wave that Elmey Sammis Trimmer and her family moved from Genoa, New York, to Townsend, Ohio. By the time they arrived in 1839, the township and surrounding areas were beginning to develop economically. The canal from Lake Erie to nearby Milan had just been completed in July 1839, making a harbor at Milan and increasing its commerce. Norwalk, a town adjacent to Townsend, had several factories and businesses and, indeed, Townsend had its own post office whose postmaster was Elmey's brother, White Sammis (Waggoner 40, 42-43)[6].

While the area showed an increase in population and economic growth, it still took a tremendous effort to clear the land and acquire necessities of life. During their early years as pioneers, families had spartan lifestyles not unlike those of the first settlers in this country. Of course, one of the greatest needs was for cloth for household use and clothing. One particularly sympathetic historian noted in the early twentieth century that, "the pioneers were industrious people. The situation required that the men must chop and grub and clear the land ere they could plow and sow and reap. And the women had to card and spin and knit and weave and make garments for their families, in addition to household work" (Baughman 91).

Flax and sheep were farm produced and the fibers were prepared at home or, in the case of wool, taken to a professional carder if one was available. Yarn was then spun from the prepared flax or wool, dyed and sent to a weaver or woven on the household loom. At times the process of cloth making called for "fulling" or "kicking" parties since wool cloth for men's wear needed to be fulled (actually shrunk) to produce a thicker, warmer fabric. During these social gatherings the woven cloth was "stretched out on the puncheon floor and held at each end while men with bared feet sat in rows at the sides and kicked the cloth, while the women poured on warm soap suds" (Baughman 91). When families became more forehanded, that is when they had more sheep and goods they could sell in the market, they could acquire more finely prepared all-wool broadcloth which had been professionally fulled and dressed and have it made into clothing by a professional tailoress, tailor or seamstress.

The clothing of pioneer children usually was not tailor made or even hand-me-down ready-made clothing, but rather the result of the household preparation of linen or woolen yarns. During a roll call of the Firelands Historical Society in 1906, Mr. Perrin reminisced about pioneer days in East Milan. He recalled that the boys all dressed alike in "their identical butternut [a common dye] suits of clothes their mothers had made them, with their skull caps with the tassels on top, looking very much like Commanche Indians." He described the clothes he wore to Sunday School as "tow linen pants my mother made me and a blue round-about [jacket]." Although he wore no shoes, he was especially proud of a speckled hat he had bought with 18 cents earned for hoeing corn ("Records of Proceedings..." 1229). Children were not always so well dressed, for there were times when wool was in short supply. In a letter dated 1839 a Clarksfield, Huron County, mother noted "not having wool of late, we are destitute of clothing," and the children look quite ragged (Baughman 108).

It was necessary to produce cloth in the home because the cost of purchased cloth was prohibitive. Fulled cloth, for instance, was $2.00 per yard. If a gentleman had a very plain suit made from a more expensive satinett the cost would be approximately $24.75, which was more than three month's labor. Most pioneers would not consider doing this and so wore deerskin pants, home-made flannel and linen for suits and coats, and wool hats or coonskin caps. Fulled cloth was common for dress coats. Women's dresses were made from tow and linen cloth, handmade plaid and flannels, and calico for special occasions (Smith 35; Sommers 74-75).[7]

In her reminiscences of life in the Firelands of Ohio, Emma Brown noted that after the fleeces were washed, scoured and cleansed they were sent to the carding mill at Clarksfield, Huron County, to be made into rolls. The average amount of wool spun in a day was forty knots (80 yards). Some of it was doubled and twisted for knitting, and the rest went to the loom. She noted that some of the yarn was colored and woven in fancy stripes for dresses and that gingham was popular for aprons. Another pioneer woman, "Aunt Debby" Stevens of New London, Huron County, followed the trade of weaving and spinning: reeling, dyeing, weaving or knitting for her own family and her neighbors. She was one of the few who could spin flax fine and even enough for sewing thread (Brown 193; "Mrs. Deborah Stevens" 155).

Elmey S. Trimmer as Pioneer Weaver

After moving into the pioneer environment of Huron County it was only natural that Elmey Trimmer would adapt her weaving and sewing skills to the needs of the community, just as Aunt Debby was doing in New London. Apparently soon after their arrival the Trimmers began to clear the land. The account book reveals that in September, 1839, they sold several oak trees for staves at one dollar each and purchased seed wheat. Since Elmey noted that the Trimmers did not raise the house, that is the living room, until 1843, it is possible that they lived in a simple log house during their first few years of residence. Elmey did, however, begin to weave a few months after their arrival in the fall. Her first Ohio entry for weaving was on December 4, 1839. She wove woolen yardage for Wm. Whipple, a Townsend neighbor.[8]

In her Ohio years Elmey's account book reveals that her work concentrated on weaving rather than tailoring. The clothing she recorded for Ohio between 1839 and 1875 amounted to an income of only $4.46 for knitting socks and mittens and making a pair of pantaloons, suspenders and a pair of shoes. Although she apparently curtailed her tailoring business, Elmey continued to sew her own clothing, for a passage in her account book reveals the cost of making two black silk dresses for herself and Sally Sammis, her sister. The materials were bought in 1863 and made up in the spring of 1864. The cost was:

Silk asst.	$34.75
Skirt lining	4.00
Waist [blouse] lining	.75
Velvet	2.50
	$47.00

During her Ohio years Elmey earned $469.38 from weaving. In 1839, the year of her marriage to Isaac Trimmer and her first year in Ohio, she earned only $2.50 from weaving. Her gross earnings from weaving increased to $66.11 in 1840. In 1841 she made only $30.69, and in 1842, $25.40, a low amount which may relate to pregnancy and childbirth. In 1843 she again earned a respectable $52.06. Between 1844 and 1846 her productivity dropped. For those years she earned $34.35 (1844), $24.96 (1845), and $23.12 (1846). Yet, in 1847 and 1848 Elmey again earned $57.66 and $53.11, respectively. In 1849 her earnings from weaving dropped to $37.92. She has entries for each year after that until 1856 which together total only $55.50. In 1866 she recorded only $5.00, and then a final entry in 1875 reveals that she wove a rag carpet for herself valued at $3.60. The latter amount would not be considered earnings.

Of all the items woven by Elmey the most popular probably was a woven bed cover called a coverlid, or coverlet. Elmey wove many of these during her lifetime and clearly she took pride in the number she produced. Her account book reveals this sentiment, for she entered a separate list of "all the 'floured' [flowered] coverlids I ever wove" which totalled 142. She added a note: "16 for self."[9] Because coverlids were very colorful finished products and prized by her customers, Elmey's pride is understandable.

The popularity of coverlets may have kept the individual weaver, such as Elmey, in business. These were woven throughout Ohio in the nineteenth century, at first on a multi-harness loom in farm homes or shops and later in small factories on a Jacquard or similar loom. Coverlids were colorful as well as functional. As a traditional bedcover they filled the need for warmth and aesthetics (Figure 2). The designs on many of them relate to traditional patterns associated with the cultural backgrounds of migrants and immigrants. This is especially true of Jacquard-type coverlets popular with the Pennsylvania-Dutch migrants and German immigrants in Ohio in the nineteenth-century. And many of these coverlets have designs and symbols which reflect American popular culture as well (Cunningham "The Woven...", "Ohio's Woven...").

As noted earlier, coverlets were only one of the many types of fabrics Elmey produced. Types of cloth she included in the account book in her Ohio years which did not appear in the account book during the years she lived in New York were:

Textile Item	Price
	(per yard unless stated otherwise)
flannel	8 cents
fulled cloth	10 cents
check	9 cents
plaid	9 cents-11 cents
check (apron)	9 cents
shawls	62.5 cents each
wide cloth	10 cents
striped fabric	— —
gray cloth	10 cents

Generally, the prices for woven goods in Ohio were similar to those Elmey charged in New York. An exception was in 1875 when Elmey placed a value of 18 cents per yard on carpet which she wove for herself, a charge which may reflect inflation. Another exception to these prices are the fees she charged Allen and Dennis Canfield for weaving between July 15 and October 13, 1843. The price for their coverlids was $6.00 rather than the usual $1.50. Fulled cloth was $1.00/yd. rather than 10 cents/yd., a cearsay blanket was $3.00 rather than $1.00, and flannel was .50/yd. rather than 8 cents/yd. While it may not be possible to know why such a large price discrepancy occurred, one explanation is that Elmey provided the yarns for the coverlids and other textiles. Indeed, on another occasion she charged extra for finding rags for a customer's carpet, charging 15 cents per yard rather than the usual shilling, 12 1/2 cents. She also charged extra for dyeing yarns. In 1845 and 1848, after Allen Canfield married, Elmey charged Allen's wife, Maria, the usual one shilling per yard for weaving rag carpeting. In this case Maria Canfield may have provided rags.

As one would expect, Elmey's customers were relatives and neighbors who lived in Townsend and Wakeman Townships and the major towns nearby, Norwalk and Milan. Allen and Maria Canfield lived in Milan where Allen was a farmer and carpenter. Maria Canfield was a sister

Fig. 2 Coverlets were woven in the home and by professionals. The types include a variety of weaves such as twill, overshot, double weaves.

of Almena Clark Sammis, the wife of Elmey's brother, White Sammis. According to the U.S. Census records of 1850 and 1860 Dennis Canfield was a farmer in Townsend Township. An 1873 *Atlas of Huron County* places a D.K. Canfield in Section 4 of the township.[10]

It is not surprising that the same atlas includes names of many of Elmey's customers and shows the proximity of her home to theirs. In addition to Dennis Canfield, the familiar names are Burdue, Pinney, Denman, Sammis, French, Gerow, Lockwood, Lowe and Phillips. Other customer names are apparent in the 1840 U.S. Population Census for Huron County. In fact, clustered around the name of Isaac Trimmer in the 1840 Census for Townsend Township are the names of Elmey's brother, White Sammis, who owned the adjacent farm, as well as Benjamin Benson, Watson Baldwin, Levi Chapman, William Whipple, [Abijah] Church and Marten Denman. Other Townsend customers who appear in the 1840 census are Alpha Lowe, Wm. Babcock, Benjamin Trumble, Peter Bailey, G. W. Westfall, Cyrus Waggoner, Alber Pinney and Seth Barber. The 1840 Census also lists several Wakeman customers: Joseph French, Peter Sherman and the families of Todd, Bryant, Walden, and Brewster.[11]

In addition to the Canfield families some of Elmey's biggest customers included her brother, White, and sister-in-law, Almena Sammis. "Almena's peaces," as she often noted in the account book, amounted to $8.26, and White's came to $17.79. These included striped fabric, linnen plaid fabric, cearsay, mix, diaper, and woolen. Although White Sammis died in 1858, Almena continued as Elmey's neighbor, living in the Sammis residence with her son Anson and his family until her death in 1884 (Dean 107-108).

Other neighbors who depended on Elmey's skills as a weaver were Mr. and Mrs. Watson Baldwin, who had linnen, woolen, cearsey linnen, cotton and wool and coverlids from Elmey's loom which amounted to $16.35. Still another important customer for Elmey was Cyrus Waggoner, one of her earliest Ohio patrons and a Townsend resident. For the $14.04 Elmey earned, Waggoner received goods such as woolen, cotton and wool, linnen and 34 yards of "Red and coperas color" fabric, the only reference made to color in the weaving records. Another Townsend resident and neighbor, Marten Denman, had a coverlid woven as well as shawls, check, and cotton and wool. Elmey's earnings from Denman's patronage was $12.12. According to the account book Elmey accepted credit from Denman for hens, wool and peaches, as well as cash. As is true of many customers, little is known about Q.P. or Q.B. Brown. Yet between them Elmey earned a substantial $41.13 by producing a variety of products: aprons, blankets, mittens, cearsay linnen, socks, carpet, plaid and even pantaloons. In all, she produced goods for 74 individuals.

Judging from her productivity Elmey needed certain types of equipment and materials. The fabrics suggest that her loom had at least four harnesses (a diaper weave would require a minimum of four harnesses). She made several references to weaving "wide cloth" and on one occasion described the width as "5 qtrs. wide." Her loom, therefore, would have been at least 45 inches wide (unless, of course, she wove a double cloth which would be opened up to a single layer). She would need other tools for weaving as well, such as a warping device, and shuttles, spools, hooks, and a swift. It is likely that she had tools, such as hand cards and a spinning wheel, to prepare yarns. She also dyed yarns, for her account book includes recipes for coloring yellow, orange, blue, green, and black as well as formulas to restore the color of goods and remove dirt.

While the Ohio years reveal greater productivity in weaving than in sewing or tailoring, on the average these years were far less productive than the New York years. This may be explained by the increased demands of pioneer life, motherhood after 1842, an improved economic position after 1850, or perhaps the competition from residentiary factories in the nearby Huron County towns of Monroeville and Peru.

The first cloth-making factory in the area was built in 1830 by Timothy Baker in Monroeville (a town just West of Norwalk) on the bank of the Huron River (now Mechanic Street). Little is known of this factory, but Mr. Baker carried on a carding business as well as weaving. In 1835, B. Stetson offered to sell a wool carding and cloth dressing establishment with two good carding machines which was located in the township of Florence. On December 14, 1836, in Venice, Huron County, Samuel Smith held a public sale of his carding machine and picker. In May of 1836 Richard Bennett and David Gauff set up a carding, cloth dressing and weaving manufactory in Monroeville, apparently taking over the Baker factory. In September of 1837 Bennett dissolved the partnership with Gauff and formed a co-partnership with Weaver, offering to card, dress cloth and weave—accepting, of course, produce of all kinds in payment for their work (Williams 267; *Norwalk Experiment* 11/4/35, 1/4/37, 5/11/36, 9/27/37; *Huron Reflector* 10/3/37).

Not all carding establishments were set up in rudimentary factories which included weaving. Indeed, it was common to have a separate wool carding and cloth dressing business. Charles Gardner of Peru in Huron County advertised such a service in the local newspaper on May 31, 1838. Gardner presumed that area residents would first bring their wool to his mill for carding and then after it was spun and woven the same customers would return it to Gardner for dressing, that is for fulling (shrinking), steaming, brushing and pressing (*Norwalk Experiment* 6/6/38).

Although homespun and handwoven cloth was popular with rural residents, it is apparent that weavers had competition from local merchants who sold Ohio factory goods as well as textile products manufactured in the eastern states and Europe. The impact of imports on small factories may be apparent in a hand bill promoting the sale of a variety of fabrics and trimmings, as well as fans, collars, shawls and shoes, at the Woolen factory Store in Monroeville on May 1, 1844. It appears that rather than fight the stores that sold cheaper imports, the woolen factory joined their forces.[12]

The threat from imports was always a factor in the success of a factory. And the early factories likewise were competition for the individual weaver because even a small manufactory could provide more services than someone like Elmey Trimmer who had fewer resources on which to draw. History reveals, of course, that in the end factory goods almost completely replaced homespun and hand woven cloth, even in rural areas. But not before it became economically sound to do so. Apparently after 1850 either economic or personal factors kept Elmey's weaving business to a minimum. The changing times are reflected in an almost poignant entry made by Elmey in 1870:

"Fall River Bristol Co. = Massachusetts
1870 June 4th bought an Ingrain
carpet and put it on the parlor floor

It cost just 28 dollars
binding and all.   E.T."

The account book which Elmey Sammis Trimmer kept between 1836 and 1876 provides context for the objects she produced. It has given specific information about her personal life and family as well as her tailoring and weaving business and reveals how the two were intertwined. For these years we know who her customers were, what she produced for them, the value she put on each product, and the items she took in trade. Other sources have confirmed that many of her customers were relatives and neighbors. The value of property stated in the U.S. Population Census gives us an indication that the Trimmer and Sammis families were fairly well off. That White Sammis was an early postmaster and Justice of the Peace for 12 years suggests that he held a somewhat prominent position in the community. Obituaries of his wife Almena, and Elmey's mother-in-law, Mrs. Trimmer, appeared in the *Firelands Pioneer* and a biography of Isaac Trimmer was in Williams' *History of Huron County*. These notices also suggest that the families were respected in the community.

However, we have more than a knowledge of Elmey's business and position in society. The range of textile items she produced for her relatives and friends in New York and Ohio and the items taken in exchange for them gives us an understanding of their needs and tastes. It is clear that assorted woven fabrics, rag carpeting, blankets and coverlids as well as check aprons and shawls were popular in Ohio. And in Genoa, New York, the community appeared to depend on Elmey for clothing as well as textile products. Unfortunately there are no extant garments or textiles to examine; hence we do not have a sense of Elmey's expertise or aesthetics, the affective side of her accomplishments. Yet we do have a sense of the pride she took in them.

Indeed, as has been suggested from Elmey's book, we have a detailed view of how the economic life of an early nineteenth-century pioneer community in Ohio depended on the expertise of women skilled in the textile arts. Elmey Trimmer and women like her were important links in the productivity of their families and communities. They turned farm produced fibers (flax and wool) into fabrics needed for clothing and household use—colorful blankets, coverlids and carpets needed for warmth as well as aesthetics. And for some of them, like Elmey Sammis Trimmer, this expertise became an important and significant source of family income and a vital business worthy of an account book.

Notes

[1]See Hindle (464). Written primary sources often are not available concerning ordinary people, whereas the objects they created and used survive. Tools and textiles are examples of such everyday objects. Sometimes these artifacts are the only information available.

[2]*Cearsay*, for instance, is a heavy fabric, often a wool or wool mix, in plain or twill weave with a smooth surface and used especially for coats. *Diaper* is a fabric weave with a distinctive all-over pattern of small repeated units of geometric design. The structure has more surface area than a plain weave and, hence, is a faster absorber of moisture, particularly if woven in cotton or flax.

[3]There were 12 pence in a shilling; a shilling was worth 12 1/2 cents.

[4]Bits of information about Elmey Sammis Trimmer's life appears throughout her account book. While Elmey's notes and records make up the major portion of the information found in the book, there are entries of a geneological nature in at least two other handwriting styles which give further information about the Trimmer family. A biographical sketch of Isaac Trimmer is in Williams. The house, which became the property of Elmey's daughter, who married Joseph O. Burr, still stands on Rt. 20 in Townsend, Ohio.

[5]An examination of the early New York years of Elmey's life has not been undertaken by this researcher, but it is quite likely that public records, county and local histories, plat maps, etc., would reveal further information about the Sammis and Trimmer families.

⁶See also Weeks (40-41).

⁷The cost of the suits was itemized as follows:

satinett for pants	$4.50	trimming	and	
		making	6.00	
satinett for coat	6.00	2 shirts	4.00	
satinett for vest	1.25	shoes, hat	3.00	
		Total	$24.75	

⁸In the 1840 U.S. Population Census for Townsend, Ohio, William Whipple's name follows that of White Sammis.

Elmey's account book includes her record of other farm improvements as well: "in 1847 built the Barn, 1857 built the Cellar, 1859 painted the House 2nd time, 1860 rebuilt Store house, 1874 build Woodhouse and Garage [and] 1879 built Granary."

⁹Since the dated entries for coverlids in the account book (1836-1876) total only 56, it is quite possible that Elmey's grand list of coverlids includes those from a pre-1836 record or from her memory. There is no indication of when she compiled the list.

¹⁰Further information on the Canfield family is available in "The Geneological Records of the Jared Canfield Family" compiled by Florence Gossard Adams (Wood County Chapter, O.G.S.).

¹¹The population of Townsend over 20 years of age in 1840 was 862; in 1850 it was 1432. Wakeman township had 710 households in 1840; by 1850 the number had dropped by six, to 704.

¹²Taken from a factory handbill on display at the Monroeville Museum, Monroeville, Ohio 1984.

Works Cited

Baughman, Abraham J. *History of Huron County, Ohio; Its Progress and Development.* Vol. I. Chicago: S.J. Clarke, 1909.

Brown, Emma L. "Reminiscences." *Firelands Pioneer* N.S. 25 (June 1937) "Mrs. Deborah Stevens" [obituary], *Firelands Pioneer* N.S. 9 (October 1896).

Cunningham, Patricia A. "The Woven Record: Nineteenth-Century, Coverlets and Textile Industries in Northwest Ohio." *Northwest Ohio Quarterly* 56 (1984)— "Ohio's Woven Coverlets: Textile Industry in a Rural Economy." *Ars Textrina* 2 (1984).

Dean, R.C. "Mrs. Almeda [sic] Sammis." *Firelands Pioneer* N.S. 3 (Jan. 1886).

Hindle, Brooke. "Technology Through a 3-D Time Warp." *Technology and Culture* 24:3 (July 1983).

Norwalk Experiment, Wednesday, June 6, 1838.

Norwalk Experiment, Wednesday, November 4, 1835; January 4, 1837; May 11, 1836; and September 27, 1837. *Huron Reflector*, October 3, 1837.

"Records of Proceedings of the Forty-Eighth Annual Meeting," *Firelands Pioneer* N.S. 16 (May 1907: 1229.

Schlereth, Thomas J., ed. *Material Culture: A Research Guide.* Lawrence, Kansas: University Press of Kansas, 1985.

Smith, Fannie. "Fire Lands Reminiscences." *Firelands Pioneer* 1 (March 1859).

Sommers, Benjamin. "Early Times and Incidents in Vermillion." *Firelands Pioneer* 4 (June 1863).

U.S. Population Census, Huron County, Townsend Township 1840, 1850, 1860. Lake, D.J. *Atlas of Huron County, Ohio.* Philadelphia: Titus, Simmons & Titus, 1873.

Waggoner, Clark. "Second Historical Period of the Firelands." *Firelands Pioneer* N.S. 1 (June 1882).Weeks, F.E. "Posts, Post Offices and Postal Facilities in the Firelands, A Century and More Ago." *Firelands Pioneer* N.S. 25 (June 1937).

Williams, William W. *The History of the Firelands.* Cleveland: Leader Printing Co., 1879.

Quilt Documentation: A Case Study

Ricky Clark

The burgeoning number of state-wide quilt documentation projects testifies both to an enormous body of available and previously unstudied artifacts, and to a growing appreciation of quilts as cultural documents. At this writing researchers in twenty-nine states have been involved in studying and documenting their states' quilts, quiltmakers and quiltmaking traditions. In addition several regional surveys have been conducted. Although researchers certainly enjoy looking at beautiful quilts, the purpose of state-wide and regional quilt projects is invariably social-historical, rather than aesthetic: "Quilts are valuable historical documents in which we can read a part of the past..." (Arkansas); "A particular quilt can be examined or 'read' to reveal some of the traditional values of the community in which it was made" (South Carolina); "A great deal can be deduced about [quilt] makers from the evidence incorporated in the design organization, fabric selection, workmanship, etc." (Kentucky); "The goal of this study was to come to an understanding of [quilts'] roles as symbolic artifacts" (Delaware Valley); "a realization of...their significance as cultural documents expanded the project to include a symposium on 'quilts as visual language' " (Ohio).

Typically state quilt documentation projects sponsor *Quilt Discovery Days* to which the public brings quilts to be examined, recorded and photographed. Information thus collected is stored for the benefit of current and future researchers, and the project culminates in a representative exhibition and a publication on the particular state's quilt heritage. During a Quilt Discovery Day approximately 100-200 quilts are documented, and such meetings may be held weekly over a two- or three-year period. Thousands of privately-owned quilts are thus being made available to researchers.

Since these quilts may never again be brought out for study it is important to record as much information as possible. A lack of standardized documentation procedures, however, has hampered researchers' attempts to compare data gathered in one state with those gathered in another. Not all groups record the same information or use the same terminology, although all are dealing with the same kinds of artifacts. To solve this problem the Kentucky Heritage Quilt Society brought together twenty-five researchers involved in state and regional quilt documentation projects in October 1984 to establish a standardized methodology and develop a set of comprehensive, computer-compatible forms to record information contained within the quilt, as well as written, oral and photographic material provided by a quilt's maker or owner. These forms are currently being tested and revised by the Ohio Quilt Research Project and will eventually be made available to quilt researchers nationwide.

No matter how well designed these research projects and documentation forms are, however, their material will be only a beginning—although a substantial one—to thorough study. If the researchers are properly trained, reliable information gleaned from the quilt itself can be collected at a Quilt Discovery Day. But compiling information on the quilt's history and determining its social significance require further work. Quilt owners may be uninformed or misinformed about their quilts' history or may present as facts assumptions they have made about quilts or their makers. In addition, a large body of romantic mythology, frequently presented as indisputable fact, permeates the quilt world.

Before the data gathered by a quilt documentation project can be evaluated and published researchers must consult a variety of primary and secondary sources to verify information already collected. This kind of investigation cannot occur in the course of a Quilt Discovery Day, no matter how well planned. Researchers need more time to identify, locate and use census and institutional records, journals, diaries and other resources that will confirm or refute information acquired during a Quilt Discovery Day, and those sources will differ with each quilt.

Information thus gathered will help the researcher "read" the quilt as an informative document of the culture in which it was produced. Not every quilt brought to a Quilt Discovery Day will receive this kind of exhaustive research. But every quilt communicates something about its maker and her world. Every quilt contains clues that can be examined, and a thorough investigation increases our understanding of the quilt and greatly expands our appreciation of its cultural context. A rigorous and extensive methodology is required for this kind of documentation. Fortunately such a methodology exists. In his landmark article "Artifact Study: a Proposed Model," E. McClung Fleming presents a comprehensive, interdisciplinary approach to studying artifacts. The case study he uses as an example is of a seventeenth-century American court cupboard, but his system of analysis is designed for the study of any artifact and is ideal for quilt research.

Fleming first establishes a classification system whereby anything known about an artifact can be categorized as one of five basic properties: history, material, construction, design, and function. In terms of quilts, history deals with when and where the quilt was made and by whom, and its subsequent owners. Material involves the kinds of fabrics, threads, and batting used. Construction includes techniques such as piecing and appliqué, and whether the quilt was hand or machine-made. Design refers to its colors, decoration and motifs. Function covers both the purposes intended by its maker (utility, gift, fund-raising) and its unintended roles (social bonds, recreation, therapy).

Fleming then identifies four operations to be performed on each of these five properties: identification, evaluation, cultural analysis, and interpretation. Each operation is applied to any or all of the quilt's basic properties, and the operations must be performed in order, since each builds on what has gone before it. These operations will yield answers to all the most important questions we should ask about a quilt, and will lead to unanticipated insights into the quiltmaker and her culture. In the case study that follows, for example, this orderly and progressive process culminated in two related interpretations of significance to quilt researchers, sociologists and students of women's history: that the quiltmaker used her quilt as a metaphor for family, and that her community defined the quiltmaker and her step-children by their roles within a family that had ceased to exist eight years earlier. Both interpretations broaden our understanding of the nature and significance of family for the mid-nineteenth-century quiltmaker and her culture.

Fleming's first operation, identification, includes classification (what is it?), authentication (is it genuine?) and physical description (what does it look like?). This operation would seek to determine, for example, whether the Saltonstall quilt was really made in 1704, as was believed for many years, until its materials were discovered to date from the nineteenth century. The second operation, evaluation, involves two kinds of judgment. One deals with aesthetics (is this quilt well designed and constructed?), the other with contextual significance. This second kind of evaluation, usually involving comparison with other quilts, might determine whether the quilt was characteristic of the Depression era, or whether another quilt made by Rose Kretsinger had just been discovered. Cultural analysis relates the quilt to the culture in which it was made, and might involve researching the history and membership of a religious group, as Dena Katzenberg did with the Methodist church in her study of Baltimore album quilts, or investigating New England women's attitudes toward westward migration. This operation has enormous potential and should be of particular interest to quilt researchers. Interpretation relates the quilt to the concerns of contemporary culture and will vary with the researcher. For example, today's students of women's history might be concerned with the ways in which Victorian crazy quilts reflect the values of their makers or the role of quilts in the work of the U.S. Sanitary Commission. Art historians might concentrate on the transmission of style. My own interest in quilts as visual language leads me to investigate the various roles of quilts in the lives of their makers, particularly their communicative functions.

To illustrate the importance of the Fleming model for quilt researchers I offer the following analysis of a quilt in the collection of the Allen Memorial Art Museum in Oberlin, Ohio (acc. no. 85.24, fig. 1). In 1984 the quilt's owner, Joyce Troup, brought it to a Quilt Discovery Day in San Francisco organized by Julie Silber, quilt curator of the Esprit Corporation and well-known quilt researcher. Knowing that I live in Oberlin, Ms. Silber kindly told me about it, and eventually it was purchased for the Allen Museum's collection. Ms. Troup had brought the quilt at a house sale in Eugene, Oregon, in 1982 and was told that it had belonged to an unmarried woman then in her nineties. In the following analysis I will detail some of the primary and secondary sources used in studying this quilt, in an attempt to give an idea of the breadth of resources useful for quilt research and to show how this kind of progressive analysis helped to discover this quilt's function as a metaphor for family.

Identification

The artifact being considered is a signature quilt, a classification based on function and design. A quilt is a bedcover (function) composed of two layers of fabric with batting between them (materials), whose layers are joined together by running stitches (construction). This definition distinguishes a quilt from a tied comforter, woven coverlet, or feather bed, all of which are bedcovers sometimes confused with quilts. A signature quilt is one composed of signed blocks, a definition based on design.

This secondary classification is deliberately broad and simple to avoid the confusing and overlapping categories found in many publications. For example, in a chapter of *Quilts in America* the authors classify quilts as Victorian crazy (a category based on history, construction and design), pants quilts (materials), Yo-Yo (construction) and memory (function), to mention only a few. Within the category of "album quilts" the authors include Presentation (function), Baltimore (region), and autograph, scripture and quotation (design) (Orlofsky 225-244). In the case of the last three categories it is the content of the inscriptions that determines classification. Two other researchers further subdivide signature quilts according to construction of the component blocks (identical or different)

Fig. 1 Quilt made by Laura and Sarah Mahan
Oberlin, OH, c. 1847-1851.
Coll. Allen Memorial Art Museum
Oberlin College, Oberlin, OH.

but assign these categories names based on function ("friendship" and "album") (Lipsett 19; Nicoll 5). A third writer defines album quilts differently and includes both signature quilts and quilts with no inscriptions at all (Katzenberg 13). Systematic classification and consistent nomenclature are badly needed.

Having classified the quilt we procede to authentication, which will seek to determine whether the quilt is genuine. Fraud is not as much of a problem in the quilt world as in the worlds of documents, furniture and paintings, but dating and provenance are. This particular quilt provides a wealth of names, dates and places (see Appendix A). Authentication, therefore, begins by attempting to verify the information inscribed on the quilt. Dates on the quilt are either 1850 or 1851. Are these the dates when the quilt was made? This might seem a reasonable assumption, but some quilts are inscribed with earlier dates, such as birth or marriage dates of the quiltmaker or of the person for whom a quilt was made. Are the materials and construction techniques consistent with a mid-century date of fabrication, or does the quilt include materials made after 1851?

To authenticate this quilt we will look first at its history. One block in particular (e-1) provides so many clues in this respect that it is worth repeating here (fig. 2). It reads as follows:

This quilt, commenced by our dear Laura & finished by me, principally from fragments of her dresses, I give & bequeath unto her sister Julia M. Woodruff, or in case of her death to her sister Hila M. Hall, if she survives, otherwise to the oldest surviving granddaughter of their father, Artemas Mahan deceased.

Sarah Mahan.

Oberlin Feb. 6, 1851

This block provides us with the names of the quiltmakers; the source of materials; the fact of Artemas Mahan's death before 6 February 1851, and the intimation of Laura's; the names of Laura's two sisters; and a location, Oberlin. Other inscriptions on the quilt locate Oberlin in Lorain County, Ohio. Sarah's place in the Mahan family is unclear.

Since census records are indexed by heads of household (male, except in the case of an unmarried or widowed woman) a search for Artemas Mahan in those records is a reasonable place to begin. He is not listed in the 1850 census for Ohio or the other states inscribed on the quilt. His name appears in the 1840 census for Marion Township, Livingston County, Michigan, and in the 1820 and 1830 census records for Orangeville, Genesee (now Wyoming) County, New York. The 1840 census is most likely to include information about Artemas Mahan's wife and children, since it is the most recent. According to it, the Mahan household in 1840 consisted of Artemas, aged 40-50; one male aged 10-15; and three females aged 40-50, 5-10, and 15-20. Further information

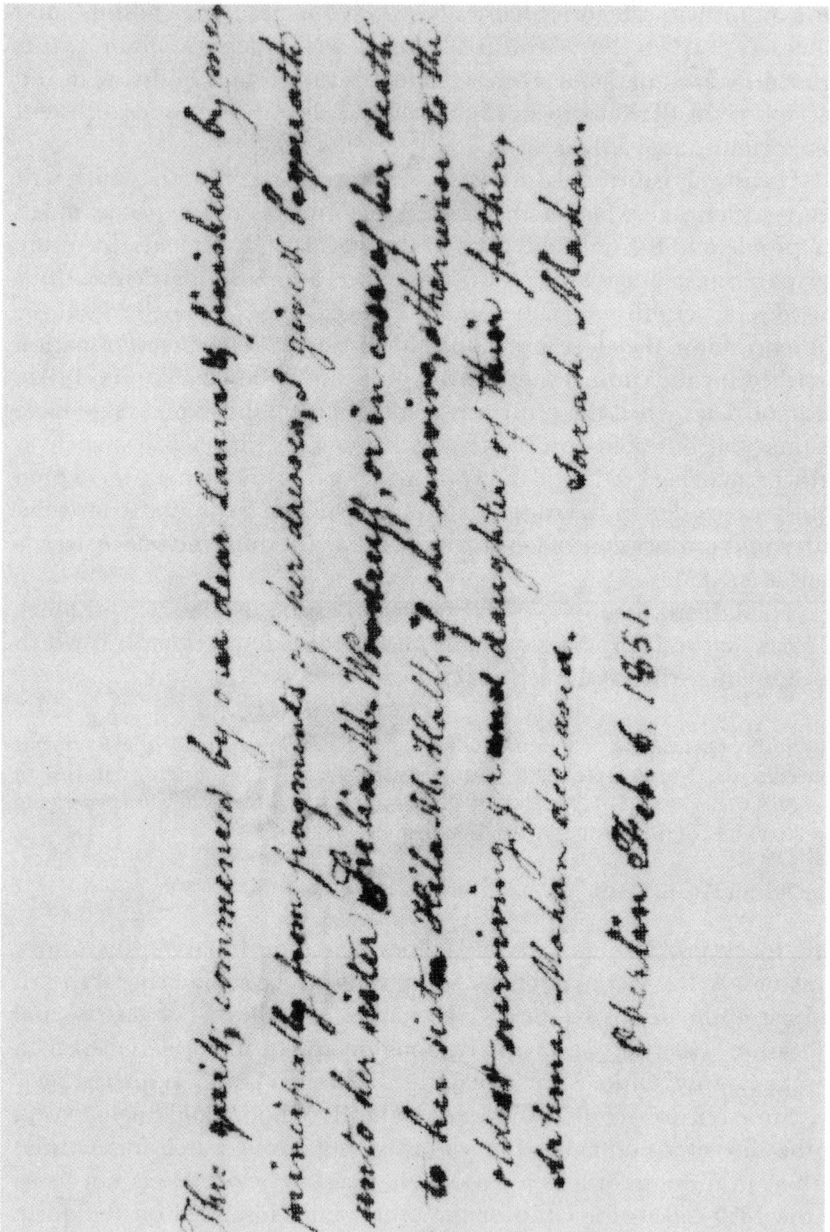

Fig. 2 Mahan quilt, detail. Quilt block e-1 (Sarah Mahan).
Coll. Allen Memorial Art Museum
Oberlin College, Oberlin, OH

is found in *The History of Livingston County, Michigan* (Ellis 348), which states that Artemas Mahan came to Marion in 1836 from Washtenaw County, Michigan, as one of the town's first settlers.

Since two of Artemas's daughters had different surnames and "M" had become their middle initial when this quilt block was inscribed, they were probably married by 1851. Marriage records for Livingston County, Michigan, indicate that Hila Mahan was born in 1821 in Orangeville, New York, and was married 20 December 1839, to Augustus Reuben Hall of Washtenaw County, Michigan. Similar records for Washtenaw County report Julia Mahan's marriage to Francis Woodruff of Pittsfield on 30 March 1847, at the home of her sister Hila. A search in the Livingston County Probate Court disclosed extensive records of the settlement of Artemas Mahan's estate (Docket #280). The earliest document in this file is dated 31 May 1843. According to these records, by that date he had died intestate, his debts exceeded the proceeds of his estate, and his property had been sold at auction. The file includes a letter from Sarah Mahan which identifies her as the wife of Artemas and the stepmother of his children.

Records of First Church in Oberlin, now in the Oberlin College Archives, document Sarah Mahan's move to Ohio. Those records indicate that on 9 July 1843 Sarah, Julia and Samuel N. Mahan joined First Church. The same records state that Samuel left First Church 5 May 1844, that Julia left 12 September 1846, and that 1 September 1851 Sarah transferred membership to Belle Prairie, Minnesota. Using the *Directory of Historical Societies and Agencies* published by the American Association of State and Local History, I identified several historical societies in Minnesota that I hoped could help trace Sarah Mahan and wrote to all of them. My inquiry to the Minnesota Historical Society Research Center's Division of Archives and Manuscripts disclosed an article, "One of Minnesota's First Schools," by Elisabeth Ayer, director of the school, and a letter from Mrs. Ayer's sister (Elizabeth Taylor Ayer Papers). These documents provided the information that Sarah Mahan became a teacher and assistant to Mrs. Ayer at this newly established mission school in Belle Prairie. She probably decided to go there in 1850, when Elisabeth Ayer visited Oberlin to recruit teachers.

From records of the Oberlin Collegiate Institute (renamed Oberlin College in 1850) we learn that Julia Mahan attended the Institute in the Preparatory and Literary Departments from 1844 to 1846, that Sarah attended the Institute during the 1846 spring term, and that Laura attended the Preparatory Department from 1847 to 1848 and died 5 June 1848 (*General Catalog* 635). Laura's obituary, published in *The Oberlin Evangelist* (8 June 1848), reports her age as 15 years 7 months and includes the information that she was the niece of Oberlin Collegiate Institute President Asa Mahan. These sources confirm the information recorded on Sarah Mahan's quilt block: the deaths of Artemas and Laura, married names of Laura's sisters, and Sarah's presence in Oberlin by 6 February 1851. They provide additional information as well: Sarah's relationship to the people whose names are recorded on her quilt block, confirmation and date of Laura's death, and names of family members listed only by sex and age groups in the 1840 census. They further suggest two probable reasons for the family's move to Oberlin: loss of economic support and the children's kinship to President Mahan.

According to Sarah Mahan's inscription this quilt had been "commenced by our dear Laura." Probably Laura had not progressed very far on it before her death, since only one cheerful inscription (d-10), written by an adult, mentions childhood. Fourteen blocks bear dates two and three years after Laura died and others, referring to death and bereavement, seem more appropriately directed to Sarah. Almost all the names on the quilt have been identified. Sources most helpful here include early annual catalogs of the Oberlin Collegiate Institute, which list students and their home residences by town, county and state; published genealogies; county histories; and a hand-written document entitled "Reminiscences of the Class of 1850," probably written by Thomas H. Robinson of that class (g-5). These sources also support the probability that the quilt blocks were signed on the inscribed dates. For example, Franklin Arnold (f-4), "destined for West Africa," in fact went there as a missionary 10 December 1850, two and a half months after the date on his quilt block. Two other students, Ann Jane Gray (a-3) and Mary E. Cone (f-6) changed their names by marriage shortly after the dates inscribed on their blocks (Alumni Records file 28/6). Having confirmed from its history that the quilt is genuine, we will look at its other properties—materials, construction, design and function—to further identify it.

Although materials can be identified through increasingly sophisticated laboratory analysis, in this case they were determined by visual and tactile inspection supported by familiarity with textile technology and quiltmaking practices in America c. 1850. The quilt top is made of a variety of cotton fabrics, both plain and patterned, and from Sarah Mahan's quilt block we learn that her fabric sources were "principally...fragments of [Laura's] dresses" (e-1). Identification of specific fabrics is difficult because overwhelming numbers of printed cottons were available at that time. However, by consulting works on mid-century fabrics and costume in the United States as well as newspaper advertisements and estate inventories (particularly of dry goods merchants), we can confirm that similar fabrics were, in fact, in use in northern Ohio at that time (Montgomery).[1] Inscribed blocks are all white, but the pieced blocks are made from both solid-colored and printed cottons. Floral prints in small, medium and large scales and plaids and stripes, primarily in shades of red, blue, white and brown are used. All are fairly light-weight. The quilt binding is in a pink-and-white print. The filler, which can be seen in several places where the fabrics in the top have deteriorated, is a thin layer of raw cotton, known as "batting." The quilt backing is cotton but is much coarser than the cottons used on the top. Cotton thread is used throughout. Inscriptions on this quilt are in ink, which will be considered a material. The ink used throughout was non-corrosive and can therefore be dated to the 1840s or later. Ink used in the early nineteenth century contained iron and tannin, which quickly rotted the fabric. After the mid-1830s more permanent inks were developed (Lipsett 17-18).

Sarah Mahan's quilt measures 87 1/2" by 76 1/2" and is pieced. It is composed of ninety square blocks, each approximately 8" on a side, and a 4"-wide pieced border. The edges of the quilt are encased in a binding 3/8" wide, measured from seam to fold. Half the blocks are plain white squares with inked inscriptions. These alternate with blocks constructed of geometrically shaped fabric pieces joined together to form a square (pieced blocks), all in a "Star of LeMoyne" pattern (Rehmel #1, 800). Some of the structural units that comprise the "Stars of LeMoyne" are made from two or more pieces of fabric sewn together before being cut to the shape of the piecing template (fig. 3). Blocks are joined in ten horizontal rows of nine blocks each. Borders repeat the alternation of pieced and plain blocks and are half as wide as the full blocks. Binding is cut on the grain, and corners of the binding are butted in two cases, rounded in the others.

The quilt back is pieced from eight rectangles of different sizes. One small triangular patch cut from the same material and applied to the back probably repaired a tear that occurred before the fabric was used in this quilt, suggesting that the back as well as the front was made from recycled material. Woven edges (selvages) are exposed on some pieces. Construction is entirely by hand. Although sewing machines had been invented by 1850, a satisfactory machine was not developed until later and not in common use until the 1860s. Quilting stitches are of uniform length and average nine per inch.

The design is geometric and shows planning. Although clothing scraps were used, the pieced blocks are arranged according to a visual plan based on color. Pieced blocks are quilted in diagonal lines, a simple and traditional quilting pattern. But the quilting design used in the signed blocks is unique. Each is quilted in a leaf pattern, and at least eight kinds of leaves can be identified: elm, sweet gum, red oak, maple, chestnut, ash, black walnut, and lilac (Crockett). All are indigenous to the Oberlin area.

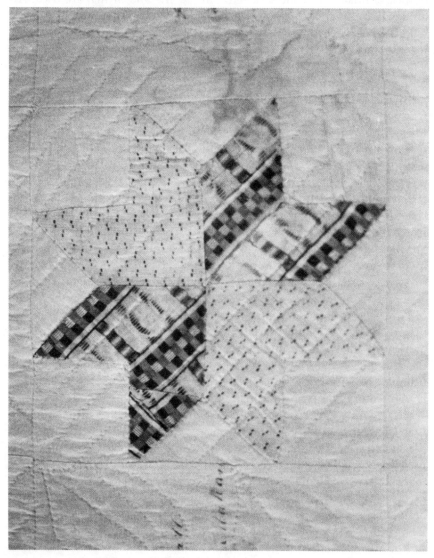

Fig. 3 Mahan quilt, detail. Quilt block d-3, showing scrap construction of pieced
    star. Photo: Chronicle-Telegram (Elyria, OH)

Inscriptions on the quilt are from different hands, and a comparison of Sarah Mahan's block (e-1) to her letter in the Livingston County Probate Records indicates that she probably inscribed the quilt block bearing her name. A similar comparison of the writing on Asa Mahan's block (c-3) to examples of his handwriting in the Oberlin College Archives indicates that he also signed his quilt block. This suggests that each block was signed by the individual whose name appears, although other comparisons were not possible. Personally autographed blocks are not uncommon. However, some makers of signature quilts had all inscriptions written by one person whose handwriting was particularly admired (Katzenberg 14). Some of the inscriptions are hard to read due to illegible handwriting or faded ink. Those including Biblical quotations are easily deciphered by looking up key words in Robert Young's *Analytical Concordance to the Bible....* An illegible town name in Licking County (c-9) was identified by consulting a nineteenth-century atlas, which also provided information on Timothy Ward, whose name is on the quilt block (fig. 4).

The quilt is in fragile condition. Some fabrics have deteriorated badly, in part due to corrosive dyes. A large rectangular area of the back is brown, suggesting that the quilt had been folded and stored on an unsealed wooden shelf or chest. This kind of damage results from age, fabric dyes and acidic wood, rather than use. The quilt is fairly clean and unstained, and the binding (which is original, since it matches fabric used in the pieced blocks) is in good condition. Usually the binding is the first part of a quilt to wear out from use. This suggests that the quilt was rarely, if ever, used.

The functions of Sarah Mahan's quilt are so important that they will be discussed more fully in the section on cultural analysis. Briefly, however, since a quilt is a bedcover we can assume that this quilt had a utilitarian function. Sarah Mahan's inscription suggests two other functions: commemoration of Laura's death and generational continuity. A fourth function, to reify community at a time of social upheaval, is supported by two inscriptions (g-9, h-10) referring to Sarah's impending departure from Oberlin (Records of First and Second Congregational Churches 33). We have determined that the quilt is what it purports to be: a pieced quilt made c. 1847-1851, primarily by Sarah Mahan of Oberlin, Ohio, and signed by identifiable people accessible to the quiltmaker. We have confirmed the quilt's functions as stated or implied by Sarah Mahan and are now ready to proceed to the next operation, evaluation.

Evaluation

A quilt can be evaluated in two ways. One kind of evaluation deals

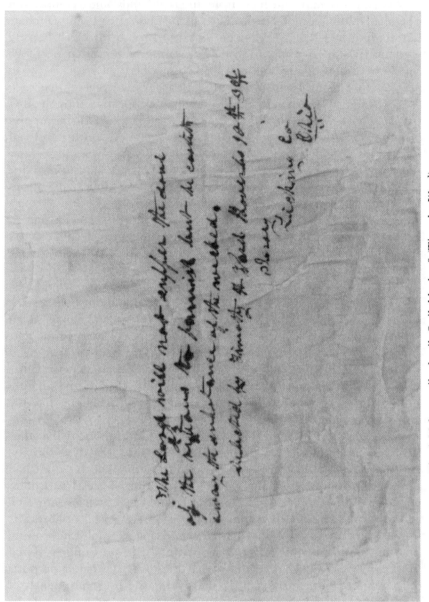

Fig. 4 Mahan quilt, detail. Quilt block c-9 (Timothy Ward).
Photo: Joan Anderson

with the aesthetics of the quilt; the other places it in historical and cultural context through comparison to other quilts. When researchers in a state quilt project tag certain quilts for possible inclusion in an exhibition, they may be using both kinds of evaluation. On the one hand they might be considering a quilt for exhibition because it is a beautifully designed and expertly crafted object in good condition and with considerable aesthetic appeal; on the other, they may select it as a representative of that state's quilting tradition within a particular time period. Because of the rather deteriorated condition of the Mahan quilt it is not aesthetically outstanding. It is, however, a representative example of mid-century signature quilts in a particular style. Signature quilts were made prolifically during the 1840s and 1850s. By that time white fabric, an appropriate background for inscriptions, had supplanted the dark chintzes favored by earlier quiltmakers, and signatures were written, stamped or embroidered on these open areas. Quiltmakers retained the same styles for signature quilts as they were using in their other quilts, and these fall into only a few categories.

The first consists of repeated blocks (usually pieced) identical in construction but made in a variety of plain and patterned fabrics. Pieced blocks sometimes alternate with plain ones. Central and background patches of the pieced blocks and any plain blocks are frequently white, and in these areas the signatures are located. This style was widely dispersed, from the middle Atlantic states to northern Vermont and westward through central New York and Ohio. Although not limited to one geographic region this was the style exclusively preferred by quiltmakers in the Connecticut and Merrimack River valleys of central New England, and in areas settled by New Englanders, such as western New York and Ohio's Western Reserve.[2]

A second style is made of blocks decorated with printed motifs, usually floral, cut from chintz and applied to a white or off-white background in a technique sometimes called *Broderie Perse*. These quilts were most popular in the middle-Atlantic and southern states during the 1830s and 1840s. Broderie Perse signature quilts, in their use of appliqué and representational imagery, were the forerunners of a far more elaborate style associated with a network of Methodist women in Baltimore (Katzenberg 58-60). Baltimore-style signature quilts are usually appliquéd, although they may also contain pieced squares. Cotton fabrics, both solid-colored and patterned, are used, and the color scheme is predominantly red and green on a white background. In contrast to the repetition of abstract patterns that characterizes the repeated block style, each square on a Baltimore-style quilt contains a different design, and most are representational. Realistic motifs are so finely detailed that specific birds, flowers and buildings can be identified. Some details are drawn in ink; others are achieved by skillful manipulation of the fabric pattern or with additional needlework techniques such as embroidery and ruching (gathering). The Baltimore style is less widely diffused than the repeated block style and is rarely found west of central Pennsylvania.

A fourth style is reminiscent of Baltimore quilts in its use of large, appliquéd, non-repeated motifs and its predominantly red and green palette. This style is found primarily in the Delaware Valley, where it coexists with the repeated block style.

According to data from regional and statewide quilt research projects in Ohio, isolated examples of Ohio-made mid-century signature quilts in the repeated block style exist, primarily from communities settled by New Englanders. Other signature quilts in several styles have been found in some concentration within Quaker settlements in southeastern and southern Ohio. Ohio Quaker quilts, like those made by Delaware Valley Friends, are in a variety of styles ranging from extreme simplicity (plain, drab blocks with inked signatures) to highly elaborate, Baltimore-style appliqué. The Quaker stress on community and historical propensity for record-keeping probably account for the popularity of signature quilts within this group (Nicoll 15).

Signature quilts in all styles may be made by a single quiltmaker whose friends signed various blocks on her quilt or constructed from a group of blocks made and signed by several people. Sarah Mahan's quilt, in the repeated block style so popular in New England, was "commenced" by Laura and finished by her stepmother, with friends signing muslin squares probably provided by both.

Sarah Mahan lived in the Western Reserve, the only portion of Connecticut's claim to western lands retained by that state when Congress created the Northwest Territory in 1787. Almost a century later this 120-mile-long tract of land in northeastern Ohio was described as "more thoroughly New England in character and spirit than most of the towns of New England" (Garfield 28). After 200 years it still retains its New England flavor, with communities of Greek Revival homes and churches surrounding town commons and bearing New England names: Norwalk, New Haven, Danbury, Pittsfield, Litchfield. Most of the land in the Reserve was sold to New Englanders or New York State immigrants originally from New England. The Oberlin Colony, which settled in a swampy area of Lorain County in 1833, was just such a community of western New Yorkers with New England roots.

A comparison of Sarah Mahan's quilt to other signature quilts from this part of Ohio indicates that it is among the earliest extant signature quilts made in the Western Reserve, that it is in the repeated block style, and that this style of signature quilt continued to be made in the Reserve well into the twentieth century. Similar quilts were made in Newburgh, Cuyahoga County, thirty miles northeast of Oberlin, in 1850; Lyme, Huron County, thirty-five miles west of Oberlin, in 1870; and Columbia,

Lorain County, fifteen miles east of Oberlin, in 1894. A quilt in a modified repeated block style was made in Austinburg, Ashtabula County, as late as 1941 by women in the earliest church in the Western Reserve.[3]

Evaluation of the Mahan quilt has concentrated on placing it in historical and cultural context. We have discovered, by comparison to other mid-nineteenth-century quilts, that it is a signature quilt in a style popular at that time in New England and New York, the source of most residents of Oberlin and its surrounding area. Knowing these facts we are ready to proceed to the third operation, cultural analysis.

Cultural Analysis

Cultural analysis seeks to discover the significance of the quilt within the culture that produced it. This may involve a consideration of its materials, construction and design, but primarily deals with its functions. A quiltmaker may select materials, construction techniques and iconography on the basis of one or more of the quilt's functions, whether consciously articulated by the quiltmaker or not.

Signature quilts, as defined above, were made throughout the nineteenth and into the twentieth centuries. Those made during the 1840s and 1850s were textile versions of the autograph album popular in America at the same time. They were made to commemorate personal relationships and, in the context of the history of nineteenth-century American women and their handwork, were the logical product of a society that divided its members into gender-oriented "spheres" and romanticized friendship. Although many of the inscriptions on such quilts were not original but came from popular published sources like *Godey's Lady's Book*, the nature of the inscriptions selected by the signers makes these mid-century quilts extremely personal. Signature quilts made after 1880 were quite different in materials, construction, design and function from those made earlier and will not be considered in this discussion.

Some mid-century signature quilts were made simply as records of friendships within a stable community, but many were made for or by women torn from their roots as they accompanied husbands to establish new homes in the West. It is hardly coincidental that signature quilts were most popular during the period of America's westward expansion. This was an era of rapid social change and domestic dislocation when women needed concrete affirmation of community ties. One study finds a high correlation between family mobility and the production of signature quilts (Nicoll 26). I believe Sarah Mahan's quilt fits this model.

When we apply the operation of cultural analysis to the materials, construction and design of the Mahan quilt we gain some insight into Sarah Mahan's society. By comparing materials, construction and design to similar quilts from the same era we have already learned that the Mahan quilt is a characteristic signature quilt in a style favored in New England and central New York, the source of many Oberlin residents. This was Sarah Mahan's background as well. According to published genealogies of the Wadsworth family her parents, identified on the quilt as Joseph and Mary Wadsworth (e-7), came from a long line of New Englanders and had emigrated from Lebanon, Connecticut, through central New York to Beloit, Wisconsin, where they both died in the 1850s. Two of Sarah's brothers settled in New York, one in China (Wyoming County), only a few miles from Orangeville, where Asa and Artemas Mahan grew up (Archer; Wadsworth; Bureau of the Census 354). Sarah Mahan's quilt thus reflects her New England heritage.

By studying the fabrics we further learn of some of the dress goods that were in use in Oberlin, Ohio, in the 1840s. Sarah's inscription states that the quilt was made "principally from fragments of [Laura's] dresses" (e-1). These fabrics are striped, checked and printed cottons. The construction of the quilt, while characteristic of those in the repeated block style, is frugal. As noted, the star motifs made from patterned fabrics are cut from previously joined fragments, and the quilt back is made of recycled material. Although Sarah Mahan's inscription indicates that this quilt was made as a family heirloom and intended to be handed down through the generations, this is very much a scrap quilt. Comparable quilts include fabrics that may indeed be dress scraps, but typically each quilt patch is cut from a single piece of cloth, rather than from two or more sections sewn together before cutting. The backs of most similar quilts, furthermore, are typically made from several narrow loom-widths joined to create a wider quilt back. With the possible exception of the white muslin squares making up half the quilt top, the Mahan quilt appears to be constructed entirely from recycled fabric scraps.

In view of the stated significance of this quilt to its maker, we may ask why Sarah Mahan was so thrifty in acquiring materials and constructing her quilt. One possibility is that she simply couldn't afford to purchase new fabric. However, her inscription indicates that using scraps from Laura's dresses was a deliberate choice unrelated to economics, and most 1840s dresses were full enough to include ample material for quilt patches without the necessity of joining smaller fragments first. Another possible reason for the scrap nature of this quilt is that Sarah Mahan valued frugality and plainness more than visual delight. The fact that she didn't seek out an expert calligrapher to write all the inscriptions supports this possibility. But can we really discern the value system of a woman who lived 130 years ago and left almost no written record? Perhaps not entirely, but we are studying a signature quilt, by implication a social document. Since Sarah Mahan presumably chose the people who signed her quilt, an investigation into her well-documented community is in order.

"Lamenting the degeneracy of the Church and the deplorable condition of our perishing world," the Oberlin colonists established their utopian community philosophically and geographically mid-way between John Humphrey Noyes's millenarian Oneida Community in New York and Robert Owens's social New Harmony settlement in Indiana (Klukas 6). Oberlin colonists intended both to create a model Christian community and to reform the "perishing world" in its image. Central to their plan, and a part of the Oberlin Covenant signed by each colonist, was the observation of "plainness and durability in the construction of our houses, furniture, carriages and all that appertains to us" (Fairchild 5). Vanity, selfishness, and the use of money to indulge these frivolities were considered cardinal sins. This ethic of spareness and simplicity strongly influenced Oberlin's early architecture, in which ornament was almost entirely eliminated. Even Sarah Mahan's brother-in-law, although he was president of the Oberlin Collegiate Institute, was criticized by a fellow colonist for including $40 worth of "unnecessary" architectural detail in two rooms in his home: five windows at four dollars each, five doors at two dollars a piece, and two fireplace mantels totalling ten dollars (Maxwell 15).

There is evidence that Sarah Mahan indeed shared the values of the Oberlin Colony. Her husband was the brother of President Mahan, and she had chosen this Christian perfectionist community as the place to live and raise her stepchildren. In her 1843 letter to Judge Kneeland of Livingston County, Michigan (Probate Court Docket, #280), she mentions her "anxiety to provide for [the children's] education," and her trust in God. She found support for these educational and religious values in Oberlin, where she joined First Church and attended the Oberlin Collegiate Institute, along with the children. Her support of Oberlin's values is further substantiated in the final disposition of Artemas Mahan's estate, which includes the payment of $8.55 to the editor of the *New York Evangelist*. This newspaper was the organ of noted evangelist Charles Grandison Finney, who joined the Oberlin faculty in 1835 at the same time as Asa Mahan and succeeded him as president (Fletcher 183). Information on the masthead of the *New York Evangelist* during the 1840s indicates that this amount would have covered the cost of three years' subscription. Sarah Mahan's quilt, then, appears to reflect her community's values. Just as plainness and frugality were made concrete in the community's early architecture, so the moral implications of style are reflected in the construction of the quilt.

The design of her quilt, which reveals her awareness of the quilt style preferred by New Englanders, also reflects changes that had occurred in the Oberlin community by 1850. This quilt is not simply utilitarian, since it includes forty-five inscriptions purely decorative, in terms of design. In 1850, when this quilt was being made, the community was on the brink of a new era. Oberlin had grown from 1,398 inhabitants in 1842 to 1,700 in 1847, and the town had become increasingly separated from the Institute, contrary to the vision of its settlers. The year after this quilt was apparently completed the first railroad tracks would be laid in Oberlin, thus opening the way to greater infiltration of the "worldly" ideas so feared earlier by the critic of Asa Mahan's exorbitant house. But the advent of the railroad was welcomed in Oberlin since it would bring in more people from diverse backgrounds and thus contribute to the community's "spirit of brotherhood" (Elrod 24). An aesthetic style of architecture was now increasingly embraced by Oberlin residents, and "taste" as well as morality became an accepted component of style. Sarah Mahan's quilt with its many inscriptions is an example of this new acceptance of aesthetics. In 1843, when Sarah Mahan joined the Oberlin community, decorating a quilt with forty-five unnecessary inscriptions would probably have been considered as frivolous as her brother-in-law's "unnecessary" windows.

Applying the operation of cultural analysis to the design of the Mahan quilt we concentrate on those forty-five inscriptions. Of these, 80% include locations in nine states and two foreign countries: Connecticut (1), Illinois (2), Indiana (2), Maine (1), Michigan (10), New York (6), Ohio (9), Pennsylvania (2), Wisconsin (1), England (1) and West Africa (1). This is an unusually wide geographic spread when compared to locations inscribed on other signature quilts. Since Oberlin had a boarding school, however, an investigation of the Institute's students is in order. This indicates that thirty of those signing the quilt (67%) were either local residents or out-of-state students at the Oberlin Collegiate Institute (*General Catalog*). Oberlin residents not registered as staff or students (there were only three) were family members of Institute personnel. Of those residing in Oberlin or attending school there, twenty-two (49%) were members of First Church in Oberlin (First Church Records). Major networks represented by the signers of the quilt, therefore, were Oberlin-related: residents, students in the Oberlin Collegiate Institute, and members of First Church, the only church in Oberlin at that time. This accurately reflects the nature of the utopian community, in which town, school and church were equal partners.

Compared to many signature quilts this one includes an unusually large number of male names (twenty-five, or 56%). In many comparable quilts most or all of the names are female. Most of the males named on this quilt are students, and it is possible that some had been part of Sarah Mahan's household during their student years. Almost everyone in Oberlin housed students, providing not only living space, but also the Christian family environment envisioned by its founders (Gurniak

31). An 1850 map of Oberlin in the Lorain County Engineer's Office locates Sarah Mahan's residence on lot 72 on South Main street, only a block from classroom buildings and conveniently situated to house students. The Oberlin Institute catalog of 1843 further identifies one student as residing at "Mrs. Mahan's" (6). Since students living with Asa and Mary Mahan were usually identified as living with "President Mahan," it is probable that "Mrs. Mahan" was Sarah, rather than her sister-in-law Mary, and that Sarah supported herself and the children by housing students.

Another important network reflected in the signatures on this quilt is family. Of the signers eleven (24%) were relatives of Laura Mahan (*Woodruff Chronicles*). Only two (her parents) were related by blood to Sarah Mahan (e-7). The largest family group represented is the Woodruff family into which Julia Mahan married. Six Woodruffs signed the quilt, five of them from Michigan. The *General Catalog of Oberlin College 1833-1908* indicates that several of those had been Oberlin students. The remaining four signatures from Michigan are either Hila Mahan Hall's family (two) or students at the Institute. There are no signatures from Marion, Michigan, where Sarah and the children lived for seven years before coming to Oberlin.

The most important properties of this signature quilt are its functions. As Fleming suggests, most artifacts have three functions: utility, delight, and communication. All are functions of the Mahan quilt, in differing degrees. Because a quilt is by definition a bedcover, we might assume that the Mahan quilt had a utilitarian function. However, the facts that the original binding, usually the first section to deteriorate from wear, is still on the quilt and in good condition, and that the damage to the quilt is due to aging and adverse storage conditions rather than to use, suggest that this quilt was rarely, if ever, used. This is true of many signature quilts, which suggests that utility was not their primary function.

A second function of many quilts is visual delight. Certainly Sarah Mahan organized her pieced blocks in an arrangement based on color and repetition, and her quilting design was unique. However, she probably could have cut the component pieces of both the stars and the quilt back from whole cloth, had technical "perfection" in the quilt's construction been important to her. The fact that she cut the stars from previously joined pieces of cloth and the back from eight rectangles of different sizes suggests that visual delight was a minor function of the quilt.

From the quiltmaker's own statement on her strategically located bequest block and from the identification of other signers of the quilt we know that the most important functions of this quilt for Sarah Mahan are the commemoration of her stepdaughter's death, the affirmation of family-based interpersonal bonds, and the preservation of the female family over time. The common denominator here is family, apparently highly valued by the quiltmaker. The significance of the family and of woman's role as mother in nineteenth-century America are well documented in prescriptive literature. That Sarah Mahan shares this value system is substantiated by evidence from other sources: her concern for the children, as stated in her letter to Judge Kneeland, cited above; her move to a community where the children's relatives lived; her membership in the Oberlin Maternal Association (Records of the OMA). Further, according to data collected by the Ohio Quilt Research Project, among nineteenth-century quiltmakers matrilineal descent was common practice. Less common, but not unprecedented, was the custom of using a quilt to memorialize the dead.

Quilts made to commemorate a death are usually called "mourning quilts," a classification based on function. Several mourning quilts have been authenticated, but such a function is difficult to verify since identification is usually based entirely on oral family tradition. Mourning iconography is included in some quilts, most notably the well-known "Graveyard Quilt" made c. 1839 by Elizabeth Mitchell of Lewis County, Kentucky, now in the collection of the Kentucky Historical Society (acc, no. 59.13), and imagery certainly helps determine a quilt's purpose. In this case an implied memorial function has been confirmed by establishing the date of Laura's death. Further support exists in the inscriptions on the quilt, particularly quotations from the Bible.[4]

Of the inscriptions on the quilt, 69% are Biblical quotations, 7% sentimental verses, and 13% personal messages. Four inscriptions (9%) include only names and a location. The predominance of Biblical quotations further reflects the religious nature of the community. Quotations inscribed on quilts warrant close study, since they are selected for a particular purpose and often reflect the circumstances under which the quilt was made. The signers of this quilt knew it was being made by a bereaved woman to mark the death of "our dear Laura." Of the 31 Biblical quotations on the quilt 21 are messages of comfort, such as " 'Cast they burden upon the Lord, and/He shall sustain thee.' Psalm 55:22" (e-3) and "Come unto me all ye that labor and/are heavy laden and I will give you rest [Matthew 11:28]" (i-3). Four inscriptions, both Biblical and from other sources, refer specifically to death, including the death of a child: "Oh! Memories of the past! Close, Rose, your tendrils twine/my heart... From earth departed - yet: how near to mine!" (a-9); "Sweet heavenborn Spirits are not/to earth confined" (f-4); "Blessed are the dead which die in the Lord...[Revelations 14:13]" (h-8).

Sarah Mahan named the deceased Laura, her living sisters and their daughters—some not yet born—on her quilt block. Members of additional families and other social networks are also represented on the quilt, and the quiltmaker arranged their inscribed blocks in family-oriented groups. In Baltimore-style signature quilts and some in the repeated block style, signed blocks are bright, colorful and highly decorated. The way in which the quiltmaker arranges these blocks on her quilt is dictated by color and design rather than by the inscriptions. By contrast, the signed blocks on the Mahan quilt are visually similar: plain white muslin inscribed in black ink. This uniformity allows the quiltmaker considerable freedom in arranging the blocks on her quilt, since color and design become minor factors, and Sarah Mahan made use of this flexibility (fig. 5).

Disregarding for the moment the pieced blocks which alternate with the signed ones, we see that Asa Mahan and his wife Mary are placed next to each other in row 3 (c-3 and e-3). Laura Mahan's sisters are in adjacent blocks, flanked by their husbands (the faded first name in b-8 is almost certainly Augustus Reuben, husband of Hila Mahan Hall), and constitute an entire horizontal row (b-8, d-8, f-8, h-8). Of the four signed blocks in row 2, three are Woodruffs. These blocks include initials instead of first names, so they cannot be identified with certainty, but "C. Woodruff" of Ypsilanti, Michigan (b-2), may be Charles Woodruff, brother of Julia Mahan Woodruff's husband Francis. "F. Woodruff" of Pittsfield, Michigan, in the adjacent block (d-2) is probably their mother, Freelove Woodruff, a resident of Pittsfield, according to the 1850 census for that city.

Other family groups are represented by their proximity on the quilt top. Three Grey sisters—Margaret (a-1), Ann Jane (a-3) and Eliza (a-7)—adjoin each other in the first vertical row, separated only by Amos Dresser (a-5) who married Ann Jane Grey 21 May 1851. Charles H. Breed (d-6) and Mary E. Cone (f-6) were apparently single when they signed their undated adjacent quilt blocks, but they married 27 August 1850 (Alumni Records file 28/6). Dates of the Breed and Dresser weddings are terminal dates for the signing of the brides' quilt blocks, since they assumed their husbands' names after they married.

Still other relationship patterns appear in row 4, which includes three missionaries. Since the Institute was a missionary training school this is not surprising, but James Cutler Tefft (d-4) and Franklin L. Arnold (f-4), whose adjacent blocks are dated "May 1850" and "Sept. 30, 1850," sailed together to the Kaw Mendi mission in Sierra Leone in December 1850 (Thompson 330). Arnold knew of his impending departure when he wrote "Destined for West Africa" on his block, and the young men had been in Sierra Leone for several months by the time Sarah Mahan assembled the quilt.

Except for Asa and Mary Mahan the only other families who were permanent residents in Oberlin are grouped in the bottom two rows of the quilt. These families include Abigail Warren (b-10) and her daughters Adelaide (a-9) and Calista (f-10); and Mrs. A. Corlett (d-10)

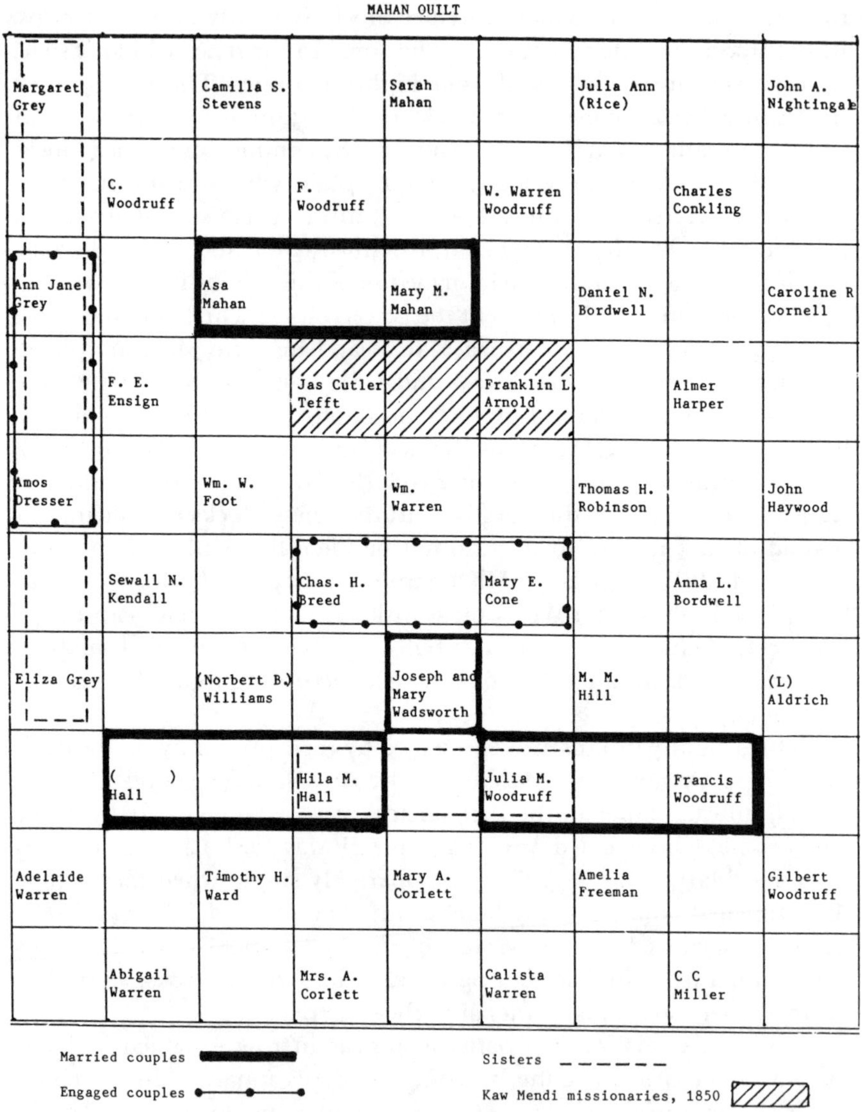

MAHAN QUILT

Margaret Grey		Camilla S. Stevens		Sarah Mahan		Julia Ann (Rice)		John A. Nightingale
	C. Woodruff		F. Woodruff		W. Warren Woodruff		Charles Conkling	
Ann Jane Grey		Asa Mahan		Mary M. Mahan		Daniel N. Bordwell		Caroline R Cornell
	F. E. Ensign		Jas Cutler Tefft		Franklin L Arnold		Almer Harper	
Amos Dresser		Wm. W. Foot		Wm. Warren		Thomas H. Robinson		John Haywood
	Sewall N. Kendall		Chas. H. Breed		Mary E. Cone		Anna L. Bordwell	
Eliza Grey		(Norbert B) Williams		Joseph and Mary Wadsworth		M. M. Hill		(L) Aldrich
	( ) Hall		Hila M. Hall		Julia M. Woodruff		Francis Woodruff	
Adelaide Warren		Timothy H. Ward		Mary A. Corlett		Amelia Freeman		Gilbert Woodruff
	Abigail Warren		Mrs. A. Corlett		Calista Warren		C C Miller	

Married couples ▬▬▬   Sisters – – – – –

Engaged couples •—•—•   Kaw Mendi missionaries, 1850 ▨

Fig. 5 Social Networks Arranged by Sarah Mahan

and her daughter Mary (e-9), identified from the records of First Church. Also at the bottom of the quilt are the only two inscriptions that refer to Sarah Mahan's imminent departure from Oberlin (g-9 and h-10). These two blocks also include the latest dates inscribed on the quilt.

The overlapping networks represented on the quilt and Sarah Mahan's arrangement of signed blocks in family-based groups suggest that of the many social organizations in Oberlin, Sarah ranked family first. In this regard, she might be speaking through her quilt on behalf of her entire community. The Oberlin colony was organized as a family, a concept spelled out in all its activities, and the various social networks within the colony overlapped. It is not simply for the sake of convenience that early records of the town, schools and churches are housed together in the Oberlin College Archives. Distinctions among these three components of the community were blurred, reciprocal and familial. Not until 1846 was a town council established. Prior to that time Oberlin's business affairs were handled by the Collegiate Institute.

As has been pointed out, Collegiate Institute students were housed primarily in local homes, thus linking education to the family. Asa Mahan's home was a prime example of the reciprocal relationship between family and school. According to the 1840 census his household numbered seventeen. Of those only seven were family members and the rest Institute students. In 1843, when Sarah and the three children came to Oberlin (and probably lived at first in the Mahan home) Asa Mahan rented a parlor in his already crowded house to the local school board for use as a classroom, thus bringing the school directly into the home (Records, Russia Township Board of Education). The relationship between church and home was complementary as well. Most Oberlin residents who signed the quilt were members of First Church and worshiped there each Sunday, but daily family Bible readings and worship within the home were an accepted part of family life as well.

Relationships portrayed on Sarah Mahan's quilt are almost entirely between living people and might thus be considered lateral (as most are literally arranged on the quilt). Those detailed in her own quilt block (e-1), however, cut across this horizontal timeline to span three generations, and therefore represent lineal continuity. The descendents cited are all women. The importance of the female family to nineteenth-century women is well documented (Lasser, Melder, Motz, Smith-Rosenberg) and Sarah's experience offers one explanation for this.

At the time Artemas died in 1843 Sarah was ill-advised by friends that she could handle his estate and settle his debts without going through the courts. When an alleged creditor complained to the court that his claim had been rejected, Sarah explained in a letter that she had hoped to settle her husband's debts by selling the crops and material goods not needed by the family (Probate Court Docket, #280). She hoped to save the farm and enough money to provide an education for the children. The settlement of the estate was taken over by the court, and E. F. Gay of Howell, father of two Oberlin students and a friend of the Mahans, was appointed administrator, at Sarah's request. Unhappily, Artemas's debts were considerable; the farm and household goods were sold at auction, and very shortly Sarah brought the children to Oberlin.

Sarah had brought some money to her marriage, but by Michigan law this was part of Artemas's estate; married women had no property rights at that time. Ironically, within a year the state of Michigan passed a Married Woman's Property Act, which would have allowed Sarah to keep the money she had brought to her marriage. Had this money been exempted from Artemas's estate she might have been able to save the farm for the children. Since the estate was in litigation until 1848 and Hila Mahan Hall still lived in Michigan, Sarah must have been aware of the new law and of the irony of her own legal situation.

Sarah knew as well as any other nineteenth-century woman the economic insecurity of marriage and its often brief duration. She had experienced first-hand the inequity of laws affecting women but created by men. If Sarah made quilts during her marriage those too would have been considered part of Artemas's estate, even if Sarah had made them for the children. Although Sarah was head of household when she made this quilt in 1851, she wanted to ensure that this family icon would go to specific women in the Mahan family. This is probably the reason she wrote her bequest on the quilt itself, a rare occurrence. Even if she left a formal will (none has been found) this inscribed bequest clarifies her intent with regard to her quilt.

Although when she made the quilt Sarah intended to leave it to her Mahan stepdaughters or their daughters, in fact it descended through women in Sarah's own family, the Wadsworths. A conversation with members of the family in which it was found, confirmed by genealogical research, indicates that Sarah Mahan gave the quilt to Sarah Wadsworth, wife of her nephew Edward. Sarah Wadsworth, who had no children, passed it on to her niece, Sarah Wadsworth Getchell of River Falls, Wisconsin, who gave it to her granddaugther, Josephine Getchell (Troup). While the line of descent changed, the quilt remained within the quiltmaker's family and was passed through female descendents, three bearing the same name.

Interpretation

The many and rich roles this quilt played for its maker indicate that for Sarah Mahan it was far more than a utilitarian bedcover. But an analysis of the quilt is not complete until we investigate its significance to Americans in the 1980s. This is the purpose of Fleming's final operation, interpretation. Through interpretation we relate facts we have discovered about the Mahan quilt to our current values. Interpretation will vary with the interests of the student; there is no single "correct answer." This operation consummates the progressive analysis proposed by Fleming, makes meaning of the process of artifact analysis and enriches the knowledge of the interpreter. If the operation of interpretation answers a single question, it is "So what?"

The existence of this volume and an article in it proposing systematic quilt documentation are evidence of the value we place today on the studies of women and of material culture. Twenty years ago a book entitled *Making the American Home: Middle Class Women and Domestic Material Culture*, 1840-1940 would not have been conceived, let alone read. Ten years ago the idea of a systematic, large-scale quilt research project did not exist. The recently developed fields of women's history, material culture, and the "new" social history have changed all that. Now scholars from many disciplines consider it not only acceptable but mandatory to study "ordinary" people and their apparently mundane activities, and these studies lead to exciting insights. History is made, we now acknowledge, not simply by kings and conquerors, but by ordinary men and women, the majority of the population at any given time. Key words in the title of this volume—American, home, women, domestic, material culture—reflect these new values. We can interpret many of the facts discovered about the Mahan quilt in their light.

Those interpreting the quilt by concentrating on its history might see it as an example of geographic dispersal of a favored New England style through one New England-based region (the Connecticut Western Reserve) to another (the Minnesota Territory) during the period of westward expansion. For Oberlin historians its importance may lie in the image of Oberlin asceticism it projects, as well as by stylistic encroachment of American popular culture on a community that had condemned it. Students of women's history might focus on its matrilineal descent, noting that the quiltmaker redirected it from the Mahan to the Wadsworth family.

Textile historians and quilt researchers who compare this quilt to others might raise questions about its materials and construction that could lead to an economic interpretation. Sarah Mahan and makers of other quilts in this style typically used commonly available cotton fabrics and simple construction techniques. By contrast many Quaker quiltmakers used more expensive silks, and makers of Baltimore appliqued quilts worked in a time-consuming and technically demanding technique. Do these factors reflect the comparative affluence of quiltmaking societies?

A consideration of materials, design and construction of repeated-block style quilts might also lead to religious and political interpretations. Jonathan Holstein relates the development of this favored nineteenth-century style to English design influence, availability of materials, working space and "the American genius for developing innovative work methods" (16-27). But might it also symbolize the egalitarianism that characterized both Jacksonian democracy and revivalistic Evangelicalism? We have already noted the popularity of these quilts in New England and its daughter communities, and the frequency of Bible verses on repeated-block signature quilts. What were the religious affiliations of those who wrote Bible verses on quilts? Some, Sarah Mahan among them, were part of an Arminian, pietistic Evangelical tradition largely centered in New England but epitomized in its best-known leader, Oberlin College president Charles Grandison Finney. This tradition stressed egalitarianism, rejecting heirarchical church governance and supporting anti-slavery, the involvement of women in church and the world, and other social reforms (Dayton). On the other hand, were these quilts in fact made primarily in New England settlements, or are those simply the areas where research has been done? Questions like these can be answered only after studying large numbers of repeated-block quilts and their makers as well as quiltmaking practices in all areas of America from 1800 to 1850. Such massive studies have not yet been undertaken.

Those interpreting the quilt from a standpoint of design may focus on the inscriptions. Viewing it as a cultural document, social historians might concentrate on the networks it represents—town, church, school, family— and the individual members of more than one of these networks. Of interest to Oberlin researchers will be the people who signed the quilt, especially the Mahan family. Further investigation into the records of voluntary associations in Oberlin, such as literary, moral reform and anti-slavery societies, can round out the picture of each signer and will reveal other overlapping social networks, thus enlarging our understanding of the Oberlin community.

My own interpretations of the Mahan quilt concentrate on its functions in the life of Sarah Mahan and her community. This is a particularly rich document of women's history: a record of social networks, of the significance of the female family to nineteenth-century women, of attitudes toward family, of individuals' roles within the family—even after death. And family, for Sarah Mahan, included its deceased members. Her quilt bridges the chasm between the living and the dead.

Laura's death was the impetus for the quilt. By completing it Sarah marked the final event in Laura's life and ritualized her own mourning with a uniquely appropriate symbol of comfort and nurture: a domestic textile traditionally associated with women. By completing Laura's unfinished quilt Sarah joined her in a communal project, continuing their relationship in spite of Laura's death. Their bonds were further strengthened by Sarah's use of scraps from Laura's dresses, materials so personal that the quilt became as much a part of Laura's identity as her dresses had been. By specifying that the quilt should descend through women in the family Sarah forged a chain connecting the deceased Laura to Mahan women not yet born.

But Laura Mahan is not the only deceased family member whose life and influence are perpetuated through this quilt. There is some indication that the quilt commemorates the death of Artemas Mahan as well. Two inscriptions refer to widows and orphans (b-6, d-6), and these inscriptions revealingly reflect the Oberlin community's perception of Sarah Mahan and her step-children. Nineteenth-century women often defined themselves by their roles within their families: "mother," "daughter," "sister," "wife" (Cott; Motz; Smith-Rosenberg). The terms "orphan" and "widow" also refer to family roles, albeit within a fractured family. By 1851, when the quilt was completed, the orphans in the Mahan family were either married or dead, and the widowed Sarah had lost her husband eight years earlier. Other written documents in Oberlin refer to Sarah as "Widow Mahan," which helps distinguish her from her sister-in-law, the only other Mrs. Mahan in the community (Records of OMA; E.M. Leonard to Prudential Committee). Artemas Mahan, whose death defined these family roles for Sarah and the children, never lived in Oberlin. The signers of the quilt and other documents who wrote of Sarah as a widow and her children as orphans had never even met Artemas, since he died several years before those people came to Oberlin. Yet the inscriptions suggest that Sarah is still mourning for her husband as well as for her stepdaughter, and that death did not always obviate a man's role as head of household.

Finally, the quilt chronicles one woman's way of coping with domestic dislocation, an important aspect of so many women's lives then and now. In 1850 Sarah's family was fractured. Artemas and Laura had died, and Laura had been the last child at home. All the students who signed Sarah's quilt, some of whom had been Laura's classmates, completed their Oberlin education in 1850 or 1851 and then left the community. In 1850, after finding himself increasingly at odds with his faculty, Asa Mahan resigned as president of the Oberlin Collegiate Institute and moved with his family to Cleveland (Fletcher 472-488). As a relative and community member Sarah must surely have been aware of the controversy leading up to his resignation and uncomfortable because of it. Perhaps because of the cumulative effect of these experiences, Sarah accepted Elisabeth Ayer's invitation to teach in Belle Prairie, Minnesota, and in the summer of 1851 left Oberlin (Ayer). At this point in her life, when her family and family-based community were disintegrating, Sarah Mahan needed a tangible reminder of those people most important to her. Her quilt, whose utilitarian purpose was to provide warmth and comfort, assumed added significance as a metaphor for family.

Sarah Mahan's quilt is a powerful document recorded in a domestic language spoken by quiltmaking women for generations. The quilt's matrilineal descent and preservation within the same family for 130 years bespeaks the continuing significance of intergenerational continuity for women and confirms that the language spoken by a woman through her quilt over a century ago is still understood.

Appendix A:

Mahan Quilt Inscriptions

Letters indicate vertical columns, a-i; numbers indicate horizontal rows, 1-10.

a-1

a-3

Margaret Gray, Albany, N.Y./"Peace I leave with you."
Ann Jane Gray Oberlin O 1851./"Thou art ever with

a-5

me & all I have is thine."
Amos Dresser, Oberlin O/1851/When thou passest through the waters, I will be with thee; and through the/rivers they shall not overflow thee; when thou walkest thro' the fire, thou shalt not/be burned, neither shall the flame kindle upon thee, for I am the Lord thy God./Holy one of Israel, *thy saviour,* . . . fear not, for *I am with thee.* Isa 43:2, 3 & 5.//Isa 40:28-31/ 41:10-20//Heb. 15:5/[unreadable] 28:20//Isa 2:40/Zech 9:90/Hoseah 7-2:18//

a-7

a-9

[unreadable]33:17/Is 48:14-40/Ezra 11:21-23, 36.
Eliza Gray - Albany, NY./Walk in the spirit.
Oh! memories of the past!/Close, Rose, your tendrils twine/My heart—and, with your touches cast,/Light forms are blithely round me fast,/From earth departed—

b-2

yet: how near to mine!/Adelaide Warren/Oberlin.
"apres se travail, il y a repos."/C Woodruff/Ypsilanti,

b-4

Aug. 6, 1850.
The wise shall inherit/glory. Prov. 3:35/Farmer Ohio/

b-6

F.E. Ensign.
What human soul can know -/A widow's joys and tears? Her, that hath felt them Sewall N. Kendall/Litchfield

b-8

NY/June 17th, 1850.

b-10

[unreadable] Hall/Ann Arbor/Mich.

c-1

Abigail Warren/Oberlin.
May the peace of the righteous/Attend thy path, Sarah,/

c-3

Litchfield, Mich., Camilla S. Stevens.
"Now the just shall/live by faith."/Asa Mahan/Oberlin

c-5

June/19th 1850.
Commit thy way unto the Lord;/Trust also in him; and he shall/bring it to pass. Ps. 37:5/Morgan, O. Wm. W.

Foot.

c-7   As thy days so shall thy strength be.—Michigan City Ind
Norbert [?] B. Williams.

c-9   The Lord will not suffer the soul/of the righteous to
famish but he casteth/away the substance of the wicked./
Selected by Timothy H. Ward./Proverbs 10th 3rd/Jersey/
Licking Co/*Ohio.*

d-2   "Prove all things; hold fast that which is good."/F
Woodruff/Pittsfield.

d-4   Rejoice evermore/Jas Cutler Tefft/Cambridge/NY/May
1850.

d-6   "Leave thy Fatherless children I will preserve alive,/and
let thy widows trust in me." Jer. 49:11/Chas. C. Breed/
New Haven/Ct.

d-8   They that trust in the Lord shall be/as mount Zion which
cannot be removed/but abideth forever/Hila M. Hall/
Ann Arbor, Mich.

d-10   "At books, or work, or healthful play,/Let my first year's
[sic] be past;/That I may give for every day/Some good
account at last."/Mrs. A. [?] Corlett/Oberlin.

e-1   This quilt, commenced by our dear Laura & finished by
me,/ principally from fragments of her dresses, I give
& bequeath/ unto her sister Julia M. Woodruff, or in
case of her death/to her sister Hila M. Hall, if she survives,
otherwise to the/oldest surviving granddaughter of their
father,/Artemas Mahan deceased./Sarah Mahan./Oberlin
Feb. 6, 1851.

e-3   "If ye keep my commandments/ye shall abide in my love."
John 15:10//"Cast thy burden upon the Lord, and/He
shall sustain thee." Psalm 55:22/Mary H. Mahan/Oberlin
Ohio, June 19th 1850.

e-5   In the bosom of Sarah's God/there is Everlasting rest./
Wm. Warren—Maine.

e-7   Fear not, little flock, it is your/Father's good pleasure
to give you/the kingdom.—/Joseph and Mary Wads-
worth/Parents of Sarah Mahan/Acts 58 and 87/1850.

e-9   The fear of the Lord is a fountain of life. Prov. XIV,
27/Mary A Corlett [?]/Oberlin/O.

f-2   It doth not yet appear/What we shall be./Blessed are the
pure in heart,/for they shall see God./W. Warren
Woodruff/Platteville, Wis./Nihil desperandum Christi
[duce]./May 27, 1850/W.W.W.

f-4   Sweet heavenborn Spirits are not/to earth confined/Sept.
30 1850 Franklin L. Arnold/Destined for West Africa.

f-6   "I was a *stranger*, and ye took me in."/Inasmuch as ye
did it to one of the least/of these, ye did it to me."/Bristol,
Ill./Mary E. Cone.

f-8   Man is like to vanity: his days are/as a shadow that passeth
away./Julia M. Woodruff/Pittsfield, Michigan.

f-10   Calista Warren/Oberlin.

g-1   I ask for thee/that while you live,/You may not live in vain,/But live to cheer the aching heart,/And soothe the woman's pain./Julia Ann [Rice]/Oberlin Ohio.

g-3   The work of righteousness shall/be peace and the effect of right-/eousness quietness and assu-/rance forever Is 32, 17/Eckford Mich/Daniel N. Bordwell.

g-5   Endure as seeing Him who is invisible./Thomas H. Robinson/North East. Erie Co. Pa.

g-7   The blessing of thy God, it maketh rich/And he addeth no sorrow with it./M.M. Hill/Perryville/Madison Co.,/ N.Y.

g-9   Remember me when/far far away/Amelia Freeman/ Pittsburgh/Pa February 11th 1851.

h-2   Love is the fulfilling of the law/Charles Conkling/Le Roy Illinois/June 1850.

h-4   Excelsior/Michigan City, Ind./Almer Harper.

h-6   Let not mercy and truth forsake thee,/Bind them about thy neck: write them/upon the table of thy heart/Anna L. Bordwell/ Eckford, Mich.

h-8   Blessed are the dead which die in the Lord,/from henceforth: yes saith his spirit,/that they may rest from their *labors*/and their works do *follow* them./Francis Woodruff/Pittsfield, Michigan.

h-10   Shall we meet again?/Cleveland Ohio CC Miller/May 8th 1851/JCL

i-1   They that trust in the Lord shall be/as Mount Zion which cannot be removed/John A. Nightingale,/Attica, Mich.

i-3   Come unto me all ye that labor and/are heavy laden and I will give you rest./Caroline [R] Cornell/Liverpool, Eng [Oct] 10

i-5   Rejoice in the Lord, all ye righteous/for praise is comely for the upright./John Haywood/Salem. Chattauqua Co. N.Y.

i-7   Search the scriptures for in/them ye think ye have/eternal life/Romeo, Mich/[L Aldrich].

i-9   We have an advocate with the Father/Jesus Christ, the righteous/Gilbert Woodruff/Augusta Mich.

Appendix B:

Social Networks Represented on the Mahan Quilt

Name	Oberlin Resident	Ob. Col. Institute	Classmate Laura Mahan	Member 1st Church	Mahan family and relatives
Arnold, Franklin		x	x	x	
Aldrich, L. [?]					
Bordwell, Anna					
Bordwell, Daniel		x*		x	
Breed, Charles		x		x	
Cone, Mary E.		x			
Conkling, Charles		x		x	
Corlett, Mrs. A.	x	x			
Corlett, Mary A.	x			x	

Cornell, Caroline		x			
Dresser, Amos	x	x*		x	
Ensign, F.E.		x			
Foot, William W.		x		x	
Freeman, Amelia		x		x	
Gray, Ann Jane	x			x	
Gray, Eliza		x			
Gray, Margaret	x			x	
Hall, (Augustus)					x
Hall, Hila					x
Harper, Almer		x		x	
Haywood, John		x		x	
Hill, M. M.		x			
Kendall, Sewall N.		x*		x	
Mahan, Asa	x	x*		x	x
Mahan, Mary	x			x	x
Mahan, Sara	x	x		x	x
Miller, C.C.		x			
Nightingale, John A.		x			
Rice, Julia Ann	x	x			
Robinson, Thomas H.		x		x	
Stevens, Camilla S.		x			
Tefft, James Cutler		x		x	
Wadsworth, Joseph/Mary					x
Ward, Timothy					
Warren, Abigail	x			x	
Warren, Adelaide	x			x	
Warren, Calista	x	x		x	
Warren, William		x	x		
Williams, (Norbert)					
Woodruff, C.					x
Woodruff, F.					x
Woodruff, Francis					x
Woodruff, Gilbert					x
Woodruff, Julia	x	x		x	x
Woodruff, W. Warren		x		x	?

*Oberlin Collegiat, Institute Faculty/Staff

Notes

[1]See estate inventory, Moses Beach, New Haven, Huron County, Ohio, 1827; estate inventory, John Johnson, New Haven, Huron County, Ohio, May 1826. The inventories include yardages and detailed lists of fabrics from Beach's and Johnson's stores.

[2]For examples of signature quilts in the repeated block style see Ricky Clark, Jane Bentley Kolter, Linda Otto Lipsett, and Jessica F. Nicoll.

[3]Western Reserve Historical Society, Cleveland (acc. no. 75.22.1); Historic Lyme Village, Bellevue, OH (Helen Nims Wood quilt); Lorain County Historical Society, Elyria, OH (acc. no. K49). The Austinburg quilt is privately owned.

[4]Biblical quotations are frequently found on signature quilts from this period, and some of these quilts have been identified with Methodist and Quaker women, as indicated above. An investigation into the religious affiliations of the makers and signers of other quilts should be informative. Were these people predominantly Christians, or were Jewish women also involved? If most signers were Christians what percentage were Protestants? Were most associated with one denomination?

Works Cited

Alumni Records file, 28/6. Oberlin College Archives.

Archer, Cathaline Alford. *Becket Sons in a Massachusetts Settlement of New Connecticut.* New Haven: L.W. Gibbons, 1953 [1954].

Ayer, Elisabeth. "One of Minnesota's First Schools," Elizabeth [sic] Taylor Ayer Papers, Division of Archives and Manuscripts, Minnesota Historical Society Research Center.

Bureau of the Census. 1820, 1830, Census Population Schedules for Wyoming County, New York; 1840, 1850 Census Population Schedules for Livingston and Washtenaw Counties, Michigan; 1850 Census Population Schedule for Lorain County, Ohio.

Catalog of the Officers and Students, Oberlin Collegiate Institute, 1843-4. Oberlin, OH: The Evangelist.

Clark, Ricky. *Quilts and Carousels: Folk Art in the Firelands.* Oberlin, OH: Firelands Association for the Visual Arts, 1983.

Cott, Nancy F. *The Bonds of Womanhood: "Woman's Sphere" in New England, 1780-1835.* New Haven: Yale University Press, 1977.

Crockett, James Underwood. "Flowering Shrubs" and "Trees." *The Time-Life Encyclopedia of Gardening.* New York: Time-Life Books, Inc., 1972.

Dayton, Donald W. *Discovering an Evangelical Heritage.* New York: Harper & Row, 1976.

Ellis, Franklin. *History of Livingston County, Michigan...* Philadelphia: Everts & Abbott, 1880.

Elrod, Diana R. "From Asceticism to Aestheticism: Domestic Architecture in Oberlin, 1833-1883." *Building Utopia: Oberlin Architecture, 1833-1983.* Exhibition catalog issued as *Allen Memorial Art Museum Bulletin.* Oberlin, OH: Oberlin College, 1983-84. Vol. XLI, No. 1.

Fairchild, James H. *Oberlin: Its Origin, Progress and Results.* Oberlin, OH: R. Butler, 1871.

Fleming, E. McClung. "Artifact Study: a Proposed Model." *Winterthur Portfolio* 9 (June 1974): 153-173.

Fletcher, Robert Samuel. *A History of Oberlin College from its Foundation Through the Civil War.* 2 vols. Oberlin, OH: Oberlin College, 1943.

Garfield, James Abram. *The Discovery and Ownership of the Northwest Territory, and Settlement of the Western Reserve,* Western Reserve and Northern Ohio Historical Society of Cleveland, Historical and Archaeological Tracts no. 20. Cleveland: Leader Printing Company, 1881.

General Catalog of Oberlin College 1833-1908. Oberlin, OH: Oberlin College, 1909.

Gurniak, Miriam R. " 'Heaven Begun Below': Student Housing in Oberlin." *Allen Memorial Art Museum Bulletin.* Oberlin, OH: Oberlin College, 1983-84. Vol.

XLI, No. 1.

Holstein, Jonathan. "The American Block Quilt", in *In the Heart of Pennsylvania: Symposium Papers.* Ed. Jeannete Lasansky. Lewisburg, PA: Oral Traditions Project, 1986.

Katzenberg, Dena. *Baltimore Album Quilts.* Baltimore: The Baltimore Museum of Art, 1981.

Klukas, Arnold. "Introduction." *Allen Memorial Art Museum Bulletin.* Oberlin, OH: Oberlin College, 1983-84, Vol. XLI, no. 1.

Kolter, Jane Bentley. *Forget Me Not: A Gallery of Friendship and Album Quilts.* Pittstown, NJ: The Main Street Press, 1985.

Lasser, Carol. " 'Let Us Be Sisters Forever': Antoinette Brown Blackwell, Lucy Stone and the Sororial Model of Nineteenth-Century Female Friendship." *Signs: Journal of Women in Culture and Society* 13 (1988), forthcoming.

Leonard to Prudential Committee, 10 July 1845. Oberlin College Archives.

Lipsett, Linda Otto. *Remember Me: Women and Their Friendship Quilts.* San Francisco: The Quilt Digest Press, 1985.

Mahan, Sarah to Judge Kneeland. Livingston County (Michigan) Probate Court Docket #280.

Maxwell, Fiona F. "The Aesthetics of a Moral Architecture: Oberlin 1833-1883." *Allen Memorial Art Museum Bulletin.* Oberlin, OH: Oberlin College, 1983-84. Vol. XLI, No. 1.

Melder, Keith E. *Beginnings of Sisterhood: the American Woman's Rights Movement, 1800-1850.* New York: Schocken Books, 1977.

Montgomery, Florence M. *Printed Textiles: English and American Cottons and Linens.* New York: The Viking Press, Inc., 1970.

Motz, Marilyn Ferris. *True Sisterhood: Michigan Women and Their Kin 1820-1920.* Albany: State University of New York Press, 1983.

Nicoll, Jessica F. *Quilted for Friends: Delaware Valley Signature Quilts, 1840-1855.* Winterthur, DE: The Henry Francis Du Pont Winterthur Museum, 1986.

Orlofsky, Patsy and Myron Orlofsky. *Quilts in America.* New York: McGraw-Hill Book Company, 1974.

Records of First and Second Congregational Churches, First Church membership records, 31/4/1, Box 17. Oberlin College Archives.

Records of the Oberlin Maternal Association, Vol. I, 3 July 1843, Box 13. Oberlin College Archives.

Records, Russia Township Board of Education, 1843, 31/11. Oberlin College Archives.

Rehmel, Judy. *Key to a Second 1,000 Quilt Patterns.* Richmond, IN, 1979.

Robinson, Thomas H. "Reminiscences of the Class of 1850." Class files, 0/2, Box 1. Oberlin College Archives.

Smith-Rosenberg, Carroll. "The Female World of Love and Ritual: Relations Between Women in Nineteenth-Century America." *Signs: Journal of Women in Culture and Society* 1, no. 1 (1975): 1-29.

Thompson, George. *Thompson in Africa: or, An Account of the Missionary Labors, Sufferings, Travels and Observations, of George Thompson, at the Mendi Mission.* Dayton, 1859.

Troup, Joyce. Telephone interview with author, 18 October 1986.

Wadsworth, Horace Andrew. *Two Hundred Fifty Years of the Wadsworth Family in America...* Lawrence, MA: Eagle Steam Job Printing Rooms, 1883.

Woodruff Chronicles: a Genealogy. Glendale, CA: The Arthur H. Clark Company, 1967.

Young, Robert. *Analytical Concordance to the Bible.*_____ *22nd Am. Ed. New York: Funk and Wagnalls Company, 1955.*

The Domestic Mission of the Privileged American Suburban Homemaker, 1877-1917: A Reassessment

Mary Corbin Sies

Historians have often placed the privileged turn-of-the-century American suburban homemaker between an ideological rock and a historiographic hard place. Despite the recent efforts of scholars like Marlene Wortman, Ruth Cowan, and Gwendolyn Wright to claim for these women a place as independent historical agents, the suburban housewife is often depicted simply as a misguided object of oppression or a lady of leisure defined in terms of her pursuit of "unproductive" activities. Since her husband's wealth allowed her to hire servants to manage her household and children, she was free to make social calls, consume conspicuously, or perhaps enjoy one of the fashionable sports like golf or tennis at the country club—all activities calculated to advertise her husband's status and promote his career. When historians have turned their attention to the suburban woman's forays into more "useful" pursuits like charity and reform activities, they have often found themselves uncomfortable with her adherence to the 19th century "cult of domesticity". As a result, she has been lambasted for contributing to social oppression, for failing to practice feminist principles as we define them today, or for advocating policies defined to preserve the social foundations of American capitalism.[1]

When we have given the privileged suburban woman credit for venturing outside the home to engage in public service—social housekeeping, it is usually labeled—we have suggested in the very next breath that her primary motive was self-interest—the promotion of her own political agenda or sublimated career ambitions. Architectural historians have been especially vehement in condemning the suburban housewife, claiming that it was principally she who was responsible for bringing about the demise of progressive domestic architecture just before WWI. They have argued that when she began to participate more actively in architectural design decisions—after 1910, they say—she had the bad taste to prefer the fashionable and historically imitative "period styles" of houses rather than the more original and functional designs offered by architects wishing to promote an indigenous American architecture. The result was an infusion of Babbitry into the design and decoration of houses, and the loss of livelihood for those few original architects striving to reform popular architectural taste. Nearly all of these interpretations have characterized the suburban woman's activities as highly circumscribed private endeavors, conceived and conducted entirely within her very privileged separate domestic sphere.[2]

The suburban homemakers whose activities I learned about when I chronicled the design and development of four pre-WWI planned, exclusive suburbs did not conform very closely to any of these images.[3] Although they were privileged women who adhered in many ways to the tenets of the cult of domesticity, they also departed from that traditional canon in significant ways. Rather than the idle, ornamental, and smug social-climbers of the common stereotype, most were public-spirited women who stepped decisively outside of the traditional private circle to address pressing issues in the urban public sphere. During the forty years preceding WWI, they played an increasingly important role in domestic architectural decision-making, but their influence more often supported than undercut progressive architectural principles. As a group, suburban homemakers had a profound impact on the nationwide consensus concerning the proper form of the ideal home environment that emerged around 1900—a consensus that has come to define the American dream over the course of the 20th century. In this essay, I would like to present a profile of these "new suburban women," indicate briefly both the issues and the activities that engaged them, summarize the domestic ideal that they promoted, and then draw a few conclusions concerning their position bridging public and private spheres.

There was a remarkable degree of similarity in social background among the adult women residing between 1877 and 1917 in Short Hills, NJ; St. Martin's, Philadelphia; Kenilworth, IL; and Lake of the Isles, Minneapolis. Nearly 90% belonged to the new Professional-Managerial Stratum (P-MS) of the urban upper-middle class that emerged as a result of the business and technical revolution occurring in post-Civil War business and industry. They were the wives or widows of men whose occupations fell into one of three categories: 1) business managers, 2) professionals, and 3) producers or transmitters of culture. A minority—perhaps 15% in some planned, exclusive suburbs—were single women. Of these, approximately one-third supported themselves with careers of their own—as teachers, musicians, artists, realtors, or physicians. In addition, a few married women—but no more than one or two in each suburb—continued their careers after marriage; they were generally schoolteachers, artists, or speculators in real estate.[4]

Nearly all of these suburban women could be called privileged although only a few could be termed wealthy or even financially secure— and these by means of their husbands' occupations rather than inherited money. Most had the equivalent of high school educations and a few had attended colleges. Over 95% belonged to Protestant religious denominations with the majority joining the Episcopal Church as adults. They also shared many common social affiliations. In each location, a majority of female residents were founders or active members of their local Women's Club, and a significant minority—perhaps 5%—also maintained their former memberships in the Women's Club of the city where they resided before moving to the suburbs. As a group, they were interested in, and many participated quite actively in, the domestic science movement; a substantial minority were also members of Arts & Crafts societies. Their names filled the membership lists of church auxiliaries, Sunday school staffs, and mission boards. Most belonged, along with their families, to the local country club. They generally maintained their interests and subscriptions in the major cultural institutions of the city— the orchestras, public libraries, and art academies. At home, they attended a brisk round of amateur theatricals, musical evenings, lectures, sporting activities, and informal social gatherings at each others' houses.[5]

Most P-MS residents of planned, exclusive suburbs adhered to a common belief system that was bifurcated—split between the traditional values of mid-century domesticity, Republicanism, and Christian virtues, and the emerging modern values of professional service, efficiency, and occupational ambition. The new suburban woman held fast to the tenets of the "cult of domesticity," but she also adapted that canon in ways which suited her contemporary circumstances. The central convention of the cult of domesticity was a set of gender stereotypes that assigned men to the public and increasingly urban realm of economic activity while women performed domestic duties centered exclusively in the private realm of the home. The P-MS homemaker continued to concentrate upon activities that nurtured and maintained the family circle. She considered the private home the locus of family unity and character formation, and her special role as moral educator of her children a serious trust upon which might rest the ongoing stability of the American polity. But at the same time, she recognized that in turn-of-the-century metropolitan society, P-MS families could no longer effectively isolate the domestic household from the worldly influence of the city. The P-MS' ability to sustain the family's status into the next generation, for example, depended upon the housewife's cultivation in her sons of more than the traditional Christian virtues; she had to impart the social skills and business acumen necessary for occupational success as well.[6]

The mid-century cult of domesticity, by designating women the moral curators of society, had emphasized the importance of the activities that she performed within her separate sphere. In the reasoning of the new turn-of-the-century business values that associated self-worth with professional or occupational achievement, however, woman's domestic vocation no longer appeared to warrant much respect. To remedy this loss of status, many P-MS homemakers, influenced by the domestic science movement, promoted the elevation of traditional household responsibilities to the status of a profession. The new "domestic scientists" would be trained to apply all of the resources of science and technology to the improvement and more efficient management of the home. In this new professional capacity, the suburban homemaker moved beyond the supervision of simple housekeeping tasks and interior decoration to influence architectural design decisions formerly the prerogative of architects alone. Her assumption of responsibility for decisions concerning the interior planning, kitchen design, sanitary engineering, landscaping, and even aesthetic expression of her home is well documented in the comments and complaints of architects faced with an ever more demanding feminine clientele (Cott, 74; Ehrenreich and English, 8-10, 17-25; Weigley, 94; Wright, *Building the Dream*, 159).[7]

But the female residents of Short Hills, St. Martin's, Kenilworth, Lake of the Isles, and other similar planned suburbs extended their new professional expertise to domestic problems in the public sphere as well. In light of the challenging social problems that threatened the quality of life for all those who were tied by occupation to the city, P-MS women felt a strong responsibility to apply those special skills peculiar to their gender to achieve the cultural and social uplift of the entire urban family. They based their increased social activism on the conviction, intrinsic to the domestic science movement, that a properly designed home environment could shape moral character and uplift human behavior. Many suburban homemakers felt a genuine moral obligation to serve to upgrade the abhorrent residential conditions that they observed all around them in the city. They also shared their husbands' fears of the social conflagration and moral degeneration that would surely come if these deleterious conditions were not alleviated. Thus, in countless women's clubs, civic improvement organizations, social agencies, and domestic reading groups, suburban women devised and attempted to disseminate strategies for the improvement of urban residential neighborhoods and their occupants. In substantial numbers, they moved outside of the private domestic circle to devise solutions for some of the most serious urban public policy problems of the day.[8]

The majority of women residing in the four planned exclusive suburbs of my research defied our stereotype of frivolous and status-seeking suburbanites intent upon escaping responsibility for the social problems of the city. But neither were they radical thinkers inclined to seriously question the social and economic circumstances that underlay the conditions which they were determined to address. Although there were a few flamboyant and significant exceptions in each suburb—usually single women—the typical P-MS homemaker did not think of herself as a feminist, did not campaign actively for suffrage, nor did she promote the "grand domestic revolution" that Dolores Hayden has written about so well.[9]

Ella Gibson Russell, who moved with her husband and firstborn from Brooklyn, NY, to Short Hills, NJ, in 1878, typified the first generation of P-MS women who ventured out to the suburbs. Her husband, William I. Russell, presided over a small metals brokerage in New York City; his business fortunes, which fluctuated wildly over the course of their long marriage, underscored the precariousness of P-MS social and economic standing. In 1879, a year in which Russell's income reached $12,000, the young couple bought "Sunnyside," their first home, for $4500. In 1881, a "banner year" in which her husband cleared $28,000, the Russells sold "Sunnyside" and commissioned their own home in Short Hills—a grand, 12-room red sandstone dwelling costing $20,000, that they christened "Redstone." According to her husband, Ella Russell's vision of the suburban lifestyle determined in broad outlines the kind of dwelling that they sought for the family home:

my wife's fertile brain would paint to me in pleasing colors what the country home should be—the cottage and its coziness, the garden, the lawn and flowers, my health restored, the benefit of country life to the boy...

She also managed—quite admirably, in an architectural critic's opinion— the interior decoration and furnishing (Russell, 63).[10]

"Redstone"—a sumptuous 'though architecturally progressive suburban dwelling by P-MS standards—represented the chief means by which the Russells indulged themselves during their most prosperous decade. In all other ways, the couple led a modest, family-centered lifestyle; Mrs. Russell, in particular, was not socially ambitious nor given to conspicuous display. She "had no difficulty keeping busy" caring for the house and looking after her children—six in all—tasks that she took very seriously during her years in Short Hills. The amount of domestic assistance she could count on varied with her husband's fortunes. During the years of William Russell's greatest prosperity—from 1887 until 1892, shortly before he lost his shirt in business—she had a maid of all works and a governess for the children in addition to a coachman and gardener for the outside chores. During their unexceptional years, however, she was assisted only by a single maid (Russell, 70 and 67; *Moffatt's Directory*, *Baldwin's Directory*).

Ella Russell enjoyed socializing within the community of Short Hills; her "desire...for neighbors, pleasant, cultured people whose society we could enjoy" had been an important factor in the decision to settle in a planned, exclusive suburb. The couple often attended the card parties or amateur theatricals followed by dancing at the Short Hills Casino, but seemed to favor "the frequent pleasant little dinner parties of four to six couples," and the informal family gatherings in the evenings that they shared with the Hortons and the Roots, their most intimate neighbors. Although they didn't participate in sporting activities, they did enjoy weekend family outings touring the country in a carriage drawn by their matched pair of Vermont Morgan horses. Despite her busy daily schedule of housekeeping, socializing, and caring for the children, Ella Russell still found considerable time to pursue her charity and social reform interests. She was known locally as a veritable "Lady Bountiful to the poor of a neighboring village," and she helped to organize and staff the "Neighborhood House," a non-resident settlement house for the needy and immigrant families of the industrial town of Millburn. The Russells, when financially able, also contributed generously to several New York City charities, including the Fresh Air Fund, St. John's Guild, and a home for crippled children (Russell, 77, 83-84, 96, 126, 141, 167).

Helen Barry Sears and her two daughters, Helen Abigail (b. 1877) and Dorothy (b. 1885), fairly represent the range of interests and activities that occupied the female residents of Kenilworth, IL, a lakeshore community founded north of Chicago in 1891. Helen Barry Sears was married to Kenilworth's founder, Joseph, a successful business manager with the N.K. Fairbank & Co. until he retired in 1887 to begin a second career as the developer of his model suburb. At the time of Sears' retirement, he may have possessed a net worth approaching $500,000, the greater sum of which he invested in land and improvements for his model community. Although the Sears family never experienced the dramatic financial ups and downs of W.I. Russell, they had to cope with periodic cash flow crises because of Joseph's investment of most of his principal in the unprofitable 'though personally gratifying development of Kenilworth. The family lived modestly in a 2 & 1/2 story lakeshore residence that cost between $6,000 and $12,000 to build, and was assisted in chores and housekeeping by a black family for whom they remodeled an old farmhouse nearby.[11]

Helen Barry Sears met her husband through their common membership in the Swedenborgian Church of New Jerusalem, an organization that profoundly influenced her values and guided her interest in charity and social reform activities. Her long record of social service began in 1871, four years after her marriage, when she devoted herself to relief work, organized by the New Church on behalf of families made destitute by the Great Chicago Fire. The mother of six children, Helen

Sears had direct experience of the tragic consequences of urban residential conditions when, in August of 1882, she lost her nineteen-month old daughter, Marion, and her nephew, Samuel Barry, to one of the diptheria epidemics that periodically swept the city. After moving to Kenilworth, she worked hard to see that the suburb developed into a model community that might inspire a dramatic improvement in residential conditions throughout the Chicago metropolitan area (Kilner, 57-63, 72, 103).

Helen and Joseph Sears' Swedenborgian beliefs—an interesting combination of conservative, progressive, and scientific values—set the tone for the social mores of Kenilworth society. Although they encouraged social gatherings and permitted dancing among the young people, they prohibited the consumption of alcohol and urged that socializing be conducted within the church and the local community. Mrs. Sears enjoyed vigorous physical activities like swimming and horseback-riding, more passive pursuits like vegetable gardening (the Sears' melon patch was the pride of the suburb), and opportunities for intellectual and artistic interaction. During the 1890s, she spearheaded many of Kenilworth's social welfare activities. She assumed the leadership of local charity efforts organized through the Kenilworth Union Church, and, as a co-founder of "The Neighbors", Kenilworth's women's club, she became involved in social reform campaigns and charity fundraising for various projects in the city. Helen Sears was described as having surprised her former social acquaintances in Chicago by supporting the woman suffrage movement, but her advocacy of women's causes was more characteristically reflected in her encouragement of each daughter's career (Kilner, 86, 279-81).

Helen Abigail, the Sears' eldest daughter, typified the "new woman" described by Henry Blake Fuller in his 1897 essay, "The Upward Movement in Chicago;" she was intelligent, artistic, and very involved in "activities of high civic and intellectual merit." Although she trained in Europe for a career as a concert pianist, she was forced during her mid-20s to abandon performance for music composition because of her weak physical constitution. Nevertheless, she achieved a modest national reputation as a composer, and several of her pieces were performed by major orchestras in Chicago and in the eastern U.S. Just before WWI, she joined two close friends, Agnes Pillsbury and Alma Birmingham, to live at Jane Addams' Hull House where she became involved with the settlement's Music School. An admirer of the more radical social activist, Ellen Gates Starr, Helen Sears joined her fellow residents in supporting striking women workers, marching at the head of a mass protest on behalf of the Amalgamated Garment Workers held on the Chicago Midway. Her photograph with the marchers, published in the next day's newspaper, raised a stir from her father, and a few months later she returned to Kenilworth to live. There she continued her social reform interests in a less prominent manner and assumed her former place in the rich musical life of the community. Throughout her life, she advocated the rights of less privileged women to develop artistically, contributing her money and time to musical education efforts, to Sigma Alpha Iota, the national music sorority, and to the Women's Symphony Orchestra of Chicago. (Kilner, 100-103).[12]

Dorothy Sears who, like her sister, never married, pursued a career in childhood education. After graduating from the Lee School, a three-year college in Cambridge, MA, she attended a training course in children's education offered by Dr. Maria Montessori. In 1916, she opened her own Montessori school in nearly Winnetka, which she ran until her retirement, just prior to WWII. Dorothy Sears believed very strongly in the influence of early training and environment upon a child's subsequent development. Thus, she was involved in a number of child-related activities in Kenilworth, directing the Junior department of the Kenilworth Union Church, organizing Bible classes, and participating in social welfare efforts sponsored by the Church Guild on behalf of needy children. A very civic-minded person, Dorothy devoted herself during WWI, for example, to the Kenilworth Emergency Bureau formed to provide civilian assistance for the war effort (Kilner 107-110).

Between 1877 and 1917, in P-MS suburbs nationwide, women from the political mainstream of suburbia, like Ella Gibson Russell and Helen Barry Sears and her daughters, dedicated their time and their money to a variety of social welfare and social reform activities. Their efforts were most commonly of three kinds: charity, educational activities, and positive environmental reform. In most planned suburban communities, charity was coordinated through the women's club, Ladies' Benevolent Society, church auxiliary, or similar organization. Through these institutions, women sought simply to distribute food, fuel, clothing, and other necessary items like eyeglasses or medical supplies to the urban needy. Occasionally, handouts were given by friendly visitors who also dispensed advice to the recipients, as with the Everready Sunshine Club of Minneapolis that formed to "scatter sunshine and cheer in the distribution of food, fuel, clothing, and friendly counsel." Fundraising to support these activities included the mounting of domestic science or arts & crafts exhibits, as in Kenilworth, or, more commonly, the sponsoring of charity balls or entertainments, as was the custom in Short Hills (Kenilworth Historical Society, 71-73; Kilner, 279-280; Foster, 100, 140, 230).[13]

Among the most popular educational efforts promoted by suburban homemakers were educational reform campaigns e.g., the Montessori and urban Kindergarten movements, and the promotion of domestic science and manual training in public schools. In Lake of the Isles, women successfully lobbied for the construction of a building at the

University of Minnesota to be devoted to research and training in domestic science. In Kenilworth, residents insisted that manual training and domestic science be included in the local school curriculum, the latter discipline taught by Miss Edith Allen, the well-known Chicago domestic scientist and reformer. To supplement the educational resources of less privileged urban residents, suburban women's clubs routinely organized and managed travelling libraries for parts of the city not served by branch libraries, donated works of art and musical instruments to city schools, and sponsored evening lecture series for adults. In St. Martin's, Lake of the Isles, and Kenilworth, local organizations established playground, vacation, and/or Bible schools for needy children. In Short Hills and Lake of the Isles, residents also raised money for scholarships to enable less privileged female students from the city to attend local colleges. (Kilner, 275-301; Kenilworth Historical Society, 71-77; Foster, 58, 185, 202, 206, 284).[14]

In all four of the planned, exclusive suburbs of my research, suburban homemakers demonstrated a special interest in positive environmental reform activities. These efforts aimed to redesign the urban residential environment in ways that would repair urban dwellers' physical constitutions and subtly but effectively evoke in them the character traits of morally upstanding citizens. Positive environmental reform efforts generally sorted themselves into three categories: 1) Many suburban women involved themselves in public health surveys and campaigns; their efforts resulted in the passage of smoke abatement and street cleaning ordinances, tenement reform and building inspections laws, and the establishment of pure water commissions. In Lake of the Isles, for example, female activists working through the Women's Club successfully lobbied for a charter reform act that created the Board of Public Welfare, and funded a Visiting Nurse Association to conduct medical inspections of public schoolchildren. In 1914, the suburb's residents founded the Minneapolis Housewives' League to work solely for the betterment of food conditions in the city.[15]

2) The second category of positive environmental reform concerned the establishment and staffing of urban neighborhood centers offering social, cultural, and educational programs for their foreign-born or underprivileged residents. An alternative strategy that served the same purpose endowed schools or vacation cottages in the suburbs to remove young urban dwellers for a few weeks at a time from their harmful surroundings. The suburban homemakers of my four case study communities supported the following institutions: Ella Russell's "Neighborhood House" in Millburn, NJ; "Buttercup Cottage," a vacation cottage for working girls operated by women from St. Martin's; Chicago's Hull House and College Settlements as well as the "Park Ridge School for Girls" near suburban Kenilworth; and the "Mary Davis Sunshine

Lodge," a "fresh-air" cottage for working girls from Minneapolis (Foster, 149; Kenilworth Historical Society, 73-74).[16]

3) The third category of environmental reform activities was more widely-ranging and engaged the greatest number of suburban women in some capacity. In planned, exclusive suburbs across the nation, women led the effort to discover the design principles that would produce for Americans of all social classes the "ideal home environment." By codifying and disseminating those principles across the urban landscape, P-MS homemakers hoped to effect a positive transformation of the urban residential setting and all those who lived there. Both men and women contributed to the consensus for the ideal home environment that quickly became the American residential standard after 1900. But scholars have not adequately recognized suburban homemakers' central role in this accomplishment. It was women like Ella Gibson Russell and Helen Barry Sears who, drawing ideas from domestic science instruction, domestic design manuals, and their own understanding of the function of the domicile, fueled the pre-WWI debate concerning the nature and design of the home. Armed with increased knowledge regarding technology, planning, and the design of domestic work spaces, P-MS women firmly intruded on the formerly male preserve of client-architect negotiations, often insisting upon an efficiency and logic in design features not welcomed by the profession. Using their own homes and, indeed, their own suburban styles of living as a model, they promoted an economically-constructed but technologically-sophisticated single-family suburban dwelling as the residential standard toward which all Americans should strive (Aronovici, 1-7).[17]

The suburban homemaker's expanding role in architectural decisions concerning the design of her own home was grumbled about by architects and championed by domestic scientists as early as the 1880s; it did not occur suddenly between 1910 and 1917 as some architectural historians have suggested. Moreover, the consensus about the proper form of the ideal home environment to which P-MS women contributed—along with suburban developers, housing reformers, architects, and other members of the design professions—embodied a number of very progressive design ideas. In lectures and discussions on the subject sponsored by women's clubs, and, more tellingly, in the design of their own homes, the suburban women of Short Hills, St. Martin's, Kenilworth, and Lake of the Isles emphasized simplicity, comfort, function, and economy over fashion or style. Certainly the typical P-MS suburbanite was aware of architectural fashions and conscious that the exterior aspect of her home conveyed a social statement. But the most powerful constraints on her design preferences derived from her determination to obtain a home that would stimulate the best moral, physical, social, and intellectual development of each member of her household. By offering their homes as models for urban neighborhoods, suburban activists hoped to engender a new kind of residential environment founded upon rational principles, one that would restore the human scale, stability, shared values, and democratic opportunities that they felt had been violated by urban and industrial growth.[18]

An analysis of all of the homes built in the four suburbs of my research between 1877 and 1917 suggests that the domestic design program that emerged there by consensus contained seven general principles, each calculated to produce in the inhabitants an orderly and healthful style of daily living. 1) The first principle was efficiency. By streamlining the floorplan to meet household functions and designing efficient, easily cleaned service and storage spaces, P-MS homemakers expected to facilitate hygiene, inculcate orderly workhabits, and lower the cost of owning a home. 2) Technology, and particularly proper sanitary engineering, would safeguard health and guarantee a wholesome and temperate living environment for the whole family. 3) By designing the home in close harmony with its natural surroundings—including, for example, lots of porches, sunrooms, and other indoor-outdoor spaces—residents might experience daily contact with the physically invigorating and spiritually nourishing forces of nature. 4) Family orientation was a fourth design feature of the ideal home environment. Suburban women favored eliminating the parlor and other separate sitting rooms in favor of one dominant living room designed to bring all members of the family together in one harmonious space. 5) At the same time, the model home would foster individuality by providing each child with a private second story space where he might learn independence of character and nurse his own dreams. 6) Housing reformers and social activists recognized the importance of the neighborhood as the framework within which the socialization of children would occur. They advocated a community-wide approach to urban residential improvement and pursued efforts to realize the ideal home environment on a neighborhood by neighborhood basis. In their own homes, they refrained from competitive exterior displays of status and arranged the first floor rooms in a hospitable manner in order to invite interaction with their neighbors. 7) The last principle in the design program was the desire to build with beauty, to create aesthetically pleasing environments that would inspire all that was noble and good in human character.[19]

Over the course of the years 1877 to 1917, the privileged homemakers of Short Hills, St. Martin's, Kenilworth, Lake of the Isles, and other similar planned suburbs steadily increased their presence in decision-making regarding the proper design of the domestic environment. Their concern for providing a home that would strengthen the American family and inspire the best development in each individual set the terms of the debate concerning the ideal home environment nationwide. In addition, their ideas about the shape that the American home should assume formed a vital component of the progressive domestic design consensus that emerged from that debate just prior to WWI.

The suburban woman's domestic accomplishments had as powerful an impact on urban public policy as they did on her own negotiations with the architect of her family home. In endeavoring to secure a safe and uplifting residential environment for all urban dwellers, she campaigned for pure water commissions, child-labor laws, public health ordinances, building inspections, municipal greenspaces, and a variety of other issues calculated to counter the unwholesome atmosphere of the city. Her efforts had far-reaching implications. The championship of the model suburban home as the solution to urban housing problems enabled thousands of families to upgrade their living standards by populating the suburban subdivisions that proliferated after WWI. At the same time, suburbanization prevented the development of more penetrating reform alternatives directed at improving the physical and human fabric of the city that suburbanites left behind. (Aronovici, Hue, Marcuse).

For better or for worse, the much-maligned suburban homemaker played a decisive role in determining many of the basic cultural forms that continue to structure our everyday lives. We must acknowledge that her historical agency at the turn of the century extended well beyond the limits of a private domestic sphere. But perhaps we ought to question also any definition of the public sphere that is limited to wage-or salary-earning activities. When we insist that the privileged P-MS homemaker who engaged in no wage- or capital-accruing activities filled her days, therefore, with meaningless (domestic) activities, we perpetuate a materialistic bias of the most insidious kind. Hundreds of suburban homemakers, in defiance of just such a judgement, relied upon their moral suasion and domestic expertise to bridge the public/private dichotomy in order to address some of the most challenging public policy issues of their day.

Acknowledgment

This essay is a revised version of a paper presented to the Seventh Berkshire Conference on the History of Women on June 21, 1987, in Wellesley, MA. I would like to express my gratitude to the Horace H. Rackham School of Graduate Studies of the University of Michigan and the American Institute of Architects Foundation for their generous support for the research on which this article is based. I also owe thanks to Margaret S. Marsh and Marilyn Ferris Motz for their thoughtful comments on earlier drafts.

Notes

[1]See, for example, Faye Dudden, *Serving Women;* Barbara Ehrenreich & Deirdre

English, "The Manufacture of Housework;" and Ann Douglas, *The Feminization of American Culture.* Willie Lee Rose's thoughtful observations concerning contemporary historians' discomfort with 19th century female reformers' traditional domestic beliefs is worth reading; see Rose, "Reforming Women." Both Mary Ryan and Aileen Kraditor exhibit this discomfort in their scholarship; see Ryan, *Womanhood in America,* esp. ch. 4, and Kraditor, *The Ideas of the Woman Suffrage Movement, 1890-1920.* For sources which provide alternative appraisals of the privileged woman's lifestyle at the turn of the 20th century, see Marlene Stein Wortman, "Domesticating the 19th Century American City;" Gwendolyn Wright, "Sweet and Clean: The Domestic Landscape of the Progressive Era;" Ruth Schwarz Cowan, *More Work for Mother;* Marilyn Motz, *True Sisterhood: Michigan Women and the Kin, 1820-1920;* and Daniel Scott Smith, "Family Limitation, Sexual Control, and Domestic Feminism in Victorian America."

I use the term "homemaker" instead of "housewife" to describe my actors in order to indicate that I am including the substantial percentage of adult females residing in planned, exclusive suburbs who were not married. While many were not housewives, all "made their homes" in these suburban communities.

[2]See, for example, Jill Conway, "Women Reformers and American Culture, 1870-1930;" H. Allen Brooks, *The Prairie School,* esp. 338; Leonard K. Eaton, *Two Chicago Architects and their Clients.* Gwendolyn Wright briefly refutes the view suggested by Brooks and Eaton in *Moralism and the Model Home,* 275.

[3]I am referring to my Ph.D. dissertation, "American Country House Architecture in Context: the Suburban Ideal of Living in the East and Midwest, 1877-1917."

[4]I derive my concept of the "Professional-Managerial Stratum" from Barbara Ehrenreich and John Ehrenreich, "The Professional-Managerial Class." My profile of suburban women is based upon an analysis of all adult females who were the original residents or commissioning clients of each house constructed between 1877 and 1917 in Short Hills, NJ; St. Martin's, Philadelphia, PA; Kenilworth, IL; and Lake of the Isles, in Minneapolis, MN. Occupational information was gleaned from the following county and city directories: *Moffatt's Directory of Essex County,* 1889; *Baldwin's Directory of the Oranges and Townships of Essex,* 1892; Philadelphia City Directories, 1880-1917; A.N. Marquis, ed., *Book of Chicagoans,* 1903, 1917, 1930; Minneapolis City Directories, 1880-1917. I classified the following occupations as managerial positions: bankers, brokers, upper-level managers in commerce or industry, insurance executives, directors of small business or industrial concerns, but not financiers, entrepreneurs, or owners of large business or industrial concerns. Among professional occupations, I included physicians, attorneys, ministers and members of the design professions, e.g. architects, landscape architects, engineers, and interior designers. Producers or transmitters of culture included artists, musicians, writers, editors, advertisers, and educators.

[5]This profile is a drastically truncated summary of information about the historic residents of each suburban community gleaned from major local history collections in each community: Short Hills/Millburn Historical Society Collection, Millburn, NJ; Chestnut Hill Historical Society Collection, Chestnut Hill, Philadelphia, PA; Kenilworth Historical Society Collection, Kenilworth, IL; Minneapolis History Collection, Minneapolis Public Library, Minneapolis, MN. See also, William Ingraham Russell, *The Romance and Tragedy of a Widely Known Business Man of New York;* Colleen Browne Kilner, *Joseph Sears and his Kenilworth; Blue Book of Minneapolis Clubs;* A.N. Marquis Co., *Book of Minnesotans;* Mary Dillon Foster,

Who's Who Among Minneapolis Women. For a thorough discussion of the social and cultural background of the original residents of Short Hills, St. Martin's, Kenilworth, and Lake of the Isles, see Sies, "American Country House Architecture in Context," chs. 5-8.

[6]I refer to the term "belief system" developed by Murray Murphey and described in his essay, "The Place of Beliefs in Modern Culture." For a complete discussion of the P-MS belief system, see Sies, "American Country House Architecture in Context," ch. 2. My thinking about the content of the P-MS belief system has been most influenced by the following sources: Ehrenreich & Ehrenreich, "The Professional Managerial Class"; Karen Halttunen, *Confidence Men and Painted Women*; Robert Wiebe, *The Search for Order, 1877-1920*, ch. 5; Alan Trachtenberg, *The Incorporation of America*; Steven Mintz, *A Prison of Expectations*; Emma Seifrit Weigley, "It Might Have Been Euthenics."

For the basic literature on the 19th century cult of domesticity, see Nancy F. Cott, *The Bonds of Womanhood*; Ryan, *Womanhood in America*, ch. 3; Barbara Welter, "The Cult of True Womanhood, 1820-1860." Also of importance is Kathryn Kish Sklar's biography of Catharine Beecher, whose articulation of the separate spheres ideology influenced generations of women well into the 20th century; see Sklar, *Catharine Beecher, A Study in American Domesticity*. Norma Prendergast's Ph.D. dissertation, "The Sense of Home: 19th Century Domestic Architectural Reform," contains a chapter summarizing the cult of domesticity and its relation to mid-century architectural reformers' concepts of the ideal home.

[7]Several good primary sources detail the ideas and responsibilities envisioned for the domestic scientist. See Helen Campbell, *Household Economics*; Christine Frederick, *Household Engineering: Scientific Management in the Home*; Mary Pattison, *The Principles of Domestic Engineering*; Ellen Swallow Richards, *Euthenics, the Science of a Controllable Environment*; Marion Talbot & Sophonisba Breckinridge, *The Modern Household*. The professional literature dealing with the subject of home design from the period is littered with comments from architects regarding the female client's more active participation in design decisions. See, for example, Eugene Gardner, *Homes and All About Them*, 207-215; Thomas E. Tallmadge, "The Chicago School," *Architectural Review*, 72 and *Western Architect*, 27. For secondary source discussions, see Brooks, *The Prairie School*, pp. 337-341; Wright, *Moralism and the Model Home* and *Building the Dream*, esp. ch. 9.

[8]Wright's *Moralism and the Model Home* firmly establishes the social reform agenda underlying interest in the design of the turn-of-the-century home. See also, Wortman, "Domesticating the 19th Century American City"; Wright, "Sweet & Clean: The Domestic Landscape in the Progressive Era"; David P. Handlin, "Efficiency and the American Home;" Ehrenreich & English, "The Manufacture of Housework"; Margaret Marsh, "The Suburban House: the Social Implications of Environmental Choice;" and Karen J. Blair, *The Clubwoman as Feminist*. Two primary sources on women's social reform efforts in the city are indispensable: Jane Cunningham Croly, *The History of the Women's Club Movement*; Mary Ritter Beard, *Woman's Work in Municipalities*.

[9]See Dolores Hayden, *The Grand Domestic Revolution*, for an excellent discussion of alternatives to the middle class single family home vigorously proposed but ultimately not accepted.

[10]William Ingraham Russell, *The Romance and Tragedy of a Widely Known Business Man of New York*; 63. See the *American Architect's* description of Redstone

in "An American Park," 15. Russell's memoir, lightly disguised as a work of fiction, is an insightful account of the author's career during a volatile period of American business history and a poignant chronicle of the impact of P-MS career fluctuations on the author's family and personal life.

[11]For a more full account of the Sears family, see Sies, "American Country House Architecture in Context," ch 7, and Colleen Browne Kilner, *Joseph Sears and his Kenilworth*. The cost estimate of the Sears' residence, "Waverley," is derived from figures recorded in the original Kenilworth Company Account Book held by the Kenilworth Historical Society, Kenilworth, Illinois.

[12]See also, Henry Blake Fuller, "The Upward Movement in Chicago."

[13]See also issues of the *Short Hills Item*.

[14]See issues of the *Short Hills Item* and "The Woman's Club of Millburn;" Helen Moak, "The First 75 Years: A Parish History." Information is also based on interviews with Eleanor Houston Smith (Philadelphia, PA, April 1983) and with Charles Woodward (Chestnut Hill, Philadelphia, April 1983).

[15]My understanding of positive environmental reform strategies derives from Paul Boyer's excellent *Urban Masses and Moral Order in America, 1820-1920*. On women's public health campaigns in Minneapolis, see Foster, *Who's Who Among Minneapolis Women*, 54, 202, 206, 356.

[16]Information based also on an interview with Eleanor Houston Smith, (April 1983).

[17]For a thorough discussion of the consensus regarding the model suburban home that emerged between 1877 and 1917, see Sies, "American Country House Architecture in Context," ch. 3.

[18]In "Form Follows Function or Form Follows Fashion: Women and American Suburban Architecture, 1897-1917," I refute the widely-held assumption that the suburban housewife's sudden intrusion on architectural decision-making around 1915 brought about the demise of progressive domestic architecture.

[19]My own reconstruction of the suburban domestic design program draws on the work of Gwendolyn Wright, *Moralism and the Model Home*, and Reynar Banham, *The Architecture of the Well-Tempered Environment*. David Handlin's *The American Home: Architecture and Society, 1815-1915* is best when discussing innovations in domestic technology. Other interpretations which differ from my own include Marsh, "The Suburban House: the Social Implications of Environmental Choice"; Alan Gowans, *The Comfortable House*; Clifford Edward Clark, Jr., *The American Family Home: 1800-1960*; Sally McMurray, "City Parlor, Country Sitting Room: Rural Vernacular Design and the American Parlor, 1840-1900;" Colleen McDannell, *The Christian Home in Victorian America, 1840-1900*; Richard Guy Wilson, "Arts & Crafts Architecture: Radical Though Dedicated to the Cause Conservative;" and Cheryl Robertson, "House and Home in the Arts & Crafts Era: Reforms for Simpler Living."

Works Cited

"An American Park," *AABN* 16 (July 12, 1886): 15.

Aronovici, Carol. "Housing and the Housing Problem." *Annals Am. Acad.* 51 (Jan. 1914): 1-7.

Baldwin's Directory of the Oranges and Townships of Essex. 1892. Millburn/Short Hills Historical Society Collection.

Banham, Reynar. *The Architecture of the Well-Tempered Environment.* Chicago: University of Chicago Press, 1969.

Beard, Mary Ritter. *Woman's Work in Municipalities.* Orig. publ. 1915. New York: Arno Press, 1972.

Blair, Karen J. *The Clubwoman as Feminist.* New York: Holmes & Meier, 1980.

Blue Book of Minneapolis Clubs. 1909. Minneapolis, MN: Minneapolis History Collection, Minneapolis Public Library.

Book of Chicagoans A.N. Marquis, ed. 1903, 1917, 1930.

Book of Minnesotans. Chicago: A.N. Marquis Co., 1907.

Boyer, Paul. *Urban Masses and Moral Order in America, 1820-1920.* Cambridge: Harvard Univ. Press, 1978.

Brooks, H. Allen. *The Prairie School.* New York: W.W. Norton, 1972.

Campbell, Helen. *Household Economics.* New York: G.P. Putnam's Sons, 1897.

Chestnut Hill Historical Society Collection. Philadelphia, PA.

Clark, Clifford Edward, Jr., *The American Family Home: 1800-1960.* Chapel Hill, NC: The University of North Carolina Press, 1986.

Conway, Jill. "Women Reformers and American Culture, 1870-1930." *Journal of Social History* (1976): 164-177.

Cott, Nancy F. *The Bonds of Womanhood.* New Haven: Yale University Press, 1977,

Cowan, Ruth Schwarz. *More Work for Mother.* New York: Basic Books, 1983.

Croly, Jane Cunningham. *The History of the Women's Club Movement.* New York: 1898.

Douglas, Ann. *The Feminization of American Culture.* New York: Alfred A. Knopf, 1977.

Dudden, Faye. *Serving Women.* Middletown, CT: Wesleyan Univ. Press, 1983.

Eaton, Leonard K. *Two Chicago Architects and their Clients.* Cambridge: MIT Press, 1969.

Ehrenreich, Barbara and Ehrenreich, John. "The Professional-Managerial Class." *Radical America* 11(2), (1977): 7-31.

Ehrenreich, Barbara and English, Deirdre. "The Manufacture of Housework." *Socialist Revolution* 5 (Oct.-Dec. 1975): 8-10, 17-25.

Foster, Mary Dillon. *Who's Who Among Minnesota Women.* Minneapolis: M.D. Foster, 1924.

Frederick, Christine. *Household Engineering: Scientific Management in the Home.* New York: Doubleday, 1912.

Fuller, Henry Blake. "The Upward Movement in Chicago." *Atlantic Monthly* 80 (1897): 534-47.

Gardner, Eugene. *Homes and All About Them.* Boston: James R. Osgood & Co., 1885.

Gowans, Alan. *The Comfortable House.* Cambridge, MA: MIT Press, 1986.

Halttunen, Karen. *Confidence Men and Painted Women.* New Haven: Yale University Press, 1982.

Handlin, David. *The American Home: Architecture and Society, 1815-1915.* Boston: Little, Brown & Co., 1979.

Handlin, David P. "Efficiency and the American Home." *Architectural Association Quarterly* 5 (Winter 1973): 50-54.

Hayden, Dolores. *The Grand Domestic Revolution.* Cambridge: MIT Press, 1981.

Hue, Samuel Warren. "The Problem of the Family." *St. Louis, MO: Universal Exposition, Congress of Arts & Sciences.* Howard J. Rogers, ed., 7 (1904): 709-722.

Kenilworth Historical Society. *The First Fifty Years.* Kenilworth, IL, 1947.

Kenilworth Historical Society Collection. Kenilworth, IL.

Kilner, Colleen Browne. *Joseph Sears and his Kenilworth.* Kenilworth, IL: Kenilworth Historical Society, 1969.

Kraditor, Aileen. *The Ideas of the Woman Suffrage Movement, 1890-1920.* New York: 1965.

Marcuse, Peter. "Housing in Early City Planning." *JUH* 6 (Feb. 1980): 153-176.

Marsh, Margaret. "The Suburban House: the Social Implications of Environmental Choice." Paper presented at the Annual Meeting of the OAH, New York City, April 1986.

McDannell, Colleen. *The Christian Home in Victorian America, 1840-1900.* Bloomington, IN: Indiana University Press, 1986.

McMurray, Sally. "City Parlor, Country Sitting Room: Rural Vernacular Design and the American Parlor, 1840-1900." *Winterthur Portfolio* 20 (Winter 1985): 261-280.

Millburn/Short Hills Historical Society Collection. Millburn, NJ.

Minneapolis City Directories, 1880-1917.

Minneapolis History Collection. Minneapolis Public Library. Minneapolis, MN.

Mintz, Steven. *A Prison of Expectations.* New York: New York Univ. Press, 1983.

Moak, Helen. "The First 75 Years: A Parish History." *Newsletter, St. Martin in the Fields Parish.* Chestnut Hill Historical Society Collection.

Moffatt's Directory of Essex County. 1889. Millburn/Short Hills Historical Society Collection

Motz, Marilyn. *True Sisterhood: Michigan Women and the Kin, 1820-1920.* Albany: SUNY Press, 1983.

Murphey, Murray. "The Place of Beliefs in Modern Culture." *New Directions in American Intellectual History.* P. Conkin & J. Higham, eds. Baltimore: Johns Hopkins University Press, 1982.

Pattison, Mary. *The Principles of Domestic Engineering.* New York: Trow Press, 1912.

Philadelphia City Directories. 1880-1917.

Prendergast, Norma. "The Sense of Home: 19th Century Domestic Architectural Reform" Ph.D. dissertation, Cornell University, 1981.

Richards, Ellen Swallow. *Euthenics, the Science of a Controllable Environment.* Boston: Whitcomb & Barrows, 1910.

Robertson, Cheryl. "House and Home in the Arts & Crafts Era: Reforms for Simpler Living." In *The Art That Is Life: The Arts & Crafts Movement in America, 1875-1920.* Wendy Kaplan, ed. Boston: Museum of Fine Arts, 1987.

Rose, Willie Lee. "Reforming Women." *New York Review of Books* (Oct. 7, 1982): 45-49.

Russell, William Ingraham. *The Romance and Tragedy of a Widely Known Business Man of New York.* Baltimore: W.I. Russell, 1913.

Ryan, Mary. *Womanhood in America.* New York: New Viewpoints, 1979.

Short Hills Item. Millburn/Short Hills Historical Society Collection. Millburn, NJ.

Sies, Mary Corbin. "American Country House Architecture in Context: the Suburban Ideal of Living in the East and Midwest, 1877-1917," Ph.D. dissertation, University of Michigan, 1987.

_____ "Form Follows Function or Form Follows Fashion: Women and American Suburban Architecture, 1897-1917." Paper presented at Popular Culture Association Annual Meeting, Louisville, KY, April 1985.

Sklar, Kathryn Kish. *Catharine Beecher, A Study in American Domesticity*. New Haven: Yale University Press, 1973.

Smith, Daniel Scott. "Family Limitation, Sexual Control, and Domestic Feminism in Victorian America." In *Clio's Consciousness Raised*. Mary S. Hartman and Lois Banner, eds. New York: Harper Colophon Books, 1974: 119-136.

Talbot, Marion. and Breckinridge, Sophonisba. *The Modern Household*. Boston: Whitcomb & Barrows, 1912.

Tallmadge, Thomas E. "The Chicago School." *Architectural Review* 15 (April 1908): 72 and *Western Architect* 25 (1917): 27.

Trachtenberg, Alan. *The Incorporation of America*Weigley, Emma Seifrit. "It Might Have Been Euthenics." *American Quarterly* 26 (1974): 79-96.

. New York: Hill & Wang, 1982.

Welter, Barbara. "The Cult of True Womanhood, 1820-1860." *AQ* 18 (1966): 151-174.

Wiebe, Robert. *The Search for Order, 1877-1920. New York: Hill & Wang, 1967.*

_____ Wilson, Richard Guy. "Arts & Crafts Architecture: Radical Though Dedicated to the Cause Conservative." In *The Art That Is Life: The Arts & Crafts Movement in America, 1875-1920*. Wendy Kaplan, ed. Boston: Museum of Fine Arts, 1987.

"The Woman's Club of Millburn." *The Bulletin* (Jan. 1939). Millburn/Short Hills Historical Society Collection.

Wortman, Marlene Stein. "Domesticating the 19th Century American City," *Prospects* 3 (1977): 531-572.

Wright, Gwendolyn. *Building the Dream*. New York: Pantheon Books, 1981.

Wright, Gwendolyn. *Moralism and the Model Home*. Chicago: University of Chicago Press, 1980.

Wright, Gwendolyn. "Sweet and Clean: The Domestic Landscape of the Progressive Era." *Landscape* 20 (Oct. 1975): 38-43.

Notes on Contributors

Susan S. Arpad is the Coordinator of the Women's Studies Program at California State University, Fresno. She teaches courses in Women and Popular Culture and Women's History and collects women's private writings and women's oral histories. At one time, she quilted; now she gardens and takes photographs.

Sue Bridwell Beckham teaches English at the University of Wisconsin-Stout; however, while she enjoys her students and her teaching her heart is in her research. Her book *A Gentle Reconstruction: Depression Post Office Murals and Southern Culture* will soon appear from Louisiana State University Press and she is presently beginning to research a book on Southern tourism and souvenirs.

Jane Converse Brown has degrees from Stanford Univeristy (A.B.) and the University of Wisconsin-Madison (M.S. & Ph.D). She is currently working on an introduction to design history for beginning design students.

Pat Browne is an editor with the Bowling Green State University Popular Press. She edited *Heroines of Popular Culture* and co-edited *Dimensions of Detective Fiction*. She edits the journal, *Clues, A Journal of Detection*.

Ricky Clark, an Affiliate Scholar at Oberlin College, is a quilt researcher particularly interested in quilts as cultural documents. Her articles have appeared in *Timeline, The Hayes Historical Journal, The Quilt Digest, Western Reserve Studies Journal*, and various anthologies and exhibition catalogs. As a member of the Ohio Quilt Research Project, she is currently documenting Ohio's quilts, quiltmakers and quiltmaking traditions.

Patricia Cunningham is an Associate Professor in the Division of Apparel, Merchandising and Interior Design at Bowling Green State University. She edited *Woven Coverlets: Textiles in the Folk Tradition* which was published in conjunction with an exhibiton of coverlets held at Bowling Green State University in 1984 and has published on costume and textile history in *Dress, the Journal of the Costume Society of America, Ars Textrina* and *The Northwest Ohio Quarterly*. She is currently engaged in a book length study, *Artistic and Healthy Costume: Dress Reform in the Modern Design Movements in Europe and America*. With Susan Lab, she is editing *Dress and Popular Culture* for the Popular Press.

Beverly Gordon teaches in the Environment, Textiles, and Design department at the University of Wisconsin-Madison. She is the author of numerous works on popular and material culture, including *Shaker Textile Arts, Feltmaking,* and "Souvenirs: Concretization of The Extraordinary." (*JPC* 1986).

Jean Gordon is Associate Professor of History at the University of North Carolina at Greensboro, Greensboro, N.C. She has published widely in the fields of history and women's culture.

Jan McArthur is Chairman of the Housing and Interior Design Department at the University of North Carolina at Greensboro, Greensboro, North Carolina. She has published numerous articles on material culture.

Marilyn Ferris Motz is an assistant professor in the Popular Culture Department at Bowling Green State University. She is the author of several articles. Her book, *True Sisterhood: Michigan Women and Their Kin, 1820-1920* was published by the State University of New York Press.

Beverly Seaton, a long-time member of the Popular Culture Association, teaches English at the Newark Campus of Ohio State University. Her research specialties are nineteenth and early twentieth century popular culture and garden history.

Mary Corbin Sies is an assistant professor in the Department of American Studies at the University of Maryland. She is finishing a book on the cultural and architectural history of planned, exclusive suburbs in the United States during the pre-WWI era.